D0806162

Libraries, Museums, and Archives

Legal Issues and Ethical Challenges in the New Information Era

EDITED BY TOMAS A. LIPINSKI

The Scarecrow Press, Inc.
Lanham, Maryland, and London
2002

SCARECROW PRESS, INC.

Published in the United States of America
by Scarecrow Press, Inc.
4720 Boston Way
Lanham, Maryland 20706
www.scarecrowpress.com

4 Pleydell Gardens, Folkestone
Kent CT20 2DN, England

British Library Cataloguing in Publication Information Available

Library of Congress Cataloging-in-Publication Data

Libraries, museums, and archives : legal issues and ethical challenges in the new information era / edited by Tomas A. Lipinski.

p. cm.

Includes index.

ISBN 0-8108-4085-5 (hbk.: alk. paper)

1. Library legislation—United States. 2. Museums—Law and legislation—United States. 3. Archives—Law and legislation—United States. 4. Fair use (Copyright)—United States. 5. Information technology—Moral and ethical aspects. I. Lipinski, Tomas A., 1958–

KF4315 .L53 2002
344.73'092—dc21

2001041078

∞™ The paper used in this publication meets the minimum requirements of American National Standard for Information Sciences—Permanence of Paper for Printed Library Materials, ANSI/NISO Z39.48-1992.
Manufactured in the United States of America.

Contents

PART 5: COPYRIGHT AND OTHER OWNERSHIP ISSUES

PART 6: IMPLEMENTATION OF LEGAL AND ETHICAL CONCEPTS

Acknowledgments

The editor and contributors greatly acknowledge the support of the Institute for Library and Museum Services, Washington, D.C., with whose support through a 1999 National Leadership Grant Award the initial conference was funded, and where the chapters in this volume were first presented.

The editor would also like to thank the following people at the Center for Information Policy Research, the School of Information Studies (SOIS), and the University of Wisconsin–Milwaukee: Chancellor Nancy L. Zympher, Dean Mohammed M. Aman, Assistant Dean Wilfred W. Fong, Associate Dean Judith J. Senkevitch (retired), Assistant Professor Elizabeth A. Buchanan, Rebecca Hall, Jeannine Strunk, Michael Huntsicker, Saad Akbar Khan, and other members of the SOIS faculty and staff who contributed to make the conference, the "Institute on Legal and Ethical Issues in the New Information Era: Challenges for Libraries, Museums and Archives," held May 20–26, 2000, at the University of Wisconsin–Milwaukee, a resounding success.

Foreword

The following chapters were initially presented at the "Institute for Legal and Ethical Issues in the New Information Era: Challenges for Libraries, Museums and Archives." conference. The institute was funded by a National Leadership Grant from the Institute of Museum and Library Services. The institute and surrounding events were sponsored by the Center for Information Policy Research and the School of Information Studies, University of Wisconsin–Milwaukee, and were held from May 20 to May 26, 2000, at the Edith Hefter Conference Center, University of Wisconsin–Milwaukee. The editor solicited contributions based upon the expertise—often both academic and practical—and national recognition of each contributor.

Introduction

Legal and ethical issues have always permeated the information environment. This is especially true in traditional institutional environments such as libraries, museums, and archives. Rather than simplifying, the saturation of these environments by information technology only complicates the matter. Responding to these issues is always challenging. What the "proper" response is may be clear or it may be uncertain, but in any event it is often a blend of the legal, the ethical, and the practical. Issues of information access or privacy of patron records, for example, do not exist in a vacuum. Underlying principles and overlying context of a problem must be considered side by side with the law. This collection will hopefully provide professionals and others dealing with these issues the guidance necessary to make more informed decisions, or perhaps to better balance the legal, ethical, and practical aspects of a particular problem in their daily institutional settings.

The chapters are organized by themes. Parts 1 and 2 revolve around the physical collection of the library, museum, or archive. Before everything else, a collection must be acquired. Robert J. Vanni, legal counsel of the New York Public Library, draws upon his many years of legal service to the eleemosynary community and presents a thorough discussion of the legal issues involved in acquiring items by gift. He discusses both real property concepts as well as federal tax implications of the process. Andrew McLean also draws upon many years of experience, but from the other side of the counter: Professor McLean is an appraiser and dealer of rare books and manuscripts. Part 1 also includes Tomas A. Lipinski's brief survey of the privacy and publicity issues that may arise when personal items and artifacts of contributors or other individuals may be in the collection and are used in exhibits or displays. In the last chapter of part 1, Judith Krug, director of the American Library Association's Office for Intellectual Freedom, discusses the problems public institutions, especially museums, have faced when exhibiting controversial materials.

While an issue such as copyright may apply equally to libraries, museums, and archives, special attention was necessary for the unique set of laws applying to physical, as opposed to documentary, collections residing in museums. The chapters by Marie C. Malaro and Ildiko P. DeAngelis explore these issues in detail through discussions of overriding concerns in collection policy development (Malaro) and hypothetical situations (DeAngelis). Malaro and DeAngelis bring years of experience as legal counsels to the Smithsonian and as former and current directors, respectively, of the Museum Studies Program, George Washington University, Washington, D.C.

Part 3 deals with the legal issues surrounding users of these institutions. This includes the privacy of patrons in library and archive settings, information accessibility and technology, and safety and security issues in public spaces. Professor Lipinski provides a brief survey of the patron privacy laws and suggests how a policy can augment the statutory structure of state privacy laws. Professor Minow teaches a course on legal issues in libraries and has a background in disability law, thus her chapter discusses the application of the Americans with Disabilities Act to electronic access of information, specifically relating to library, museum, and archive web sites. Also, Bruce Shuman draws from his research in library security and safety management to describe the "seven levels" of safety in public places.

Part 4 is devoted to ethical issues. Computer ethics expert Marsha Woodbury sets the stage with an exploration of the challenges facing public institutions in the advance of an Internet dominated increasingly by commercial interests. Professor Johannes Britz brings a third world perspective to his discussion of information ethics. He discusses how ethical reasoning can be applied to issues involving information access vis-à-vis public institutions such as libraries, museums, and archives. Professor Elizabeth Buchanan follows this with guidelines for putting ethical standards into practice.

A final substantive legal section, part 5, discusses copyright and other information "control" issues. Professor Shelly Warwick provides an overview of copyright law, including its historical development, recent changes to the law, and its practical application. Dwayne Buttler and Kenny Crews, recognized experts on copyright issues in educational institutions, delve into more detail, discussing the nuances, for example, of section 108 of the copyright law. And law professor David Rice presents his concerns regarding various legislative initiatives of information owners to control the free flow of public information through, for example, database reform legislation at the national level and the now infamous Uniform Computer Information Transaction Act movement at the state level.

The three chapters constituting part 6 provide resources for implementation. Jane Colwin from the Wisconsin State Law Library provides a resource list of ethical and legal materials in print and on the World Wide Web targeted at the library, museum, and archive audience. Attorney Claire Weber, who made her career drafting "legislation" at the state and local level, provides a discussion of the proper structure and elements of library, museum, and archive policy content that is the best this editor has come across. Her discussion is a superb blueprint for effective policy drafting at all levels of the institutional life cycle. Finally, Professor Thomas Walker discusses the problems and potentials of change within an information service organization.

Obviously there are issues not discussed, and of course more detail is always helpful, but this collection is broader than most and its focus on legal issues without ignoring practical and ethical issues is sure to give it a place on the shelves of interested professionals.

While many of the chapter authors have practiced law, are licensed attorneys, and have legal experience in the areas on which each is writing, nothing in this book should be taken as the provision of legal advice or legal service; such advice or service should be rendered by your institution's designated legal counsel.

PART ONE: WORKING WITH THE COLLECTION

CHAPTER 1

Deeds of Gift

CARESSING THE HAND THAT FEEDS

Robert J. Vanni

Introduction

As a result of history and law, the American republic has developed a unique approach to philanthropy, if not in philosophy, then in practice. The heterogeneity of the population, the interests each citizen brings to the "American banquet," and the intentions of the founding fathers to allow the administration of the state to proceed in an environment of guaranteed freedoms of speech, choice, religion and association have resulted in the coming together of like-minded people and the creation of institutions to espouse, protect, practice and preach their diverse interests. The law, our system's instrument of implementation, has accommodated these actions, first by providing for the creation of legal vehicles, associations and corporations, to perpetuate such interests and, later, by creating a special class of organization under the tax laws, the nonprofit association or corporation, which is largely exempt from direct taxation. This conjunction of the exercise of guaranteed freedoms and a tax regime that encourages individual support of special interests by "rewarding" philanthropy has given rise to possibly the world's most active and rich independent sectors.

In the instance of educational institutions, and in particular libraries and museums, the past two hundred years have witnessed the founding of collections that now rival those of institutions that have been acquiring materials since the Middle Ages. Indeed, within the past one hundred years alone, vast amounts, in both size and value, of educational and cultural materials have come to rest in the United States from every region of the world, a testament to the vitality of the American philanthropic model.

It is undoubtedly a truism that each of the institutions represented by the curators and librarians who attended the conference that led to the publication of this book owes much to the beneficence of its friends and donors—if not the majority, then probably its more unique and special collections, as well as many of its buildings and most of its endowment. Without these donors and their unique passions and commitments, few of our organizations would exist in such glory.

As a case in point, I offer the New York Public Library, Astor, Lenox and Tilden Foundations (NYPL). The library was formed in 1897 by the consolidation of several independent, private collections of art, manuscripts and book materials, most notably the Astor Library and the Lenox Library, with the financial boost of a significant bequest from the estate of Samuel Tilden (former governor of New York and candidate for president of the United States in 1876). All this, combined with a public-private partnership between Andrew Carnegie and the city of New York, has resulted in a private library that, within one hundred years of its formation, has developed research collections in a class with the Bibliothèque Nationale de France, the British Library, the Lenin Library and our own Library of Congress, as well as having become one of the largest circulating libraries in the country, with eighty-four branches. The most significant point, however, and one often misunderstood as a result of the institution's name, is that among these great world libraries, only NYPL is a private, nonprofit corporation and not an organ or instrumentality of a government, as one might expect. Its status among the world's leading research libraries could not have been achieved without our donors—the Bergs, the Stewarts, the Pforzheimers, the Roses, the Cullmans, the Toscanninis, Jerome Robbins, the Schomburgs and many more past and present donors.

In the early part of the twentieth century, however, life seems to have been a bit less complicated. Donors made their wishes known through simple letters or relatively uncomplicated deeds of gift or bequests to nascent institutions overseen by the local elite, with whom they shared their friends, their mores and their clubs—secure in the knowledge that their will be done! As a case in point, see appendix A, a copy of the one-page letter from Andrew Carnegie that is the foundation of the present eighty-four lending libraries run by NYPL—it is simple, direct, unequivocal. Also see an Associated Press article dated May 8, 2000, on "James Smithson's Surprising Will," the source of today's Smithsonian Institution.

By contrast, today the business of charity has become a bit more complicated. Not only has the donor base become much broader, but with it has come a more varied range of donor concerns and agendas, such as naming opportunities, political biases, managerial and philosophical concerns, visibility and publicity and fear thereof. Further, there is more competition for donor beneficence among institutions, and there are prodigious long-term efforts of donor cultivation. Add to this the cyber-revolution, the availability of more information about nonprofits and their programs through the Internet, and a national trend in law and practice for greater "transparency" concerning the transactions and operations of nonprofits, and we have defined the current environment in which our institutions must master their strategies for growth.

This is not to suggest that any of this is new, but rather, these concerns have reached new heights such that pledges or agreements from donors are no longer accomplished with a handshake or a simple note on embossed stationery. This is especially so in the modern environment of escalating costs of labor, materials, and collection acquisition and maintenance, which forces most institutions to carefully shepherd and marshal their resources to fill the gaps, and to add to their collections. As we seek to attract donors, we wish to be as accommodating as possible. And as donors have become more "sophisticated,"—or, perhaps, more demanding regarding how their donations are to be used, handled, implemented—there has arisen a dynamic tension. On one side is the institution that is trying to add to its resources, fulfill its mission as dictated by its board of trustees, and meet its objectives and strategic plans in a priority order as decided by its professional managers. On the other side is the donor with his or her own agenda, priorities and interests. To defer completely to the donor (however well intentioned he or she is) could hobble the institution or some division within it. For an institution to be too inflexible will only discourage gifts. It would be biting the hand that feeds!

Hence, it is the duty of the curator, librarian, development office, CEO or board member to understand the needs of the institution, recognize the interests of the donor, and find a common ground such that the acceptance of a gift meets, as much as possible, the interests and needs of both parties. The mechanism for this process is the negotiation and drafting of a deed of gift.

The object of this chapter, then, is to attempt to

a) demystify the legalities of drafting clear and thoughtful deeds of gift;
b) identify issues that should be addressed in deeds of gift;
c) make some comments on pledge agreements and deposit agreements;
d) offer examples of how to resolve selected issues; and
e) highlight some tax-related issues donors and donees should be aware of.

Before beginning, I will lay down some understandings or ground rules. First, by and large, there need be no legal "hocus pocus" or "magic words" in a deed of gift. Clarity, precision in drafting, and reaching a true meeting of the minds are the objectives. Remember, the document is not only to serve as a common understanding between donor and donee, but it will also be a road map for the future librarians, curators and administrators of the gift or collection.

Second, it need not be long and complicated. If it is to be a simple gift of a few discreet items with no real conditions or restrictions, then use a simple form of agreement. For this purpose see the one-page gift agreement in appendix B.

Third, lawyers sometimes refer to straightforward transactions as "vanilla deals." When it comes to large donations, with a variety of types of donated materials, with restrictions or conditions, or concerning the lives of famous or historically important individuals, there is seldom a "vanilla deal." As a result, each transaction needs to be thoroughly analyzed and each potential issue raised and responded to in the deed of gift.

Having stated these ground rules, it will be helpful to use as a template a form of agreement that we use at NYPL, reproduced in appendix C. I will go though each section, explain why it is included and highlight the issues and problems it is designed to address. I will attempt to keep my comments in "plain English." Rather than a legal treatise, this presentation is largely based on my experiences in negotiating and drafting these kinds of agreements, thus it highlights issues to be aware of and offers solutions to be considered. Again, I emphasize that this is only one format. Other solutions may resolve the issues just as well. Also be aware that this form and my comments are based on New York State law. Your individual jurisdictions might present unique issues, or might require special resolutions of issues.

Deeds of Gift

What is the objective of drafting a deed of gift? In simplest terms, it is to identify the donor, the nature of the gift, and issues that relate to the gift, some due to the nature of the material, some to the demands or restrictions placed by the donor. It creates a historical record that can be referred to over time—most donors preferring that period to be "perpetuity"—and can offer guidance in administering the material or fund. Recognize that the negotiation process is also often one of education of the donor. Demands placed on the gift may well fly in the face of good librarianship, and it is during the negotiation of a deed of gift that the donor is enlightened on the procedures and priorities of the institution and, hopefully, can be brought into line with them. As an aside, if lawyers had their way, all the deeds of gift they draw would be almost identical, for ease of drafting, but more importantly for ease of future administration. Although, as mentioned, there are few "vanilla deals" and you can seldom use a cookie-cutter agreement, you should also avoid having a large number of agreements with broadly varying terms, because it could well result in an administrative nightmare such that unintended errors in management could embarrass the institution, alienate the donors or their heirs and, perhaps even worse, make future, potential donors wary of dealing with your institution.

WHO IS THE DONOR?

In the basic form used at NYPL, the opening paragraph identifies the parties. It is very important to define properly who the donor is. Often, you are dealing with Mr. and Mrs. X, but you later find out that the gift is in fact being made through their family foundation. If the deed is not executed by the appropriate party, significant legal and tax issues can arise. You also need to identify the donor properly so that later in the document you can get the appropriate representations and warranties, and ensure that the donor has the legal right to make an enforceable gift. Types of potential donors to be aware of are an estate, acting through the executor of the Will or a named literary executor, or the administrator of an intestate estate; heirs of a deceased collector, or legally appointed conservators or guardians of an infant or otherwise incompetent donor; an individual; a corporation; a foundation; and a governmental or quasigovernmental entity. Each category of donor may give rise to a series of questions and issues relating to title, authority to make the gift, and evidence of that authority.

Be aware, too, of a growing trend across the United States to broadening the classes of persons who can sue to enforce promises of nonprofits. Usually it is a state's attorney general that is charged with overseeing nonprofits. Depending on state laws, heirs, trustees and more distant beneficiaries might be granted "standing" to sue on the enforcement of deeds of gift terms, so it behooves you to clearly and accurately identify the donor.

WHEREAS CLAUSES

WHEREAS or introductory clauses, though not controlling legally, are often helpful in explaining the history of the transaction and the motives or intentions of the parties and, in the case of the NYPL form, can be used to define the gift. This is accomplished by generally explaining the materials in the gift and referring to a more detailed, often item-by-item description or inventory, contained in an attachment to the agreement.

Just a word about legal notation. Often you will see "defined terms" in an agreement. A "defined term" is indicated by a capitalized word or words, such as ". . . Mr. X ('Donor') . . .", or, often, by referring to the gift as the "Collection" throughout the agreement. This is a useful bit of legal notation and often assists in the brevity and clarity of the document.

DECLARATION OF THE GIFT

The donor should clearly state what interest in the material is being donated. Usually it is "all my right, title and interest." It is possible that only a fractional interest is being given, with the balance going to another institution, for example. Be careful at this point, however. If the donor intends to retain certain elements of title, a "split gift" might result, which will have distinct implications as to the availability of a charitable income tax deduction to the donor. (See sections 1221 and 170(f)(3) of the Internal Revenue Code of 1986, as amended [IRS Code].)

In the agreement, it may be useful to specifically state when title passes, that is, when the institution becomes the owner of the materials. This is particularly so for collections that need to be packed and transported (especially internationally), or if, for some other reason, the physical possession of the material by the institution will be delayed. This has special significance on "shifting the risk." For example, who should insure the materials against damage or loss during transport? Donor or donee? Who has the responsibility to obtain export permits or customs clearances? If the transaction was not a pure gift, but a bargain sale or cash acquisition, the matter of when title passes can directly affect whether payment is due despite loss or damage prior to receipt by the institution.

RESERVATION OF INTERESTS

Often, when archives and manuscripts are the subject of the gift, the donor will retain intellectual property rights for himself, his family or his heirs. Under the IRS Code, this may give rise to a split gift. In general, a gift of a partial interest in property is not deductible for federal income tax purposes. (See section 170(f)(3) of the IRS Code.) A donor who makes a gift of a manuscript but retains the copyright interest generally cannot take an income tax deduction for the value of the manuscript. However, a manuscript and its related copyright are treated as separate properties for purposes of the gift and estate tax charitable deductions. (See IRS Code sections 2055(e)(4) and 2522(c)(3).) Therefore, the donor's gift will not be subject to gift tax. In addition, a donor may make a gift of the manuscript at death, retain the copyright and obtain a charitable deduction for estate tax purposes. If the donor is retaining copyright interests, it must be specifically stated, since this will affect how the collection can be used and managed by the institution.

If intellectual property rights are to be part of the donation as well, then that should be specifically stated with an understanding that the donor will execute such documents necessary to transfer such rights that may have been registered in his name with the U.S. Copyright Office.

NAMING THE COLLECTION

It is useful, in advance, to have the donor agree to how the collection will be referred to in library finding aids and scholarly works. Usually this does not raise any problems, but you should be aware that if the name is too long, when material is being credited to the collection in books or scholarly works, or credit lines are to be added beneath reproduced images, especially if the name of your division and institution are long, authors or editors may choose to inappropriately shorten, or completely omit, the credit line. If the name of the collection is lengthy, see if you can get the donor to agree to the use of a shortened version when required.

As referred to earlier, the negotiation of agreements is an opportunity to educate the donor. Often, a request may be made that the collection will be "kept together" or housed as a unit. As we know, good librarianship, conservation and space needs, institutional curatorial divisions and off-site or nonpublic storage can well make such a request inappropriate. Usually what the donor wants is that the public be made aware that specific items are part of a unique collection. Since most libraries have automated catalogs, the donor should be "educated" to the fact that the collection will be given "bibliographical unity" through the catalog and that "physical unity" may not be in the best interests of the institution or the materials.

RESTRICTIONS ON ACCESS

For a variety of reasons, a donor may wish to put restrictions on the institution's use of the collection. Of all sections of a deed of gift, this is the one to be most careful about, that may require the most diplomatic and Solomonic drafting and that may offer the greatest opportunity for the education of the donor. Beware, too, of the donor who wants to maintain too much control over the gift. Not only can this interfere with the institution's prerogatives, it can subject the donor to tax consequences that can disqualify his charitable deduction.

One of the most often requested restrictions is that all or part of the collection be closed to researcher access for a number of years. Curators do not like these restrictions, since their shelves just become storage units. Researchers learn of the collection but are frustrated by their inability to access it. Often, if this is explained, the donor can be made to understand that, especially as to large collections, seldom do all items require the same level of confidentiality. Either before the delivery, or within a *stated period* (e.g., six months, one year) of delivery of the collection to the institution, the donor should go through the material and stratify it into those materials that can be made available immediately and those that can be closed for a varying period (e.g., five years, ten years); those that must wait for the death of a named individual(s); and those that may be viewed only with the donor's or his representative's prior approval. The objective is to make as much of a collection accessible as soon as possible and to permit the exercise of good librarianship and curatorship to process, organize, catalog, conserve and preserve the material. With explanation and understanding, many donors will appreciate the logic of this stratification approach and will work with the institution to achieve this end.

Besides time restrictions, donors may require use restrictions that vary from the institution's usual rules and regulations. For example, no copying is to be permitted, access is to be restricted until an official biography has been completed and published, access is to be granted only to a named biographer. These types of restrictions may vary based on the nature of the materials being donated. By way of example, a donor of stage set designs and costume designs to NYPL required the library to agree that if a theatrical company needed to see the original designs to know accurate colors and materials, upon notice and with proper safeguards, these otherwise noncirculating items would be loaned.

When drafting restrictions, be they on use or handling, how a supporting endowment will be used or the intended "purpose" of a gift, think long and hard as to how that restriction's use or purpose statement will play out in the future. Perpetuity is a long time! Collection policy may change, buildings may be demolished, community use or expectations may change. If possible, provide for a permitted range of alternatives. For example, if a fund is being established for a stated purpose, provide that if the income is greater than the need for purpose X, it could "pour over" and be used for purpose Y. It can become very difficult for any number of reasons to continue to comply with certain restrictions one, two or more generations in the future. Well-drawn restriction or purpose clauses assist in future administration and avoid the costly and time-consuming legal undertaking to set aside or alter restrictions through a court process called a *cy pres* proceeding, when complying with the terms of the gift become "impossible or impracticable."

If the collection is the archive of a famous individual, there may be stated or implicit restrictions based on rights of publicity and rights of privacy. For example, some states, such as New York and California, recognize a right of publicity, which grants to the individual, and in some instances to heirs, the right to capitalize on the famous person's name and image. If, for example, a gift of photographs includes the copyright interest of the photographer, a patron or researcher requesting a copy of the photo should be advised that although the institution can grant permission to reproduce it, the individual in the photo must also waive any right to publicity, if the photo is to be used, for example, in an advertisement. Similarly, in states where rights of privacy are recognized (in most cases this right ends with the individual's death), there may be implicit restrictions on how certain materials may be used, relating not only to the donor, but to third parties referred to in the collection who otherwise have no intellectual or property rights in the materials. The privacy issue goes especially to images, photos and written materials such as letters or diaries. Such rights may have an impact on how a collection is administered, even if there are otherwise no access restrictions placed on the collection. The institution may wish to place its own restrictions on a collection for these reasons if none are imposed by the donor (as discussed below).

Sometimes donated materials have restrictions on access imposed by law. Such materials could include health records, adoption-related records, information on HIV status or information that might be subject to what lawyers refer to as "attorney-client privilege" or "doctor-patient privilege."

If the collection is likely to have such material, request the donor to identify it and, if possible, grant or obtain waivers of such privileges or other legal restrictions.

Sometimes the donor will request that the institution undertake to make the collection available by a given date, or give special access during processing or provide a written inventory or catalog by a certain date. This is one of the situations that can result in a reordering of institutional or divisional priorities, or the expenditure of significant time, effort and funds, at the expense of other collections. Clearly, one wants to be accommodating to the donor, but unless such dictated terms can be undertaken without compromising other needs of the division, such terms need to be carefully negotiated; again, provide an opportunity to educate the donor on institutional needs and priorities.

One balm that can often soothe such pains is, of course, money. If special processing or accessing requirements are sought by the donor, then once they are educated to the realities of maintaining an entire division, a request that the donation include a cash fund or endowment to cover, for example, the cost of hiring a freelance cataloger or a portion of a new staff member's salary, may well be met with success.

THE INSTITUTION'S RESERVATION OF RIGHTS

Notwithstanding the donor's restrictions, the institution may well want to make clear its own rights in regard to the donated materials. One reason may be to assure that both the donor and the donee have a meeting of the minds on how the institution will manage the collection to assure that the donor understands and will not later be affronted or annoyed. Another is to grant to the institution the right to manage and handle the material so as not to subject itself to potential liability or negative impacts. Yet a third reason is to clearly establish for the future the rights the institution has in using, managing and processing the materials. Often a fundamental benefit to the institution is to simplify its use of the materials by not having to get prior donor approval for certain types of use.

Notwithstanding these different types of restrictions, librarians and archivists should also be aware of how federal and state freedom of information laws might impact restricted collections, especially if your institution is a public or governmental entity.

Although under the Copyright Act there are special provisions for libraries that permit reproduction for scholarly and research purposes and preservation purposes (see sections 107 and 108), it is sometimes useful to restate and in some cases expand such rights. The following are some examples:

1. Though libraries can reproduce items for preservation purposes, it is suggested that the institution reserve the right to decide the medium or technology for preservation (e.g., CD, digitization).
2. As a corollary, if materials have badly deteriorated, the institution should reserve the right (particularly after materials have, for example, been microfilmed) to dispose of them (in accordance with the institution's deaccessioning policy), notwithstanding that the agreement might say materials will be retained "in perpetuity."

3. Although the Copyright Act permits reproductions for researchers and scholars, it is often useful to restate that so as to inform the donor. However, if the agreement requires that income produced from the collection (royalties, permission fees, etc.) be used to support the collection, then make clear that reproduction fees charged to recapture administrative costs are for the benefit of the institution, not the collection.
4. Though a fundamental right of ownership of an item is the right to display or exhibit it, a restatement of this right and the agreement of the donor that (assuming he retains copyright) the institution can, without further donor approval, make reproductions of materials for exhibition catalogs, promotional materials, brochures, reports and other educational purposes can significantly ease the administrative task of mounting exhibitions or lending materials for exhibitions by other institutions.

Often during the processing of a donated collection, the librarian or curator will find materials that, according to the collection policy or in the interest of the collection, need not be retained. A simple example is a personal archive that contains routine paid bills and cancelled checks, or perhaps tax returns. Assuming they hold no special significance, it is helpful to retain the right to offer to return or otherwise dispose of such material before the collection is formally accessioned.

Depending on the nature of the collection, the institution may want to retain the right to restrict access to certain materials in the collection. For example, it may be the donor's intent to make all the material available to the public immediately. However, during processing the curator finds that the materials include health records subject to privilege or materials that could give rise to claims of the right of privacy by third parties. To protect itself from potential liability now that it is owner of these materials, the institution should retain the right (and exercise it judiciously) to restrict certain materials until it is satisfied that law or time has relieved it of such liability.

ADMINISTERING THE COLLECTION

Once the collection has been processed and is open to researchers, it is often helpful to the administration process if certain matters are made clear in the deed of gift:

1. If the donor or some other party retains the intellectual property rights in the materials, it is imperative to know to whom a researcher or the institution itself should go to receive permission to reproduce items. This is especially true if the intellectual property rights are owned by a group of individuals, such as the heirs of the donor. In this case it can be helpful if the group can designate one person who has the authority to act on behalf of the entire group concerning such matters. If the donor is a corporation or association that may be going out of business, it would be helpful to have a successor organization named to respond to such requests.
2. Often, if there is income potential in the collection, the donor will require that the income earned be used for the benefit of the collection. If there is any sharing of the income between that purpose and covering administrative costs or between the institution and the donor or third party, those terms should be clearly defined.
3. Sometimes, donors will request an annual report on the scholarly use, maintenance, condition and expansion of the collection. It is helpful to future librarians to know what kinds of reports (written or narrative) or statistics the donor expects. Similarly, it is often helpful to reach agreement on the length of time such reports are required (e.g., a term of years, the life of the donor).
4. A donor may want to continue to donate materials over time or by bequest to the collection. Depending on your institution's collecting policies, it may be wise to make future donations subject to the terms of this same deed of gift, and require that future materials be of the same nature or format. For example, if the donation is of papers and photographs, you may wish to limit a future donation of another type of item (such as a writing desk, clothes or musical instruments) that is outside your collecting policy and might be better placed in a museum or costume institute. The NYPL form also contemplates donations by third parties that would become part of the named collection.

REPRESENTATIONS AND WARRANTIES

When accepting a gift, the institution should receive comfort that the donor has the right to donate the material and grant the rights that may be included. As much as possible, the institution should limit the potential of a future contest with a third party that could prove to be not only costly but embarrassing. This is usually accomplished by the donor making certain "representations and warranties." Such statements have significant legal import and may be relied upon for recompense should a future contest arise. Representations and warranties might include:

1. if the donor is an individual, that he is the sole owner of the material being donated; or that he is a legally appointed representative of the donor (i.e., agent, guardian, executor, custodian) legally authorized to act on the donor's behalf;
2. that there are no other claims against the materials, and that the title being transferred is "free and clear of all liens and claims and is unencumbered";
3. if the donor is a corporation, that it is validly formed and has obtained all necessary corporate actions and approvals (e.g., board vote) to make the donation; that all necessary governmental approvals or consents (e.g., from the state's attorney general) have been received.

To support some of these statements you may want documentary evidence, such as copies of letters testamentary, appointment letters or acknowledgment of corporate authority to make the gift.

In return, the donor organization will be asked to represent and warrant its own good standing, its tax-exempt status and its own ability to make a binding agreement on behalf of the institution.

If due to the nature of the donor or the material in the collection, it is acknowledged that there may be potential claims, it is not inappropriate to protect the institution by asking the donor to indemnify the institution by defending against future claims should they arise, or, in extreme cases, to permit the return of the collection to the donor should such claims be deemed too burdensome to the institution.

Finally, depending on the nature of the materials and the method and dates of acquisition by the donor, it may be wise to include disclosure or representations and warranties as to provenance. In accepting a gift the institution should not be naively stepping into a lawsuit. As the recent news reports show, there has been significant increase in claims for art, artifacts and manuscript materials resulting from illegally seized Holocaust-era assets and cultural patrimony illegally exported from its country of origin.

MISCELLANEOUS PROVISIONS

To aid in the future administration of the agreement it is helpful to include certain miscellaneous clauses so that the parties have certainty as to future action. Such clauses might include:

1. A statement that the deed of gift includes the entire agreement between the parties. You want to avoid additional terms or donor expectations that are embodied in ancillary letters or documents. If the deed of gift is meant to memorialize all the terms agreed to between the parties then say that it "contains the sole agreement between the parties concerning the subject matter hereof. . . ." Permitting for written clarifications or terms that need to be added in the future can be easily accomplished by written amendments signed by both the donor and the donee.
2. The selection of a jurisdiction and law under which disputes will be resolved. This is helpful in interstate transactions and, especially, in international transactions.
3. Addresses for notice to the parties.

FORMALITIES OF EXECUTION

It is important to have a date on which the deed of gift is effective. This may affect insurance and title issues, capacity to make the gift and charitable donation tax deductions. Usually, such a document becomes effective on the date the last party signs. Finally, it is often useful to have a notarization page where the signatories' positions and rights to execute the document and their signatures are acknowledged.

This has been a general overview of the issues to be considered when negotiating and drafting a deed of gift for an in-kind donation of significant size or value.

This is just an outline—many other issues may arise due to the special nature of the materials, the needs and unique requirements of the donor and the special concerns of the recipient. Whatever the case, your objectives should be to flush out these special issues, to be clear in defining the understandings and agreements of the parties and to try to accommodate the special needs and desires of the donor; but in so doing do not compromise the legitimate needs, interests and priorities of the donee institution and its mission, collections policy and deaccession policy, especially as they may change over time.

Pledge Agreements and Deposit Agreements

Often associated with deeds of gift are pledges to make a gift and deposit agreements. Though this chapter is not meant to cover these types of agreements, a few words about each might be helpful.

PLEDGE AGREEMENTS

A pledge is a promise to make a gift. State laws vary on the enforceability of such agreements. In New York State, if the institution is able to show sufficient reliance on the promise to make a future gift, the pledge will be enforced and the pledgor will be required to carry through with the gift. At least in New York, it is therefore important to state in a pledge agreement the nature and extent of reliance placed on the promise by the institution.

In the case of a pledge of funds, reliance might mean the institution has engaged architects to commence a building project, has forgone other opportunities for funds or has made public announcements or other public recognition of a pledged gift. The agreement should be clear and explicit, and should contain an agreed upon timetable as to when and how the donation—be it funds or materials—will be made. Recognize, though, that it may be more difficult to establish reliance on a pledge to donate a collection than on a pledge to donate cash or funds.

DEPOSIT AGREEMENTS

Deposit agreements, too, need to be clear and explicit. Of particular importance in drafting them is identifying who bears the risk of loss or damage, who insures, what use the institution can make of the deposited materials (if any), any duty the institution has to expend its own resources to conserve or preserve the materials and mechanisms for the depositor's access to or withdrawal of the material from the institution. As we all know, deposits are accepted with the hope that eventually the materials will be donated to the institution. This does not always occur. Yet in the interim, the depositor gets free storage, often in an archival environment, which is more secure from theft, fire or other damage than is the donor's home or office. Once out of sight, the materials remain out of mind while the institution is dedicating valuable space and resources to someone else's materials. As a result, it is often useful to include in deposit agreements a term of years after which the agreement will be reviewed, or the terms under which the institution may return the deposited materials. If the institution takes over more than storage responsibilities such as inventorying, organizing or cataloging materials, or placing them in acid free folders, for example, this is a use of valuable institutional resources that might only benefit the depositor and some subsequent donee institution. Perhaps a recapture of such costs can be included in the deposit agreement in the event the materials are not subsequently donated to your institution.

Charitable Tax Deduction Considerations Concerning Gifts-in-Kind

Unlike with gifts of cash or marketable securities, when gifts-in-kind are made to a nonprofit, the Internal Revenue Code and Regulations (section 170 and regulations thereunder) require special attention. In 1984, as a result of a trend toward greater disclosure and perceived abuse by taxpayers and institutions relating to the valuation of in-kind gifts for income tax deduction purposes, Congress requested that the IRS promulgate the rules making the mechanics of claiming a charitable deduction a bit more rigorous. On the part of the taxpayer, a Form 8283 is now a necessary attachment to the income tax return filed for the year in which the in-kind gift was made if the deduction of all noncash gifts is greater than $500. It contains requirements as to valuation appraisal and donee verification of the gift. Also, requirements were placed on the receiving institution in Form 8282. (See http://www.irs.ustreas.gov for a copy of forms 8282 and 8283 and instructions.)

Though the onus is on the donor to ensure he properly complies with the IRS's requirements in this regard, it is important for the donee to be aware of the possibility the donor will lose his deduction because of failure to comply. Though we all assume donative intent on the donor's behalf is the driving force for giving gifts, tax deductibility plays no small part in such beneficence. Though you should not "advise" your donor about his tax filings, it may be appropriate to recommend he speak with his accountant and attorney as regards Form 8283 and its requirements, to assure all necessary steps have been taken in timely order to permit a claim for a charitable donation to be made.

FORM 8283

In general, individuals and entities claiming an income tax charitable contribution deduction of noncash gifts (that is, gifts of property other than cash or publicly traded securities) of more than $500 must substantiate the deduction by attaching to their income tax return a completed Form 8283. Without it, the deduction will be disallowed.

The form is structured as follows:

1. Section A requires the donor to identify the donee organization, give a description of the donated property for which a deduction of $5,000 or less (per item or similar group of items) is claimed and provide other information. Note that if a donation is for the tangible property only, with the *donor* retaining for himself the copyright interests, this constitutes a "split gift" and, barring special circumstances, no deduction will be allowed (IRS Code section 170(f)(3)).
2. Section B relates to deductions of more than $5,000 (per item or group of similar items). This section requires an acknowledgment of receipt by the donee institution plus a certification by a qualified appraiser. The donor must have a written appraisal from a qualified appraiser to support a deduction of more than $5,000. If the donor's total deduction for art is $20,000 or more, then the appraisal must be attached to Form 8283 (see Instructions to Form 8283).

QUALIFIED APPRAISAL

The appraisal required in these instances must be a "qualified appraisal" as defined in Treas. Reg. section 1.170 A-13(c)(e)(i)-(ii). First, the appraisal must be made during the period commencing sixty days prior to the date the gift is made, but before the due date for the donor's tax return (including extensions). It must be prepared, signed and dated by a "qualified appraiser."

"QUALIFIED APPRAISER"

It is critical that the appraiser meets the strict definition of a "qualified appraiser." If not, the risk is great that the deduction will be disallowed. To be a "qualified appraiser,"

1. the individual must hold himself or herself out to the public as an appraiser;
2. the appraiser must state credentials showing that he or she is qualified to appraise the type of property being valued; and
3. the appraiser should be aware of penalties for overstatements of value.

The following can *never* be a "qualified appraiser":

1. the donor;
2. a party to the transaction in which the donor acquired the property, unless the property is donated within two months of its acquisition and it is appraised at no higher than the donor's acquisition price;
3. the charitable donee;
4. anyone employed by or related to any of the foregoing; or
5. anyone whose relationship to any of the foregoing would cause a reasonable person to question the appraiser's independence.

THE APPRAISAL FEE

The appraisal fee *cannot* be based on the property's appraised value in whole or in part. From the donor's point of view, the cost of the appraisal cannot be claimed as a charitable deduction, nor can it be added to the value of the gift. It may, however, be added to the donor's cost of tax return preparation, portions of which may be deductible (IRS Code section 212(3)). For more thorough guidance in valuations and appraisals, see IRS publication 561, "Determining the Value of Donated Property."

OTHER CONSIDERATIONS

Remember that if the gift is of publicly traded securities, an appraisal or summary appraisal is never required, even if the value exceeds $5,000. But, such gifts of greater than $500 must still be reported by the donor by completing section A of Form 8283 and attaching it to his return.

For gifts of closely held stock, if the value is over $10,000 then both an appraisal and an appraisal summary form are required.

As for donated works of art valued at $20,000 or more, the donor's return must include a copy of the signed appraisal itself (not just a summary), plus 8 × 10 color photos or 4 × 5 color slides of the donated property.

The Institution's Form 8282

Be aware that the charitable donee of gifts-in-kind (or gifts that, generally, are subject to the appraisal rules) must report to the IRS and the donor if it sells or otherwise disposes of the gift within two years of its receipt. There are three exceptions:

1. if the gift was not subject to the appraisal rules, (e.g., marketable securities or a gift-in-kind value under $5,000);
2. if the gift is used in furtherance of the charity's purposes (e.g., a relief organization distributing donated food or medicines); or
3. if the donor certifies in section B, part III of Form 8283 that the value of the gift is $500 or less.

Conclusion

Hopefully, this overview of negotiating and drafting deeds of gift, pledge agreements and deposit agreements, plus some highlights of the tax code as it relates to a donor's charitable gift deductions, offers the curators and librarians of collecting institutions a better understanding of the need to be careful and thorough in crafting such documents, and of other issues to be aware of when negotiating with donors. Again, the objective is clarity in drafting, preserving for the institution its prerogatives in administering its collections, while acceding as appropriate to the donors' and benefactors' wishes. This will all aid in caressing—not biting—the hand that feeds.

Appendix A

LETTER OF MR. CARNEGIE

NEW YORK, 12TH March, 1901.

DR. J. S. BILLINGS,
Director, New York Public Library.

DEAR MR. BILLINGS:

Our conferences upon the needs of Greater New York for Branch Libraries to reach the masses of the people in every district have convinced me of the wisdom of your plans.

Sixty-five branches strike one at first as a large order, but as other cities have found one necessary for every sixty or seventy thousand of population the number is not excessive.

You estimate the average cost of these libraries at, say, $80,000 each, being $5,200,000 for all. If New York will furnish sites for these Branches for the special benefit of the masses of the people, as it has done for the Central Library, and also agree in satisfactory form to provide for their maintenance as built, I should esteem it a rare privilege to be permitted to furnish the money as needed for the buildings, say $5,200,000. Sixty-five libraries at one stroke probably breaks the record, but this is the day of big operations and New York is soon to be the biggest of cities.

Very truly yours,
ANDREW CARNEGIE

Appendix B: Standard Deed of Gift—Short Form

THE NEW YORK PUBLIC LIBRARY, ASTOR, LENOX AND TILDEN FOUNDATIONS

DEED OF GIFT
and
ACCEPTANCE

The undersigned (the "Donor") does hereby unconditionally donate, give, transfer, set over and convey to The New York Public Library, Astor, Lenox and Tilden Foundations (the "Library"), as an absolute and unrestricted gift, all of Donor's right, title and interest in and to the tangible property described below:

Donor further hereby *(strike phrase which is inapplicable) transfers and assigns to the Library / specifically retains* all copyright and other intangible intellectual property rights Donor owns in said property.

Donor hereby represents and warrants that Donor is the sole owner of the above described property and any intangible intellectual property rights therein transferred hereby; that Donor's title thereto is free and clear of all liens and claims and is unencumbered; that none of said property has been unlawfully imported into the United States of America or unlawfully exported from any other country; and that Donor has full power and authority to convey good title thereto to the Library. In separate written documentation, please provide the Library with all information you have regarding the provenance of each item of said property and please indicate your preferred wording for acknowledgement of this gift in such manner as the Library deems appropriate (e.g., possible inclusion in a list of donors).

____

Signature of Donor Date
Print Donor's Name:
Address:

Tel. No.:

ACCEPTED:

The New York Public Library, Astor, Lenox and Tilden Foundations

By: ____

Name: Date
Title:

Appendix C: Deed of Gift Form—Individual Donor

DEED OF GIFT
and
ACCEPTANCE

AGREEMENT made as of the ___ day of _______, 200_ between ______________________________, with an address at

____________________, ______________, ____________

("Donor") and **The New York Public Library, Astor, Lenox and Tilden Foundations**, a New York not-for-profit corporation, with a business address at Fifth Avenue and 42nd Street, New York, New York 10018 (the "Library").

W I T N E S S E T H :

WHEREAS, the Donor is the sole owner of the ________________, as more fully described in Exhibit A attached hereto and made an integral part hereof, (the "Collection); and

WHEREAS, the Donor wishes to donate the Collection to the Library, and the Library wishes to accept such donation.

NOW, THEREFORE, in consideration of the premises and mutual covenants contained herein, the Donor and the Library agree as follows:

1. [Except as limited by Paragraph 2. below,] as of the date hereof, Donor hereby unconditionally donates, gives, transfers, sets over and

conveys to the Library all of Donor's right, title and interest in and to the tangible property constituting the Collection, and the Library hereby accepts such donation.

[2. Donor specifically retains all copyright and other intangible intellectual property rights Donor may have in the Collection.]

3. The Collection will be referred to as the [________________] in the Library's finding aids and for bibliographical purposes.

4. It is understood that the Collection will be made available for research purposes, and may be loaned by the Library to other institutions for exhibition purposes, in accordance with the Library's rules and regulations governing the use of such materials as may be in force from time to time.

5. (a) [Notwithstanding the specific reservation of rights contained in Paragraph 2. above,] it is understood and agreed that the Library may in its sole discretion and without further approval of the Donor:

(i) make copies of or otherwise reproduce in media of the Library's choice all or portions of the Collection for preservation and reference purposes and, in its sole discretion and in such manner as it deems appropriate, may dispose of badly deteriorated portions of the Collection once they have been reproduced; and

(ii) make copies of items in the Collection for researchers and scholars; any usual and standard fees received by the Library for such reproductions or other means of making the Collection accessible to its users will inure solely to the benefit of the Library; and

(iii) display and exhibit (and permit others to display and exhibit) and make copies of items in the Collection for exhibition purposes or other related purposes, including but not limited to exhibition catalogues, promotional materials and posters, brochures and reports about the Collection or the Library, and for other educational purposes.

(b) The Library shall refer third parties requesting permission to reproduce or otherwise use items from the Collection (other than for scholarly and research purposes referred to in subparagraph (a) above) to the Donor, as the holder of the intellectual property rights therein, or the Donor's successors and assigns. Any reproduction or other fees charged by the Library in connection with making items in the Collection accessible to users will inure solely to the benefit of the Library.

(c) The Library shall submit its own requests for permission to make reproductions or other uses of items in the Collection in excess of those permitted by law or pursuant to subparagraph (a) above to the Donor, as the holder of the intellectual property rights therein, or the Donor's successors and assigns. In order to help defray the cost to the Library of processing and caring for the Collection, the Donor agrees that (in addition to any reproduction or other fees charged by the Library which shall inure solely to the benefit of the Library) the Library shall receive _____% of any royalties or similar remuneration payable to the Donor (or the Donor's successors and assigns) that may result from publication, reproductions or other uses of items in the Collection.]

6. Donor, with the approval of the Library, may add to the Collection items similar in subject matter and format to those already in the Collection, and materials so added will be subject to the terms and conditions hereof. The Library may also add to the Collection materials similar in subject matter from other acknowledged sources. Should the Library identify duplicate materials or other items in the Collection that the Library in its sole discretion determines are not in its best interest to retain, [the Library will first offer to return such materials to the Donor. If Donor fails to accept such items,] the Library may dispose of the same as the Library determines appropriate in its sole discretion.

7. The Library agrees that, upon reasonable advance notice, Donor shall have access to the Collection during the regular business hours of the Library and in accordance with the Library's rules and regulations in force from time to time.

8. Donor represents and warrants that Donor is the sole owner of the tangible property comprising the Collection; that[, but for copyright and other intellectual property rights not to be transferred hereby,] Donor's title to the Collection is free and clear of all liens and claims and

is unencumbered; and that Donor has full power and authority to convey to the Library good title to the Collection. [refer to Exhibit B as needed]

9. The Library represents and warrants that it is a not-for-profit corporation duly organized, validly existing and in good standing under the laws of the State of New York; that all necessary corporate action has been taken to make this Deed of Gift binding and enforceable against the Library in accordance with its terms; and that the Library is an organization described in Sections 170(c)(2) and 501(c)(3) of the Internal Revenue Code of 1986 (the "Code"), as amended, and is not a private foundation as described in Section 509(a) of the Code.

10. This Deed of Gift contains the sole agreement between the parties concerning the subject matter hereof; shall not be altered or amended except in writing duly executed by both parties; shall be construed in accordance with the laws of the State of New York; and shall be binding upon and inure to the benefit of the Donor, the Library, and their respective successors and assigns.

IN WITNESS WHEREOF, the parties hereto have executed this Deed of Gift as of the date first above written.

____
[Donor]

The New York Public Library, Astor,
Lenox and Tilden Foundations

By: __________________________
Name:
Title:

STATE OF NEW YORK)
) ss.:
COUNTY OF NEW YORK)

On the ____ day of ______________, 200_, before me personally came ___________________________, to me known, who being by me duly sworn, did depose and say that s/he executed the foregoing instrument.

____

Notary Public

STATE OF NEW YORK)
) ss.:
COUNTY OF NEW YORK)

On the ____ day of ______________, 200_, before me personally came _______________, to me known, who being by me duly sworn, did depose and say that s/he is the ______________ of **THE NEW YORK PUBLIC LIBRARY, ASTOR, LENOX AND TILDEN FOUNDATIONS,** the corporation described in and which executed the foregoing instrument; that s/he duly acknowledged that s/he executed said instrument on behalf of said corporation; that s/he knows the seal of said corporation; that the seal affixed to said instrument is such corporate seal; that it was so affixed by order of the Board of Trustees of said corporation; and that s/he signed her/his name thereto by like order.

____

Notary Public

EXHIBIT A

[description of materials]

[EXHIBIT B]

[If applicable, certified copy of Will, etc.]

CHAPTER 2

The Appraiser and the Appraisal

WHAT MAKES A BOOK VALUABLE?

Andrew M. McLean

Collectors ride their own hobbyhorse.

I can't fathom why anyone would pay much for a bone China teacup and saucer, a set of crystal salt and pepper shakers, or some nineteenth-century political button featuring the face of an unsuccessful and now unknown candidate for the vice presidency. Yet, when riding my own hobbyhorse, I'll quickly shell out $50, $100, or $500 for a book "I have to have!" while someone nearby is aghast that I'd so eagerly pay more than a buck.

And, of course, it is the librarian, archivist, or the museum curator who often ends up with a stable of such hobbyhorses. When collectors donate their collection, on which over the years they have spent time and money, they want to have it appraised "for tax purposes." This means that when I'm asked to appraise, I have to determine what this collection is worth. How do I do it?

Well, let's begin with the question I'm asked most often: "What makes a book valuable?" There is, of course, no short answer to this question. So, allow me to give you the long answer. In doing so, I hope to lay out some parameters for placing monetary value on any object, book or otherwise, that might be donated to a library, archive, or museum. My specialty is appraising books, manuscripts, and other (mainly) literary and historical materials, but my remarks may also help to clarify procedures in valuing other kinds of donations.

My concern is to explain how an appraiser places a value on what is donated, and to comment on what the Internal Revenue Service (IRS) says about all this. In order to do this, I discuss what makes a book valuable, how one locates an appraiser, and how the appraisal is prepared. Finally, in a postscript, I offer a list of reference books and book value guides that I use frequently when preparing an appraisal.

Before I discuss all this, I want to make it clear how important it is that the appraiser maintain objectivity about value. The appraiser often feels pressure from both the donor and the recipient of the gift to exaggerate value. The donor wants a large tax write-off and the institution doesn't want to lose the collection or gift. The most ethical quality of any appraiser is resistance to these pressures, so that he can examine the object physically, represent it accurately in writing for what it is, and place a fair market value (FMV) on the item, according to the appraiser's knowledge of that market.

While I primarily discuss valuing books and manuscripts, the underlying principles apply to other kinds of objects and artifacts that are frequently donated to libraries, museums, archives, and various historical societies.

Three Kinds of Appraisals

There are three kinds of appraisals. One a dealer does for himself or herself when buying inventory for resale. This might involve a box or a roomful of books that the dealer hopes to resell. The second kind of appraisal places value on donated material at what the IRS terms "fair market value." The third kind of appraisal, done for insurance purposes, details the "replacement value" of the items (which is usually higher than a fair market value). Most librarians, archivists, and curators are concerned with having the donor of materials receive a "fair market value" appraisal, which is documented in IRS Form 8283, signed by both the appraiser and the recipient of the gift.

A Dealer Buys Inventory

As to the first kind of appraisal, when I'm buying books for resale in my bookstore, for example, how much I spend is predicated on my answers to four questions: (1) How soon can I expect to turn these books around? (2) How common are they? (3) What do I already have in stock? (4) How much money do I have to spend? These commonsense questions are answered differently by each dealer or book buyer. Keep in mind that it is not uncommon for a book to sit on a bookstore's shelf for many years before a customer buys it. A wise book buyer is always aware of overhead, storage, advertising, and the myriad other business expenses that go into owning a book. (Generally, if a book doesn't sell in a store within a few years, the dealer has made no money on the sale when the book sells.)

The IRS and Fair Market Value

The second kind of appraisal, the kind I do for a donor who gives a collection of books or related material to a university library, for example, is based on what the IRS calls "fair market value." The IRS defines "fair market value" as "the price at which property would change hands between a willing buyer and a willing seller, neither being under a compulsion to buy or sell, and both having reasonable knowledge of relevant factors" (see Income Tax Regs. section 1.170A-1(c)(2)). Essentially this means that the value of the book (or object) is approximately what it would sell for in a reputable used book (or antique) store, or in a reputable art gallery. Put another way, the item is worth what a buyer is willing to pay in the free and open marketplace.

In one sense, this rule of thumb can often make an appraisal of a large ad hoc collection of books fairly easy. One can count up how many books there are, categorize them in some way—some at a dollar a book, some at five, others at ten, fifty, or whatever group price is reasonable—and add up the value of each category. For example, someone donates one thousand books to the university's library. I determine that half of them might reasonably sell at $2 each, a quarter at $10 each and the rest between $50 and $100. If my addition is correct, this collection could be appraised at a fair market value of some $16,000. Then I fill out and sign the appraiser's portion of IRS Form 8283, send off my bill, and wait for my fee to arrive in the mail.

But if it were only so easy!

While some donations can be handled this way, that's usually not the case. In fact, a good collection of anything usually involves a myriad of the unexpected: of something not encountered before, of something "rare," "scarce," or unique (usually the reason the donor bought it in the first place), or as in many cases, a collection that has a focus or theme that makes it more interesting than just a random quantity of books or buttons or bows. It's often the "hobbyhorse factor" that makes a collection desirable for the institution to acquire after the collector's hobbyhorse has finally gone to pasture (in one way or another).

Old Is Not Necessarily Valuable

First, let me say the age of a book often has little to do with its value.

The older I get, the more I realize that "old" is relative. For example, I frequently get calls asking about the value of "really old" books printed in 1941 (my year of birth), or about "antique" books that are "over one hundred years old." How old is "old"? First, in the book trade we don't use the word "antique" to discuss or describe books. There is a cognate word we use, as in "*antiquarian* book dealer." This doesn't mean, however, that the book dealer is old. It usually means that this dealer has a selection of better quality books from the sixteenth to nineteenth centuries, and probably an assortment of more collectible books that are signed, first editions, limited printings, well illustrated, or finely bound.

These last qualities take us to the heart of the matter. What makes a book valuable is usually what makes it different from the millions of other books that have been published.

It goes without saying, but I'll say it anyway: the author and subject of the book or manuscript is always important. No library wants the drafts or notes of the books I've written, none are asking to house my voluminous correspondence as an editor of a scholarly journal for twenty-two years, and there's been no interest in my marginal notes in the hundreds of scholarly books shelved in my personal library. However, if this were the correspondence of William Faulkner, the manuscripts of early Hemingway writings, or John Milton's notes in the margins of his books, we'd have a grand auction at hand. Subject matter and author do matter, most of the time, but not always in the ways one might think.

What Makes One Book Different from Another?

Getting back to the heart of what makes a book valuable. Let's talk about how the book is made and what unique qualities a given book might have. Leaving subject matter and authorship aside for the moment, let's consider a few of these differences: bindings, limited editions, first editions, author's signatures or inscriptions, and some other ways that may distinguish one book from another.

The Paper and the Binding

A book comprises printed pages that are gathered together in groupings, sewn together, and bound over with some material. (A "gathering" is when one sheet of paper, printed on both sides, is folded and sewn through the centerfold.) Prior to around 1870, paper used in books was made of rag (cotton) as opposed to wood pulp. Rag paper has a much lower acid content and thus doesn't "brown" as quickly as wood-pulp paper does. This browning effect, known as *foxing*, is caused by some kind of acidic reaction in the paper. Since their paper is made of rag, you'll often find sixteenth- and seventeenth-century books in remarkably pristine condition. Many years ago I appraised a copy of a Koberger Bible printed in 1484. The book was in such pristine condition that at first glance I assumed it was a facsimile reproduction of the original. But it wasn't. The heavy rag paper covered in a strong vellum cover had been well taken care of for over five hundred years. (This Koberger Bible is also an example of *incunabula*, a term used to distinguish books printed before around 1500.)

A quality rag paper, often handmade, is often used in limited printings or private press books. Often there is a statement in the *colophon* at the end of the book identifying the type of paper used, the type font used in producing the book, and any limitation or signature of designer or illustrator.

Usually books are bound in paper or cloth, but they can be bound in any material. Leather bindings generally enhance the look and value of a book, but this will vary in the quality of leather used and the craftsmanship involved in binding the book. It might have an ornate spine design, or elaborate hand tooling on the cover. Books can be bound in full leather, half leather (only the spine is leather), or three-quarters in leather (the spine and corners only in leather). The bookbinder might be very famous, or this might be one of only five copies bound in leather or vellum or aluminum.

Aluminum? Well, the Limited Editions Club issued Ray Bradbury's *Fahrenheit 451* bound in aluminum, and there is a private printing of Edwin Abbott's *Flatland* also bound in aluminum. Books have been bound in plastic, linen, wood, velvet, and other materials. I have a large folio-sized sixteenth-century book the covers of which are English oak covered in leather with lovely brass studs at each corner. Books of the Victorian period often have velvet, mother of pearl, or other materials in ornately designed covers.

Limited Printings

A limited printing means that only so many copies of this book have been printed. Somewhere in the book, usually in the front or rear *endpaper* (those blank pages found at the front and rear of a book), there is a statement to this effect. The idea is that only so many copies of this book in this format are available. Clearly the size of limitation is important. "One of fifty copies" is quite different from "one of twenty-five hundred copies." The Limited Editions Club, for example, has "limited" production to fifteen hundred numbered copies signed by author or illustrator. Some of these books sell for under a $100, while others sell for thousands, especially those illustrated by Matisse and Picasso. Obviously, the smaller the limitation, the more potential value the book might have.

Illustrations

Books have been illustrated almost from the beginning of printing. They can be illustrated in numerous ways, depending on the technology of the times: by hand coloring; lithographs; wood, copper, or steel engravings; tipped-in color plates; photographs; line drawings; and other means. An artist or author might even make an original drawing in the book. Illustrations can add to a book's beauty as well as to its value. But who is the artist and what is the process? Marc Chagall's *Jerusalem Windows* (1962) is a handsome book. The trade edition sells for around $40, while the edition that includes two original Chagall lithographs sells for $1,400.

Signed Books, Presentation Copies, and Association Copies

Had Chagall presented a copy of his *Jerusalem Windows* to Picasso with a short inscription saying something like, "Dear Pablo, Thank you for telling me I couldn't paint and that I should try making stained glass instead. Always your pupil, Marc," what a unique copy we'd have. What this fictitious copy has going for it is that it is signed by a major artist, it's associated with another major figure of the twentieth-century art world, it includes original artwork, and it has a tantalizing bit of biographical information in its inscription. Generally there isn't much difference in value between a signed book (one with the author's autograph) and a presentation copy (in which the author says "To John Doe"). Unless, of course, John Doe is someone of note or importance. "To Tom, wishing you well in the presidency, John Adams," for example, would contain a wonderfully double joy for the book collector or librarian to own regardless of what the book itself was.

But we should remind ourselves that there are thousands of books signed by authors we never heard of and given to people we don't know anything about, and even though these may be nicely bound, illustrated, and limited printings, they still might have little commercial value.

First Editions and Modern First Editions

Everyone assumes, erroneously, that being a first edition makes a book valuable. A first edition of a book means the first printing of the book. Clear enough, but perhaps not really so. For book collectors, *first edition* means the *first impression*, or copies printed from one continuous operation of the press. When changes to the text occur after the book has been published, a second or later *issue* occurs. This is the stuff bibliographers thrive upon, and frequently alters the value of a given book. Determining the first printing, first issue, second issue, and so on of a book demands professional bibliographic help. We look for *issue points*, places in the text where changes were made that help us to determine which copy we have in our hand. A standard source for American authors, for example, is Jacob Blanck's *Bibliography of American Literature*, and I'll just cite some of his comments on two of Mark Twain's books.

The Adventures of Huckleberry Finn was published in London in 1884. Blanck notes a Canadian edition a few months later, and then in New York in 1885. Chronologically, the London edition is the "first" edition, but the New York "first" edition usually commands three to four times the value of the London edition. The New York edition was published in green or blue cloth (and various leather bindings), with green cloth being the most common. There are several issue points to help identify this copy. For example, the first issue has "was" for "saw" (on page 57, line 23) and "Him and another man" is given in a list of illustrations as being on page 88. Twain's *Life on the Mississippi* was published in London and New York in 1883, and Blanck describes a first state and second state of the New York edition. The first issue has a drawing of the author in flames (on page 441) and a caption (on page 443) reading, "The St. Louis Hotel," which in the second issue reads "St. Charles Hotel." And there are many more points I won't bore you with.

Enthusiasts who collect first editions often forget that most books printed only appeared as first editions. They were never reprinted. At present there is a little bit of madness in the book world about collecting modern first editions. This includes books published only a few years ago that can command prices from $300 to $1,500 or more. Some first editions of Tom Clancy, Stephen King, and Amy Tan, among other contemporary writers, for example, are selling for more than many a "classic" English or American author. Yet, when all is said and done about first editions, limitation, and signed, illustrated, and finely bound copies, the final and perhaps most compelling factor in book value is the physical condition of the book.

Condition, Condition, Condition

"Well, it's in good shape for its age" is often the novice's explanation of condition. But we've already dismissed the age fallacy for books. Recall that 1484 Koberger Bible in pristine condition after five hundred years. While it is uncommon to find a Koberger Bible in such pristine condition, it is not uncommon to find books that are hundreds of years old in very fine condition.

It's important to describe the physical condition of a book carefully. Book dealers spend a lot of time doing this and usually rate books as *mint* (as issued, but few books fall into this category), *fine* (the book is almost like new), *very good* (shows some signs of wear but no defects), *Good* (shows normal age and wear, but still no defects), and so on. There are various guidelines for such descriptions (see, for example, Shoshana Edwards on condition for abebooks.com), but the point here is how important it is in an appraisal to describe the physical condition of the book. I wouldn't do this for every book in a large appraisal, but I would take care to do it for books of some value because it affects the book's value. A binding is usually described when defects are present in terms such as "joints tender," "cover detached," and "rubbed corners."

Related to the physical condition of the modern book is whether or not it has a dust jacket (or dust wrapper), that paper cover that wraps around the binding. (Toys and dolls, for example, often increase in value if the original box is present.) The book's dust jacket is always described separately from the book, and its presence or absence can significantly affect book value. Collectors of modern first editions, for example, might pay $500 for a first edition in dust jacket and fine condition, but only $150 or less were the dust jacket absent, badly chipped, or torn.

Finding an Appraiser

I hope I have indicated a few of the many obstacles a book appraiser, or appraiser of any object, encounters when evaluating and valuing books and other objects. How does an appraiser learn to do this, one might ask, and where are good appraisers found? Unfortunately, this is not an easy question to answer, and there is both good news and bad news about finding an experienced appraiser.

The bad news (well, not all that bad) is that there is no licensing requirement for appraisers, no set curriculum to study leading to a B.S. in appraisal science (or, if linguistic skills are required, it might be a B.A. degree), and no universally recognized certificate at hand to assert an appraiser is qualified. The good news is that there are a variety of associations of appraisers that promote standards and offer some minimum qualifications to look for in appraisers. These organizations include the Appraisal Association of America, the American Society of Appraisers, and the International Society of Appraisers. This latter organization (see www.appraisalfoundation.org) annually revises its Uniform Standards of Professional Appraisal Practices, and many of these groups are teaming up with academic institutions to offer appraisal workshops and training in specific areas. There are also specialized professional organizations, such as the Antiquarian Bookseller's Association of America (abaa.org), which can refer one to dealers specializing in particular subject areas, and which have high standards for their membership.

Experience is the best quality to look for in an appraiser, and word of mouth the best reference for finding one. By talking with other archivists, librarians, or curators who have used different appraisers, or by seeking suggestions from local banks or insurance companies that have used appraisers for specific purposes, one can begin to locate qualified people. Once an appraiser is identified, one should look at the appraiser's years of experience in doing the kinds of appraisals you want done. In addition, one should examine the appraiser's educational background, publications, lecture or speaking engagements, memberships in professional societies, and above all, the references supplied.

If I may immodestly use my own qualifications as an example, I'll admit I don't fill all of my own criteria. I do not belong to any of the fine appraisal organizations mentioned above or to the ABAA; I don't speak often about appraising, nor have I published anything specifically about appraising. But while I've never attended a workshop or course dealing with learning how to appraise anything, I have given some. And I do have over twenty-five years experience appraising, and can supply some respectable references. I also own a bookstore in which I buy and sell books in the open market, and I read dealer catalogs and book auction records like kids read comic books. These activities keep me well tuned to what is or isn't "fair market value" for a given book. I also have a few educational advantages over most appraisers.

Having earned a Ph.D. in Renaissance English literature, I'm well acquainted with "old" books, the history of printing, bibliographic procedures, and how to do detailed research on a given topic. In the course of my academic research, I've worked in most major American and European libraries, I speak several languages, and I've published four books (including a bibliography). I have also written numerous articles and reviews, and done many other academically specialized activities that ensure my thoroughness and ability in approaching an appraisal. But most importantly, my academic background makes me admit rather quickly what I don't know. I am quick to recognize that frequently when doing an appraisal I need to call in the help of others who know more about this or that than I do.

Often this advice comes from archivists, curators, other book dealers, or collectors who have more concrete understanding of particular items being appraised. No appraiser knows everything, and every appraisal is a learning experience. This is why experience is the most important qualification for an appraiser, and it is the excitement of meeting a new challenge that keeps a good appraiser alert and always learning.

Appraisal Fees and the Appraiser's Liability

Appraisal fees should never be a percentage of the appraised value. This is clearly unethical. An appraiser should charge a per diem or hourly rate agreed to by whomever is paying the bill. A good appraiser can usually estimate the time it will take to complete an appraisal, although for a large collection of material, one is never certain what to expect. Generally it's a good idea for the appraiser to have a written agreement or contract that outlines the services to be provided and the purpose of the appraisal, provides for the right to examine the items, and perhaps sets a maximum fee (that might be renegotiated at a later date). For some appraisals it is appropriate to provide photographs of the items.

While the IRS does not require an appraisal for (and requires minimal documentation for) property worth less than $500, for donations between $500 and $5,000, IRS Form 8283 must be filed with the taxpayer's return with a statement about how fair market value was determined. For donations valued over $5,000, Form 8283 must be signed by a "qualified appraiser," and by a representative of the institution acknowledging receipt of the gift. Generally, for gifts over $20,000, the appraiser must attach full documentation about the determination of value.

The appraiser is liable for the value of a donation, and can be subject to penalties (including fines and imprisonment) for willfully aiding or assisting in preparing fraudulent documents to the IRS (on which see Internal Revenue Code, sections 6701 and 7206). It's legally significant for the appraiser to be accurate in determining fair market value and to provide as accurate a description as possible of what's being valued. Appraising, however, is not a science; it is clearly an art. Frequently the appraiser makes "educated guesses" based on experience and knowledge of the marketplace in order to come up with a *reasonable value* for the donated objects.

Allow me to offer one quick example. I recently appraised a collection consisting of 152 taped interviews, transcripts, and computer disks that were produced as part of the research done for a book published about the Civil Rights movement. The donation by the author conveyed his rights to these interviews, which included interviews with leading civil rights activists, and because it included interviews with many local people, the collection was a rich oral history about an important historic moment and involving major players. The contents of this collection were described in fourteen pages. When considering the value of this material, I had to consider first the question of authorship and use. Because the author donated this material, material he used in producing a commercial venture, i.e., his book, I could only value the material based on the costs the author incurred for tapes, transcriptions, and so on. One way to get at value was to determine that transcribing tapes usually costs about $20 an hour, and that it usually takes some five to eight hours to transcribe every hour of tape. Of course, if someone other than the author had donated this material, the actual appraised value would have been significantly higher.

The Qualified Appraisal

What an appraisal should include is clearly outlined in "IRS Publication 561: Determining the Value of Donated Property." It is a helpful list of considerations and I quote it here almost verbatim:

1. A description of the property in sufficient detail to determine that the property appraised is the property that was contributed.
2. The physical condition of any tangible property.
3. The date of contribution, and the terms of any agreement entered into by or on behalf of the donor.

4. Identification and qualifications of the "qualified appraiser."
5. A statement that the appraisal was prepared for income tax purposes.
6. The date(s) on which the property was valued, and the fair market value on the date of the contribution.
7. The method of valuation used to determine fair market value, and the specific basis for the valuation, such as any comparable sales transactions.

Resources for Appraising Book Values

The best guides to fair market value are dealer catalogs. and current auction prices. There are a variety of such resources mentioned below that major libraries should have. In addition, electronic sales networks for the used book market are growing (e.g., Advanced Book Exchange, at abebooks.com and Bibliofind, at bibliofind.com) and provide a kind of immediate online catalog. However, because almost anyone can get online and sell books, there is often a wide discrepancy in prices quoted for the same book, and bibliographic descriptions are often vague. I should also add a word of caution about using e-mail auctions as price guides. Again, anyone can sell at auction, and one person's honest description of an object might be totally inadequate. In addition, an auction price only reflects what someone at that particular auction is willing to pay at that moment, and this may have little to do with "fair market value." (I once bought a $1,200 [FMV] book at auction for $250 at a reputable book auction because I was the *only* bidder!) "Buyer beware" is the motto of buying at *any* auction, e-mail or otherwise.

Below is a short list of reference books and guides to book values that I find helpful and use frequently in preparing appraisals.

REFERENCE BOOKS

Balay, Robert, ed. *Guide to Reference Books.* 11th ed. Chicago: American Library Association, 1996. A cornucopia of information about books and serials often needed by the appraiser for specialized information.

Blanck, Jacob N. (continued by Michael Winship). *Bibliography of American Literature.* 9 vols. New Haven: Yale University Press, 1955–91. Detailed bibliographic accounts of books by American authors from the mid-nineteenth century to about 1931.

Buchsbaum, Ann. *Practical Guide to Print Collecting.* Rev. and expanded ed. New York: Van Nostrand Reinhold, 1975. A practical introduction to the subject, as is William M. Iviris Jr., *How Prints Look.*

Carter, John. *The ABC for Book Collectors.* 7th ed. New Castle, Del.: Oak Knoll, 1995. Surely the best volume that defines and explains terms used in the book trade and in book collecting.

Gascoigne, Bamber. *How to Identify Prints.* New York: Thames and Hudson, 1988. A readable guide to the manual and mechanical processes from woodcuts to ink jet, well illustrated, and with a glossary of terms helpful in understanding illustrations in books.

Iviris, William M. Jr. *How Prints Look.* Boston: Beacon, 1987.

Peters, Jean, ed. *The Bookman's Glossary.* 6th ed. New York: Bowker, 1983. The standard reference for all aspects of the book trade.

Zempel, Edward N., and Linda A. Verkler, eds. *First Editions: A Guide to Identification. Statements of Selected North American, British Commonwealth, and Irish Publishers on Their Methods of Designating First Editions.* 3d ed. Peoria, Ill.: Spoon River, 1995. The best current book on this subject.

PRICE GUIDES TO BOOK VALUES

Ahern, Allen, and Patricia Ahern. *Collected Books: The Guide to Values.* New York: Putnam, 1991. Read prefatory matter carefully about how to use this useful guide.

Bradley, Van Allen. *The Book Collector's Handbook of Values, 1982–83.* New York: Putnam's, 1982. The last of several volumes, it lists about twenty thousand titles and upon which Ahern develops his work.

American Book Prices Current (ABPC). New York: American Book Prices Current, 1895–. Invaluable annual gathering auction prices realized for books, manuscripts, maps, etc. Many five-year cumulative indexes are available.

Book Price Index (BPI). Detroit: Gale Research, 1964–. Invaluable guide to book prices based on prices from used booksellers' catalogs. Cumulative indexes available.

Book Prices: Used and Rare. Peoria, Ill.: Spoon River, 1993–. Useful for valuing more commonly found books, and most helpful in appraising when used in conjunction with *BPI* and *ABPC.*

Howes, Wright. *U.S.iana (1650–1950).* Rev. ed. New York: Bowker, 1962. A comprehensive list of rare and scarce ("uncommon and significant") Americana, which is graded by relative monetary value. While prices have changed, the relative values of items are about the same today.

TWO USEFUL BOOKS THAT FIT IN YOUR POCKET

Chidley, John. *Discovering Book Collecting* (1982, subsequent reprintings). It's hard to believe how much is covered in these readable and well-illustrated pages; a good read for anyone.

McBride, Bill. *A Pocket Guide to the Identification of First Editions.* 5th ed. West Hartford, Conn.: McBride, 1995. The very concise version of Zempel and Verkler.

CHAPTER 3

Tort Theory in Library, Museum and Archival Collections, Materials, Exhibits, and Displays

RIGHTS OF PRIVACY AND PUBLICITY IN PERSONAL INFORMATION AND PERSONA

Tomas A. Lipinski

This chapter discusses the application of two legal concepts, the right of privacy and the right of publicity as each concept might apply to the collections or holdings of libraries, museums and archives. The substantive legal issue is whether the law limits in some way the use, commercial (right of publicity) or otherwise (right of privacy), by the library, museum, archive or its patrons of the personal items, records, effects, or representations of a particular individual that happen to be in its collections.

Right of Privacy

The right of privacy includes four possible grounds for action: intrusion into seclusion, public disclosure of private facts, false light, and (mis)appropriation.[1] Like the right of publicity, the right of privacy varies from state to state, making a complete and accurate discussion impossible. However, several general comments may be made.

For a cause of action involving intrusion into seclusion, several elements must be present. First, there must be some sort of prying or intrusion. Second, this intrusion must be offensive to a reasonable person. Third, the prying or intrusion must be into an area in which a person is entitled to privacy. "If an action, no matter how embarrassing, is recorded or photographed in public, there can be no intrusion to seclusion because there is no protection of anything that occurs in public."[2] Obviously if the library, museum or archive, in an attempt to collect a "record" (e.g., a recording, videotape or photograph) of such private facts for its collection, intruded into a person's seclusion, a cause of action would conceivably lie. However, in most cases the item (the record of the private fact, e.g., a recording, videotape or photograph) would have been donated to the library, museum or archive. Liability would lie with the original intruder into that seclusion. This is true because "[t]he tort does not require that information be obtained or material be taken . . . or that the fruits of the intrusion be published or otherwise publicized."[3] Since the library, museum or archive did not perform the actual invasion of the privacy there should be no legal liability. Action would more properly lie against the original recorder, videotaper, or photographer.

It is important to note that the right of privacy generally does not survive death (as opposed to the right of publicity, which may in some states). If the data subject is deceased, then no claim for intrusion, or any other privacy right for that matter, is possible. Furthermore, consent is always a defense to an invasion of privacy. If the original recorder, taper, photographer, etc. obtained permission and has documentary proof of that consent, again no cause of action will exist. However, if the library, museum or archive intends to display or publish (somehow make public) the recording, tape, or photograph, then a cause of action for disclosure of private facts (if there is no record of consent and the subject is still living) may indeed lie (see the discussion about this below). In contrast, merely holding documentation (audiotape, videotape or photograph) of the embarrassing intrusion would not trigger this right (intrusion into seclusion), nor would a mere holding of the item appear to trigger an action for public disclosure (see discussion below). As stated earlier, an action would more properly lie against the original recorder of the intrusion, not against the library, museum or archive that subsequently holds the item (documentation of the intrusion) in its collections.

For the actions of a library, museum or archive to violate a person's right to privacy vis-à-vis a public disclosure of private facts requires that a public disclosure of embarrassing private facts that would be objectionable to the reasonable person be made. Suppose an item has come into the possession of the library, museum or archive: would the mere holding of the item in its research collection be a disclosure for purposes of the rights of privacy? It would appear unlikely, unless an expanded reading of the *Hotaling v. Church of Latter Day Saints*[4] decision is applicable. However, tort law (distribution under a right of privacy: disclosure of private facts) is not the same as copyright law (right of distribution). More than a simple disclosure or distribution vis-à-vis library, museum or archival collection access is needed. "The defendant's acts must *publicize* the private information in a highly offensive manner. This tort does not deal with mere *disclosure*, but offensive publicity."[5] However, once the library, museum or archive desires to display, exhibit or otherwise publish the documentation of the invasion—the disclosure of the private embarrassing fact—and actively promotes that display or exhibit, a cause of action might lie. The remaining question is whether the display or exhibit could be said to constitute an "offensive publicity." Consider a photographic exhibit entitled "American Political Maneuvers," consisting of images of famous political figures caught on film in the rapture of passion, say from Gary Hart to Ted Kennedy. If the museum, library or archive ran advertisements hawking this exhibit, not merely in bad taste, it might also constitute offensive publicity.

An exception does exist for those private facts that are of a "legitimate public interest or concern."[6] Determining the boundaries of "legitimate public interest" is often difficult. One standard often employed is newsworthiness; another is a public official standard, i.e., whether the subject is a public servant. In contrast, "the antithesis of newsworthiness is idle curiosity, prying and the resulting gossip of others. Such gossip has little if any currency (it may be passed on for years) and cannot be related in any meaningful way to the nature or functioning of society. Such idle curiosity, prying and gossip is outside the newsworthiness protective shield."[7] If an issue arises as to whether a display or exhibit of an embarrassing private fact of a living person is of "legitimate public interest," recall that consent is always a defense to an invasion of privacy. Thus it is always advisable "to seek a written release from a living subject of a photograph [or other representation] that it [the library, museum or archive] intends to exhibit, especially if the individual is readily identifiable and if the photograph could be viewed as embarrassing."[8] Furthermore, courts appear especially sensitive to disclosures based upon photographic documentation, thus obtaining permission to display (even short of publication) is always advisable.

False light also requires a highly offensive public disclosure, but differs from the disclosure "branch" of privacy invasion in that it requires the disclosure place someone in a false light with the public. Some states require an additional element: that the defendant must act with knowledge of the falsity or reckless disregard as to veracity.[9] Of the four branches of privacy invasions, this appears the least articulated or rationalized.[10] "It may be all that can be said is that false light protects against the mental upset, embarrassment or humiliation from attention and publicity that is generated by false communications to the public, or, if one is already in the public eye and not adverse to attention and publicity, the mental distress, embarrassment or humiliation resulting from the assault on dignity from false portrayal."[11] Several jurisdictions have rejected false light as an actionable tort claim.[12] Another state legislature has rejected false light right by simply not including it in its privacy statute.[13] The difference between disclosure and false light is that in false light latter facts disclosed have to be false. "[F]alse light actions deal with untruths that put a person in a false light with the public. In false light cases, it is important to remember that the facts disclosed have to be false or make false implications."[14] A classic example is *Uhl v. CBS, Inc.*,[15] in which a public official and hunter was shown in a highly edited television documentary to be shooting geese that were merely standing on the ground instead of flying.

A focus upon "[o]ffensive publicity in this context tends to consist of linking an unrelated person with controversial issues (e.g., drug use, prostitution, sexual attitudes, gambling) through the unauthorized use of photographs, attributions of opinion, or use of name on a petition or in a lawsuit."[16] Consider the facts of the *Uhl* case. If the library, museum or archive undertook the steps to create such a work (on audiotape, videotape or photograph) and then disclosed its contents within a documentary about hunting, a cause of action would lie. But what if an artist has done the same in an attempt to provide some sort of social commentary, satire or parody and the museum displayed or exhibited the work? An infamous example was the controversy generated over a painting exhibited in the School of the Art Institute of Chicago that portrayed former mayor Harold Washington garbed in women's undergarments.[17] In general, under tort law principles (defamation, for example) a publisher or republisher is as liable as the creator or original publisher, thus the library, museum or archive that displays or exhibits the work would be just as liable.[18] In response, the artist-creator or the library, museum or archive would claim protection from the First Amendment and such expressions would generally be protected.[19] However, because the information being released to the public is false in a false light claim, the protection afforded the disseminator on the basis of free speech may arguably be weaker.[20] Suffice it to say that the balance between the right of privacy and the First Amendment is delicate and still subject to judicial tinkering.[21]

The final privacy right is appropriation. While appropriation is similar to the right of publicity (discussed below) and, according to at least one commentator, eventually evolved into it,[22] appropriation nonetheless remains a separate tort right. Another explanation of the relationship between the two causes of action is that the right of privacy appropriation consists of two separate subspecies of claims: one dignitary, the other proprietary. The proprietary interest forms the basis for the right of publicity. The elements include the unauthorized use for the defendant's advantage of the plaintiff's name or likeness. Obvious prohibited takings would include the use of an individual's image of likeness in library, museum or archive promotional material without the subject's permission. Again the First Amendment (covering art, commentary, criticism, parody, newsworthiness, etc.) offers protection for publishers or republishers, including libraries, museums and archives. However, "[t]he limit of First Amendment protection is reached when the media engage in fraudulent exploitation of an individual's name, likeness or persona to sell their product"[23] or, logically, to increase membership or patronage or readership.

Right of Publicity

Another legal concept that may impact the use of materials in a library, museum or archive is the right of publicity. A scenario triggering the application of this concept would be the institution's use of the image or likeness (photographs, drawings, audio or video recording) or persona of an individual in some commercial way. In order for the right to be triggered, the name, likeness or persona (personal attribute) of the person must be used or it must be recognized as deriving from the subject individual, as in the case of a look-alike or sound-alike. That use or derivation must of course be unauthorized. The right of publicity places an enforceable property interest in the unauthorized commercial use of a person's name, likeness, or other personal attribute. The unauthorized use must also cause commercial harm. The originator (the person or persona subject) must derive an economic benefit from his or her persona and the unauthorized use must somehow detract or interfere with the economic interest the originator has in it. Using a picture of a famous model in a calendar[24] or poster of a famous sports star on a T-shirt[25] are two common examples. Use of a person's likeness or persona in a similar way, even if for the purposes of library, museum or archive promotion (arguably a "good cause") still requires the permission of the owner (the individual subject or their assignee or, in cases of descendibility, their estate).

The concept developed out of the right of privacy's prohibition against the use of a person's name, likeness or persona without permission to the defendant's advantage.[26] Over time, public fixation with celebrities coupled with the rapid development of mass media and mass communications forced courts and legislatures to slowly expand the right of privacy concept. The right of privacy doctrine of persona misappropriation was thus expanded into a special right of publicity for those persons who as a result of their celebrity status have amassed commercial value in their persona or likeness.[27] According to Nimmer,[28] "[t]he right of publicity mediates between the person and the user of the image or other identifying characteristic." Like other intellectual property laws, it creates an incentive mechanism. The incentive is established through the grant of an economic interest in the fruits of publicity or celebrity status. The enticement of an economic interest encourages individuals to enter the public mainstream, become celebrities and, though a debatable benefit to be sure, in theory, contribute to the richness of life for all members of society.

The right of publicity also has a moral or just component to it. The doctrine was created to prevent the unjust enrichment through the unauthorized use of another's goodwill.[29] "The importance and value of this right have become such common knowledge that courts have taken judicial notice of the commercial exploitation of celebrity figures."[30] The most interesting aspect is that the doctrine not only protects against unauthorized use of a photograph, but also the use of look-alikes and sound-alikes, which might create the false impression of a celebrity association.[31] The right of publicity is intended to protect "the essence of the person, his or her identity or persona from being unwillingly or unknowingly misappropriated for the profit of another."[32] The misuse of one's persona is also an unfair trade practice under section 43(a) of the Lanham Act[33] if the use creates confusion as to the celebrity's endorsement of the advertised product or service. Protectable interests have also included nicknames,[34] characters created by performers,[35] and even distinctive entertainment styles.[36] While the concept may have developed to the point that it covers a purely commercial or economic interest, there is still much it can offer the present discussion. "[M]odern case law separates private people from celebrities. One group (private people) are concerned about their own persona as something personal to them [a privacy right]. Celebrities have committed their image to the public and are concerned about controlling exploitation of the image."[37]

Recall the American Library Association (ALA) promotional "READ" posters that have become so common an appurtenance in libraries. The posters often display some celebrity in an appropriate promotional pose—reading, using the library, etc. A recent poster of actress Renee O'Connor portrays Gabrielle, the companion of Xena, on the television program *Xena Warrior Princess.* In the poster, O'Connor is posed on the set of *Xena Warrior Princess* and in costume; the caption reads, "SHARE a story the legacy," with, in small type, "Gabrielle for America's Libraries." To use the poster, the ALA had to secure the permission of the television program's creators (the owner of the fictional character Gabrielle). And in addition to the show's creators, O'Connor has as economic interest in her "realization" of the Gabrielle character, i.e., the association of Gabrielle with Renee O'Connor in the minds of fans. In other words, O'Connor could most likely prohibit the ALA from using another boyish-looking athletic blond female dressed in pseudomedieval garb, in a pseudomedieval setting, and in a similar promotion with the same caption. This is an example of the wide reach of economic rights protected by the right of publicity.

Rights of publicity cannot be disassociated from the person from whom they derive, although the right may be assigned. These rights allow one to control the commercial interest resulting from his/her popularity or prevent the exploitation of the person to whom a name, likeness or image relates.[38] While similar to the appropriation right of privacy, the right of publicity maintains a slightly different focus. At present, the right of publicity is not attributable to groups of persons or to a type of person, like a tomboy or mythical female soldier. In general, the right does not survive death. However, the type of right it protects—commercial appropriation of a valuable market interest—albeit the marketability of a living person (in most states) or their persona, is consistent with the stated goals of the protection mechanisms under discussion. Having the holder of that right, in this case a celebrity, control how others may portray his or her image to the world would also be consistent with curbing the types of harms documented earlier. A recent example is the dispute regarding the nude Nancy Kerrigan web site. Kerrigan, a figure skater, is objecting to a web site that displays pictures of her in the nude.[39] In reality the pictures are cropped or doctored. Nancy Kerrigan has never posed or skated in the nude, thus an action for false light might also lie. The point behind a right of publicity analysis as applied to these facts is that if anyone has the right to profit from nude pictures of Nancy Kerrigan, real or fake, it is Nancy Kerrigan.

The problem of descendibility occurs because when the right is applied to an individual, whose life is fixed or limited, it is logical to impose some temporal limit. As a result, few states have extended their right of publicity statutes to protect commercial persona interests after the individual is deceased[40] or have provided for transferability.[41] As with the right of privacy, the right of publicity is not without limit. As a compromise, the postmortem extension of the right of publicity requires commercial exploitation during the subject's lifetime.[42] Courts have carved out exceptions for the newsworthiness of certain representations. A recent case involved the use of a picture of radio personality Howard Stern on an online bulletin board.[43] The use was upheld because the New York misappropriation statute contained an exception for newsworthiness. Since the posting of the picture was in conjunction with the reporting of a news story that Stern was running for governor, the use of the photograph on a bulletin board service was the equivalent of a "letter to the editor" in a newspaper. Therefore, the posting was not a misappropriation of a celebrity image or likeness, but a news event exception to the statute. "Although it is clear that much in a celebrity's life is newsworthy and that publishers are therefore protected by the First Amendment, . . . if a newspaper or publisher goes beyond just publishing an article, and uses the article to increase circulation or for other commercial benefit, liability attaches."[44] In, *Eastwood v. National Enquirer, Inc.*,[45] a newspaper was prohibited from using a photograph of Clint Eastwood to boost sales of the paper. The photograph had been part of an article about the actor's relationship with actress Sandra Locke.

The legality of placing the image or likeness in a library, museum or archive display or exhibit depends on the circumstances. "The focus on unauthorized use of names and likeness for advertising and trade purposes makes the precise uses to which such names and likenesses are put a central concern in determining the applicability of this type of legislation."[46] Suppose one exhibit used the image of Renee O'Connor's Gabrielle in a piece of art, in a montage of fictional women characters. This would likely be protected by the First Amendment. Suppose another exhibit used the characters from the Xena television program to promote a new exhibit that underscores the myth and magic of the ancient Celts and the Romans (two groups often featured in Xena's adventures). Here the persona is used to promote (through attendance, patronage, friends' group registration, etc.) the library, museum or archive, and some economic benefit is derived from and traceable to the use of the fictional characters and the realizations created by the actresses portraying those characters. Such use may cross the line into prohibited promotional use. Courts appear to draw a distinction between legitimate newsworthiness and other protected First Amendment expressions and the mere promotion of economic benefit. The recommended course of action, again, is to seek permission before using the name, likeness, persona or other personal attribute in exhibits, displays and, especially, promotional materials.[47]

Conclusion

At the heart of the mission of the library, museum and archive is the provision of access to a wide variety of information through its collections, holdings, exhibits and displays. However, when the library, museum or archive provides access to information relating to individuals, the right of privacy may be implicated. Knowledge of the basic concepts involved can help an institution navigate the complex rubric of state laws.

As competition for public funding becomes greater, libraries, museums and archives are forced increasingly to adopt market-oriented strategies both in the design of their promotional activities and in conjunction with the creation of collections and exhibits. As a result, there is an increased potential for institutions to run afoul of the commercial interests of others when a person's image, likeness or persona is used beyond purposes such as newsworthiness, art, commentary and criticism. Being mindful of these concepts will help an institution to avoid this problem.

Notes

This publication is designed to provide accurate and authoritative information in regard to the subject matter covered. However, this information is NOT a substitute for legal advice. If legal advice or expert assistance is required, the services of a competent legal professional should be sought.

1. William Prosser, *Privacy,* 48 California Law Review 383, 389 (1960).
2. James S. Talbot, *New Media: Intellectual Property, Entertainment and Technology Law* § 8:5, at 8-8 (1999).
3. Harvey L. Zuckman et al., 1 *Modern Communications Law* § 4.4, at 409 (1999).
4. For purposes of the right of distribution, under copyright law, one court has held that by merely making an item available in its collections the library fulfills the requirements for distribution to the public. *Hotaling v. Church of Latter Day Saints,* 118 F.3d 199 (4th Cir. 1999) ("When a public library adds a work to its collection, lists the work in its index or catalog system, and makes the work available to the borrowing or browsing public, it has completed all the steps necessary for *distribution* to the public." 118 F.3d at 203. Emphasis added).
5. Raymond T. Nimmer, *Information Law* ¶ 8.07[3], at 8-33 (2000).
6. Raymond T. Nimmer, *Information Law* ¶ 8.05, at 8-22 (2000).
7. Harvey L. Zuckman et al., 1 *Modern Communications Law* § 4.7, at 491 (1999).
8. Marie C. Malaro, *A Legal Primer on Managing Museum Collections* 200 (2d ed. 1998).
9. James S. Talbot, *New Media: Intellectual Property, Entertainment and Technology Law* § 8:8, at 8-10 (1999); Harvey L. Zuckman et al., 1 *Modern Communications Law* § 4.6, at 450 (1999).
10. Ruth F. Walden and Emile Netzhammer, *False Light Invasion of Privacy: Untangling the Web of Uncertainty,* 9 Comm/Ent, 347, 373 (1987).
11. Harvey L. Zuckman et al., 1 *Modern Communications Law* § 4.6, at 450 (1999).
12. *Sullivan v. Pulitzer Broadcasting Co.*, 709 S.W.2d 475 (Mo. 1986); *Hoppe v. Hearst Corp.*, 53 Wash. Ct. App. 668, 770 P.2d 203 (Wash. Ct. App. 1989).
13. Wisconsin does not have a false light right of privacy. Wisconsin Statutes § 895.50. See also *Comment: Absence of False Light from the Wisconsin Privacy Statute,* 70 Marquette Law Review 88 (1986).
14. James S. Talbot, *New Media: Intellectual Property, Entertainment and Technology Law* § 8:7, at 8-10 (1999).
15. *Uhl v. CBS, Inc.*, 476 F.Supp. 1134 (W.D. Pa. 1984).
16. Kent D. Stuckey, *Internet and Online Law* § 5.02[10], at 5-12–5-13 (2000).
17. The painting, entitled *Mirth and Girth,* was removed by several Washington supporters. The artist sued under 41 U.S.C. §1983 (violation of First and Fourteenth Amendment rights) and the case was eventually settled in favor of the

artist. See Debra Cassens Moss and Stephanie B. Goldberg, *Picture This Expense,* ABA Journal, May 1994, at 44.

18. Marie C. Malaro, *A Legal Primer on Managing Museum Collections* 200 (2d ed. 1998).

19. *Time, Inc. v. Hill,* 385 U.S. 374, 387–88 (1967) (applying First Amendment guarantees to false light privacy claim).

20. Raymond T. Nimmer, *Information Law* ¶ 8.07[1], at 8-29–8-30 (2000).

21. Kimberly Wood Bacon, Florida Sun v. B. J. F.: *The Right of Privacy Collides with the First Amendment,* 76 Iowa Law Review 139 (1990); *Note, Defamation, Privacy and the First Amendment* (1976) Duke Law Journal 1016 (1976).

22. James S. Talbot, *New Media: Intellectual Property, Entertainment and Technology Law* §§ 8:9, at 8-11 ("Appropriation is also the branch of privacy that has splintered off into the right of publicity."); § 8:13, at 8-13 (1999).

23. Harvey L. Zuckman et al., 1 *Modern Communications Law* § 4.5, at 434 (1999).

24. *Brinkley v. Casablanca,* 438 N.Y.S. zd 1004 (1981).

25. *Winterland Concessions Co. v. Trela,* 735 F.zd 257 (7th Cir. 1984).

26. Raymond T. Nimmer, *Information Law* ¶¶ 6.19[1] and [2], (2000); James S. Talbot, *New Media: Intellectual Property, Entertainment and Technology Law* § 8:9, at 8-11 (1999).

27. James S. Talbot, *New Media: Intellectual Property, Entertainment and Technology Law* § 9:2 (1999).

28. Raymond T. Nimmer, *Information Law* ¶ 6.19[1], at 6-55 (2000).

29. *Zacchini v. Scripps-Howard Broadcasting Co.,* 433 U.S. 562 (1977).

30. Kent D. Stuckey, *Internet and Online Law,* § 7.05, at 7-62.7 (2000).

31. Julian S. Millstein, Jeffrey D. Neubueger and Jeffrey P. Weingart, *Doing Business on the Internet: Forms and Analysis* §11.05[1], at 11-53 (2000). ("In many states, a person's right of publicity is violated through the commercial use of look-alikes or features which, when used in the proper context, identify the person." Id., at footnote 9, and the cases cited therein.); Raymond T. Nimmer, *Information Law* ¶ 6.22[1], at 6-65 (2000).

32. See, *Onassis v. Christian Dior-New York, Inc.,* 472 N.Y.S. 254, 260 (N.Y. Supp. 1984), aff'd mem. 488 N.Y.S. 493 (1st Dept. 1985) (svelte style and appearance of Jackie Onassis).

33. 15 U.S.C. §1125 (1998).

34. "Crazy Legs" for football legend Elroy "Crazy Legs" Hirsch. See *Hirsch v. S.C. Johnson & Son, Inc.,* 280 N.W.2d 129 (Wis. 1979).

35. Cliff and Norm from the television show *Cheers.* See *Wendt v. Host International, Inc.,* 125 F.3d 806 (9th Cir. 1997); *Booth v. Colgate-Palmolive Co.,* 362 F. Supp. 343 (S.D.N.Y. 1973) (Shirley Booth's absent-minded but know-it-all housemaid, Hazel).

36. *Midler v. Ford Motor Co.,* 849 F.2d 460 (9th Cir. 1988) (Bette Midler's saucy singing style) and *Waits v. Frito-Lay, Inc.* 978 F.2d 1093 (9th Cir. 1992) (Tom Waits's raspy voice).

37. Raymond T. Nimmer, *Information Law* ¶ 6.19[1], at 6-56–6-57 (2000).

38. Kent D. Stuckey, *Internet and Online Law,* § 7.05, at 7-62.7 (2000), citing *Haelan Labs, Inc. v. Topps Chewing Gum, Inc.*, 202 F.2d 866, 868 (2d Cir.), cert. denied 346 U.S. 816 (1953).

39. Walter A. Effross, *Latest Wrinkle in Adult Web Sites: Seamless Seaminess? Fake Nudes Are "Cropping" up Online,* Multimedia and Web Strategist, December 1998, at 1.

40. But see California Civil Code § 990 (fifty years following death); Florida Statutes Annotated § 540.08 (forty years following death); Tennessee Code Annotated §47-25-1104(a) and (b) (ten years following death, renewable as long as commercially exploited).

41. But see California Civil Code § 990; Florida Statutes Annotated §§ 540.08(1)(b) and (2); Tennessee Code Annotated § 47-25-1103.

42. J. Thomas McCarthy, 2 *The Rights of Publicity and Privacy* § 9:14, at 9-31–9-35 (2d ed. 2000).

43. *Stern v. Delphi Internet Services Corp.*, 165 Misc.2d 21, 626 N.Y.S. 2d 694 (Supreme Ct. New York County 1995).

44. James S. Talbot, *New Media: Intellectual Property, Entertainment and Technology Law* § 9:12, at 9-25 (1999), referring to *Eastwood v. National Enquirer, Inc.*, 149 Cal. App. 3d 409, 198 Cal. Rptr. 342 (1983).

45. 149 Cal. App. 3d 409, 198 Cal. Rptr. 342 (1983).

46. Harvey L. Zuckman et al., 1 *Modern Communications Law* § 4.5, at 439 (1999).

47. Marie C. Malaro, *A Legal Primer on Managing Museum Collections* 201 (2nd 1998).

CHAPTER 4

Censorship and Controversial Materials in Museums, Libraries, and Archives

Judith F. Krug

I'm a librarian. My job is to bring people and information together. My colleagues and I do this by making sure our libraries have information and ideas across the spectrum of social and political thought, so people can *choose* what they want to read or view or listen to. Since libraries provide information for *all* the people in their community, librarians find, from time to time, that not all of their users agree with all of the material they have acquired. Some users find materials in their local library collection to be untrue, offensive, harmful, or even dangerous. But libraries serve the information needs of all the people in the community—not just the loudest, not just the most powerful, not even just the majority. Libraries serve all the people.

Librarians call this concept "intellectual freedom." This concept is based on the First Amendment to the U.S. Constitution,[1] particularly, the freedom of the press and freedom of speech clauses. Librarians have interpreted these clauses to mean that every person has the right to hold any belief or idea on any subject and to express those beliefs or ideas in whatever form they consider appropriate. And the ability to express an idea or a belief is meaningless, librarians believe, unless there is an equal commitment to the right of unrestricted access to information and ideas, regardless of the communication medium. Intellectual freedom, then, involves the right to express one's ideas and the right of others to be able to read, hear, or view them.

As I said, our concept of intellectual freedom finds its roots in the First Amendment to the U.S. Constitution:

> Congress shall make no law respecting an establishment of religion, or prohibiting the free exercise thereof; or abridging the freedom of speech, or of the press; or the right of the people peaceably to assemble, and to petition the Government for a redress of grievances.

That's it—forty-five words—forty-five words that go a long way toward making the United States of America unique among the nations of the world.

The *uniqueness* of the First Amendment lies not only in its guarantees, but also in its lack of proscriptions. For instance, the First Amendment guarantees freedom of speech—but it doesn't mandate that the speech be truthful, honest, equal, sensitive, tasteful, showing good judgment, respectful, or anything else. If you want to lie through your teeth or make prejudicial statements, the First Amendment gives you the right to do so. Of course, you also have to live with the consequences of your speech.

The *importance* of the First Amendment is that it is the mechanism that allows us to be a nation of self-governors. We live in a constitutional republic—a government of the people, by the people, and for the people. But this form of government does not function effectively unless its electorate is enlightened. The electorate must have information available and accessible. And it does—in our nation's libraries.

In today's world, that information is available in a variety of formats—books, magazines, films, videos, CD-ROM's, sound recordings, paintings, sculpture. To this mix, we have now added electronic communication, specifically, the Internet, the most important—and exciting—communication revolution since the invention of the printing press. But the format in which information is found doesn't matter—our role of bringing people together with information doesn't change.

The Internet has changed, somewhat, the manner in which libraries operate. Previously, librarians, limited by money and shelf space, selected the items that went into their collections. To a large extent, this still holds true, but it is no longer totally true. The Internet is allowing libraries, for the first time, to make the vast array of ideas and information available to everyone—and to permit each library user to act as his or her own selector. This has caused great anguish in certain quarters, because some people are convinced that if young people have unfettered access to the Internet, they will unerringly be drawn to web sites featuring explicit sex. There does not appear to be evidence to support such beliefs, but lack of evidence has not changed the minds of those who so believe. We have been dealing with such perceptions for a long time and, in many instances, they have been translated into legislative proposals.

The first such proposal to become law was the Communications Decency Act (CDA), signed into law by President Bill Clinton on February 8, 1996, as part of the Telecommunications Reform Act of 1996. The CDA sought to keep "indecent" material from anyone under eighteen. It said that if "merely" access was provided to the Internet, there was no liability. But if such content was provided, the provider risked fines of up to $250,000 and/or up to two years in prison—if anyone under eighteen was allowed to access "indecent" material over library computers.

The term "indecent," however, was not defined in the legislation. Examples of "indecency" could be found in various court cases. For instance, George Carlin's "7 Dirty Words" monologue was declared "indecent" by the U.S. Supreme Court; some portions of radio personality Howard Stern's broadcasts were declared "indecent" by a lower court in New York State; and yet another New York court declared the late Allen Ginsberg's poem *Howl* to be "indecent." But there is no definition that would serve as a guidepost in all cases.

In February 1996, two separate lawsuits were filed challenging the constitutionality of the Communications Decency Act. *The American Library Association v. U.S. Department of Justice* was filed after the *American Civil Liberties Union v. Janet Reno* and the cases were consolidated and decided under the title *ACLU v. Reno.* Both legal actions argued three main points:

1. The prohibition of material on the Internet that was "indecent" or "patently offensive" was unconstitutional because these terms were undefined, vague, and over broad. No distinction was made between material on the Internet appropriate for a five year old and that appropriate for a

seventeen-year-old college student. But librarians serve the information needs of the whole community—and seventeen year olds also need "age-appropriate" material. In short, government cannot limit adults (or near adults) solely to reading material that is appropriate for children.

2. There are alternate ways for parents to protect their minor children from materials on the Internet they consider inappropriate. Such ways, filters, for instance, would not violate the First Amendment rights of adults and would be more effective than the new law. These alternative measures, however, were not considered by Congress, which held no hearings, nor invited any testimony, on this issue before passing sweeping legislation.
3. The Internet is *not* a broadcast medium, like television and radio, on which courts have imposed content restrictions. Rather, the Internet is more like print—a newspaper, a bookstore, a library—because the audience is not captive. Each member of the audience has control over what he or she can access; each has a choice. Accordingly, the Internet deserves the same First Amendment protection as books and newspapers, not the lesser protection granted to the broadcast medium.

In June 1996, a lower court declared the CDA unconstitutional.[2] The government appealed, and on June 26, 1997, by a 9-0 vote, the U.S. Supreme Court upheld the lower court decision.[3]

The high court said:

1. Adults cannot be limited in their reading material to only what is suitable for children;
2. There are alternate means, such as filters for use at home, for parents to protect their children;
3. The Internet is more like print media than like broadcast media, and deserves the same First Amendment protection enjoyed by print. The Court, in fact, went a step further and said electronic communications may be entitled to even more First Amendment protection than print!

ALA's lawyer called the decision "the birth certificate of the Internet." The decision set the standard by which all future regulation of cyberspace communications would be judged by all other U.S. courts. By a unanimous Supreme Court decision, freedom of expression on the Internet and access to that expression became protected in the United States.

Despite this unanimous decision, Congress, state legislatures, and many local governments have spent vast amounts of time trying to figure out how to get around it. The first thing Congress did was pass the Child Online Protection Act (COPA), known as "son of CDA," or "CDA II.": The new act "criminalizes the *commercial* distribution of material that is harmful to minors" unless the distributor limits the access of those under seventeen years old by requiring use of a credit card or some other adult verification. The act defines "material harmful to minors" as matter that appeals to prurient interests, depicts sexual conduct "in a patently offensive way with respect to what is suitable for minors," and lacks "literary, artistic, political, and scientific value for minors." COPA also sets up a study commission.

In the attempt to circumvent the Supreme Court's CDA decision, two major changes were made:

1. The "harmful to minors" standard, not the "indecency" standard, is used.
2. The act focuses on the "commercial."

CDA II raises many First Amendment concerns, among them:

1. The act still depends on "the average person applying contemporary community standards." On the Internet, this begs the questions—What average person? Where? Whose community?
2. In striking down the original CDA, the Supreme Court ruled that efforts to regulate constitutionally protected online speech on behalf of a legitimate government interest—like protecting children—need to be pursued by the "least restrictive means." The text of the CDA II simply declares that its solution is just such a "least restrictive means," without exploring any alternative. The legislation was simply tacked onto a voluminous budget bill, without benefit of hearings, let alone extensive public debate.
3. The target of CDA II appears to be commercial publishers of free-access web sites that present sexual material some prosecutor somewhere might deem to be "harmful to minors." That could include depictions such as are found in Claude Brown's *Manchild in the Promised Land,* a work probably found in most libraries.

COPA was declared unconstitutional by a federal district court.[4] That decision was affirmed by the U.S. Court of Appeals for the Third Circuit.[5]

Simultaneously, the states also were busy. New York passed the first "mini-CDA," which ALA and ACLU challenged in *ALA v. Pataki.*[6] The law made it a crime to transmit to a minor a communication that "depicts actual or simulated nudity, sexual conduct or sadomasochistic abuse, and which is harmful to minors."

The challenge to the New York "mini-CDA" was based primarily on the commerce clause of the U.S. Constitution. Secondarily, it was challenged on First Amendment grounds. The commerce clause not only protects the nation's infrastructure of communication and trade, but also prohibits states from unduly interfering in the activities of people in other states. How do you limit the Internet when it comes into New York without limiting it everywhere? Because you cannot so limit the Internet, Judge Loretta A. Preska held the law unconstitutional. Subsequently, a similar law was challenged in New Mexico, with similar results. Currently, the issue is in court in both Michigan (*Cyberspace v. Engler*) and Virginia (*PSInet v. Chapman*).

Libraries, however, are not the only institutions affected by Internet-related legislation. In 1996, the Virginia legislature passed a law that prohibited state employees from using state-owned or leased computer equipment to "access, download, print or store any information, infrastructure files or services having sexually explicit content." Such material could be accessed on the job only for "a bona fide agency-approved research project or other agency-approved undertaking." Permission from the agency head was required.

Six professors from state colleges and universities in Virginia challenged the constitutionality of the statute. In the initial legal action, Judge Leonie M. Brinkema of the Eastern District of Virginia declared the statute unconstitutional on February 26, 1998. The state appealed. On February 10, 1999, a three-judge panel of the U.S. Court of Appeals for the Fourth Circuit reversed the district court decision in *Urofsky v. Allen* (now known as *Urofsky v. Gilmore*). The reversal in Urofsky was the first setback to litigation challenging the constitutionality of state statutes attempting to regulate the Internet.

While Judge Brinkema had found that the statute was an unconstitutional intrusion upon the First Amendment rights of the professors to access materials and voice matters of "public concern," the Fourth Circuit found otherwise. The First Amendment, it held, protects the speech of state employees only when they speak in their capacity as citizens. According to the court, the Virginia statute, by its own terms, controlled the speech of state employees acting as employees.

Indeed, the Fourth Circuit specifically said that professional research and debate in "art, literature, history and the law" are not protected by the First Amendment. It recognized that the First Amendment applies when public employees are speaking on "matters of public concern." But in an inexplicable contortion of logic, the appeals court held that no job-related speech involves matters of public concern. Therefore, the court said, job-related speech is not protected by the First Amendment.

"By the court's logic, a state university English professor has a free speech right to make water-cooler comments about the more salacious elements of the Clinton/Lewinsky scandal but a political science professor could be fired for discussing the same issue in her classroom," said Ann Beeson, staff attorney with the national ACLU.

In September 1999, the full bench of the Fourth Circuit reheard *Urofsky*. The court upheld the three-judge panel's decision. The question posed by *Urofsky* was rendered moot when the Virginia legislature changed the law. Unfortunately, that awful decision by the three-judge panel stands.

As the Internet becomes an ever larger part of the communications arena, it is important to remember that, despite the absolute language of the First Amendment (made applicable to the states by the Fourteenth Amendment), challenges to other formats in other venues have not abated. Museums and art galleries are cases in point.

In 1989, at the last minute, the Corcoran Gallery of Art in Washington, D.C., canceled an exhibition of photographs by Robert Mapplethorpe, *Robert Mapplethorpe: The Perfect Moment,* even though it had the support of the board at the time. The cancellation of the show led to staff resignations, an artists' boycott, outcries from the museum world, and demands for the director's resignation. The museum's contemporary programming and fund-raising dried up. Under the weight of public and artistic protest, the board distanced itself from the director, who resigned six months after canceling the show.

The following year, in Cincinnati—a city that casts itself as a bulwark in the war against pornography—local law-enforcement officials and antiporn groups joined together to attack the same Robert Mapplethorpe exhibit. When the retrospective of the late photographer's work was hung in the Contemporary Arts Center, sheriff's deputies and Cincinnati police officers shut down the center for ninety minutes and a grand jury indicted the gallery and its director, Dennis Barrie, on obscenity charges. At the center of the controversy were a dozen or so photographs—a rather small part of the exhibit—some depicting children with their genitals exposed and others showing adult males in explicit poses engaging in homosexual acts. Opponents wanted the most troubling photographs removed, but museum officials were bound by a contract requiring them to show the works in their entirety, and did not want to censor them. Cincinnati was the first city to try a gallery on obscenity charges. The jurors took just two hours to acquit the Contemporary Arts Center, and its director, of the charges—a resounding victory in a city with tough obscenity laws and a record of vigorously prosecuting obscenity.

Another censorship incident took place in Chicago. Harold Washington was a much-loved mayor of Chicago during the 1980s. Shortly after his sudden death in 1987, a satiric portrait of him (dressed in women's underwear) was removed from the School of the Art Institute of Chicago. After learning of the painting—which was part of a private competition on private property—several aldermen arrived with members of the police department at the institute and demanded the painting of Washington be removed. They charged that the painting was so offensive that its continued display might incite a riot. After several hours of discussions and threats of physical harm to the school—and by inference to its staff and students—and on the advice of their attorney, the school administration let the government officials remove the painting. Ironically, Washington was an advocate for free expression, and most certainly would have protected the right of the painter in this case.

December 19, 1995, was the date the exhibit, *Back of the Big House: The Cultural Landscape of the Plantation,* featuring library photographs and selected material from interviews with former slaves in the 1930s, was scheduled to open at the Library of Congress. Instead, it was taken down just hours before its opening, after about twenty black employees (of nearly two thousand library employees) complained that they found the exhibit offensive and lacking in "historical context." The District of Columbia Public Library responded by actively pursuing and subsequently displaying the exhibition in its entirety at the Martin Luther King Memorial Library.

In the fall of 1999, New York City mayor Rudolph Giuliani threatened to cut off millions of dollars in public funding to the Brooklyn Museum of Art because he disagreed with the content of an exhibit, *Sensation: Young British Artists from the Saatchi Collection.* He also threatened to terminate the museum's lease and take control of its board of directors. The painting at the center of the controversy was Chris Ofili's rendition of the Madonna. Ofili, a prize-winning British artist of Nigerian heritage, places elephant dung in his paintings "in an effort to ground them physically in a cultural as well as natural landscape," according to the catalog for the exhibit. An observant Catholic, Ofili denies that his work is anti-Catholic or antireligious.

The museum, with the support of First Amendment advocates like the Freedom to Read Foundation, People for the American Way, and the Municipal Art Society of New York, fought the city's attempts to censor artistic expression. After six months of legal battles, the case was settled. The mayor promised to restore the city's monthly payments to the museum and to drop his efforts to evict the museum from a city-owned building and remove its board of directors. The museum agreed to drop its First Amendment lawsuit against the mayor. Although the case was settled, the Brooklyn Museum clearly emerged the winner. In addition to resolving ongoing budget disputes with the city, the museum was protected from future retaliation by a provision that prevented Giuliani from imposing any funding cuts that are disproportionately larger than those affecting other city-supported museums.

On April 18, 2000, a San Diego man was convicted of child molestation and possession of child pornography. In addition to personal photographs, he was in possession of photocopies of pages from two art books from the San Diego Public Library. The books were *Twenty Five Years As an Artist,* by David Hamilton, and *States of Grace: Photographs, 1964–1989,* by Graham Ovenden. The conviction led to public debate over the books' places in the library collection. This debate was exacerbated by the judge's comments from the bench when he said, in effect, that photos such as these (Hamilton's and Ovenden's) in the hands of a child molester are child pornography. The judge made no ruling on the library books, nor did he accuse the library of any misconduct. In addition, no official complaint was made. Nevertheless, the library staff decided to reevaluate the books. The review committee confirmed that the books met the guidelines in the collection management policy and decided to retain them.

Be it in literature, visual art, music, or any other medium, we must be vigilant in the fight against censorship. While legal precedent is on our side, and the First Amendment is rather absolute, we see repeated attempts to censor ideas for the "good" of the community and its children. These battles are constant and they provide both challenges and opportunities. The challenges, of course, come from the many people and organizations who have decided how we all should act and what art, literature, and other information is suitable to this end. The opportunities lie in the chance to help all of our fellow citizens understand the importance of ideas regardless of their format, and the role ideas play in our lives as we move into the twenty-first century.

James Madison defined the situation almost two hundred years ago: "A popular government, without popular information, or the means of acquiring it, is but a prologue to a farce or a tragedy; or perhaps both. Knowledge will forever govern ignorance; and a people who mean to be their own governors must arm themselves with the power which knowledge gives."[7]

Notes

1. Bruce I. Ennis, "ALA Intellectual Freedom Policies and the First Amendment," *Freedom to Read Foundation News* 19, no. 1 (1994), http://www.ftrf.org/ennis.html.
2. *ACLU v. Reno,* 929 F. Supp. 824 (E.D. PA 1996) (3d Circ. decision).
3. *ACLU v. Reno,* 521 U.S. 844 (1997).
4. 31 F. Supp. zd 473 (E.D. PA 1999).
5. *ACLU v. Reno,* 521 U.S. 844 (1997).
6. 969 F. Supp. 160 (S.D.N.Y. 1997).
7. James Madison to W. T. Barry, August 4, 1822, *Letters and Other Writings of James Madison,* ed. Philip R. Fendall, vol. 3 (Philadelphia: Lippincott, 1867).

PART TWO: SPECIAL ISSUES IN MUSEUM COLLECTION MANAGEMENT

CHAPTER 5

Legal and Ethical Foundations of Museum Collecting Policies

Marie C. Malaro

Today many museum professionals feel overwhelmed by what appear to be endless and often conflicting rules and opinions about what they should collect and how they should manage their collections. They move defensively as though sailing through uncharted waters. This need not be. The law and professional ethical codes can be helpful guides on how to avoid problems, if one approaches them from the proper perspective. This article will explain how museum professionals can learn to use the law and ethical codes in a more positive way.

The Law As a Helpful Guide

The basic tenets of law in this country reflect wisdom accumulated over centuries of observing human nature and provide the student of law an abundance of common sense and practical guidance. In more recent years, however, many basic legal principles have been pushed into the background. As our society becomes increasingly complex, we often do not take the time to determine how the basic principles of law apply to present-day problems. Instead, we simply enact more laws. We seem to think that more laws (and, of course, more regulations interpreting those laws) will improve our society. Maybe it will, but the downside of this approach is that now we are so inundated by minute rules and regulations that many have forgotten, or never had the opportunity to learn, the basic legal principles that should guide their particular endeavors. For them the law is a mindless maze of dos and don'ts, not the practical source of direction it can be.

We have seen this very thing happen in the museum community. When it comes to the law, many museum trustees and managers see nothing but trouble, endless obstacles that must be negotiated if they hope to achieve their goals. This is certainly not a constructive approach for those who operate museums and historical societies, collecting organizations that need well thought-out policies and practices that can withstand the test of time.[1]

How, then, can those who guide museums come to view the law in a more positive way? First and foremost, they must know how a museum should operate with regard to the public it serves. Trustees and senior staff members of museums need to understand clearly what their chief duties are and where their loyalties lie. By providing them a measure for what is important and what is not so important, this information will give them the proper mind-set for carrying out their responsibilities, for making prudent policy decisions as individual situations arise. In effect, this mind-set will help trustees and senior staff focus on core responsibilities rather than becoming bogged down in minutia.

To develop this mind-set, trustees and senior staff need to understand three broad legal principles:

1. the concept of a trust organization
2. the basic duties the law imposes on those who run trust organizations
3. the importance of good procedure when making policy

Before discussing the above principles a few comments are in order. The principles are quite general and each organization must interpret them in accordance with its own situation. In particular, museums with considerable resources may have to do more to live up to the standards set by these principles, while museums with modest resources may find that what these standards require of them is not difficult to achieve. But though these principles are general, they can be effective. The *thoughtful* application of them can bring order and a clearer sense of direction to any museum, no matter what its size.

THE CONCEPT OF A TRUST ORGANIZATION

The "trust" is a concept long recognized by our legal tradition. It is a situation in which a party (a trustee) is charged with the management of property that must be administered for the benefit of others (the beneficiaries of the trust). For example, if a person becomes incapable of managing his or her affairs, a court may appoint a trustee to carry out these duties. In this case, there is one beneficiary, the incompetent person, and a single trustee. Or, take another example. Someone in his or her will leaves a large bequest to benefit the community. The court may appoint a board of trustees to carry out the terms of the will. In this case there is a whole class of beneficiaries (the residents of the community) and a group (not an individual) assuming the duties of trustee.

Most museums in the country are viewed by the law as "trust-like" organizations. The board of a museum is seen as having the role of a trustee because that board has control over the assets of the museum and is charged with managing those assets for the benefit of the public that is served by the museum, the segment of the public that constitutes the beneficiaries of the trust. (For a museum to identify its beneficiaries, it must go back to its charter or other enabling legal document and read carefully the purpose for which it was created.) It is very important in a trust situation to know just who the beneficiaries are, something museums tend to forget. When beneficiaries are not clearly identified, trouble arises when the next legal principle is considered.

BASIC DUTIES OF THOSE WHO RUN TRUST ORGANIZATIONS

The law imposes three legal duties on those who govern trust organizations.[2] These three duties grow out of the law's recognition of the fact that trustees need to maintain a relatively high standard of conduct so that beneficiaries of the trusts they control will have confidence in them. The importance of a high standard becomes apparent if you consider the practical side of trusteeship. Trustees have considerable power and beneficiaries have little opportunity to monitor closely what their trustees do. In such situations there may be temptations to misuse power as well as opportunities for beneficiaries to misjudge trustee performance. The law, therefore, has designed a standard of conduct to maintain the confidence of the beneficiaries and at the same time protect the trustees from false charges of mismanagement. All this should be borne in mind when pondering the standard of conduct. The standard is grounded in common sense and it is there to protect all concerned.

The three basic duties that make up the standard of conduct are:

- the duty of care
- the duty of loyalty
- the duty of obedience

The duty of *care* requires trustees to perform their duties in good faith, with a reasonable amount of diligence and care, and with the recognition that they are accountable to the beneficiaries of the trust. In other words, it is important for the trustees not only to operate in a responsible manner but also to be able to demonstrate that they are acting responsibly. How is this done? By seeing that essential policies are in place in the organization and by seeing that records of operations are maintained. (Without policies and records trustees cannot account for their activities, and thus they leave themselves vulnerable to questions. Having policies and records protects the trustees as well as the beneficiaries.)

The duty of *loyalty* requires trustees to put the interests of the trust organization before their personal interests and the interests of third parties. To protect themselves and their organizations in this regard, trustees should establish clear conflict-of-interest policies that require disclosure and sensible resolution of all conflict-of-interest situations that may arise. In simple language, this means that those who manage trust organizations should act so it is clear that their decision making is always guided by what is best for the beneficiaries of the trust, and they should use procedures that document this.

The duty of *obedience* requires trustees to be true to the mission of the organization.[3] Mission statements tend to be broad statements and many activities might be classified as falling within their purviews. At the same time, museums never have enough resources to do all that is possible. The duty of obedience requires trustees to make hard choices, always choosing what appears to be best for keeping the organization healthy and focused on its core work. Doing a lot poorly or favoring peripheral activities for short-term benefits calls into question proper adherence to the duty of obedience.

THE IMPORTANCE OF GOOD PROCEDURE WHEN MAKING POLICY

This last principle should give policy makers great comfort. When trustees make policy decisions, the law does not demand that, in hindsight, all those decisions be right. No, it only requires that trustees act in good faith and with reasonable care. Accordingly, trustees should feel secure (and not worry about personal liability) if the following criteria are met when policy decisions are made.

- Adequate information regarding the matter at issue is made available to the trustees.[4] And what is "adequate" information? It depends upon the importance of the matter and the resources of the organization. If the Metropolitan Museum of Art were weighing the proposed acquisition of a very costly artifact of doubtful provenance, its board would expect to receive extensive background material on the proposal, as compared with what the Cherry Hill Historical Society board might look for when deciding whether to accept the business records of the first apothecary shop established in the community. The test is one of reasonableness—what information would reasonable people in like circumstances expect.
- The trustees discussed and voted on the matter.
- The decision of the trustees is reasonably supported by the information available to them. In other words, reasonable people could come to that conclusion based on the information available.

This process is easy to follow and if done so routinely by trustees it provides the most effective protection against any personal liability for mismanagement. But the process should not be viewed as simply a shield against liability; more importantly, it establishes procedures that usually produce informed decisions.

In summary, from this brief discussion of the major legal principles that undergird the management of museum collections, these rules emerge:

- Museums are trust-like organizations and this means that policy makers in a museum must focus on what the mission of that organization is and what is best for the beneficiaries of that organization.
- Policy makers in museums must understand their legal responsibilities of care, loyalty, and obedience.
- Policy makers in a museum must establish reasonable policies and procedures concerning what is collected by the organization and how the collection is managed, and this includes the maintenance of adequate records so that good-faith adherence to established policies and procedures can be demonstrated.

Ethical Codes As Helpful Guides

Three topics will be covered in this discussion on ethical codes of conduct as they are used by professional organizations:

1. the difference between an ethical standard and a legal standard
2. ethical codes promulgated by the museum profession
3. effective use of ethical codes.

THE DIFFERENCE BETWEEN AN ETHICAL STANDARD AND A LEGAL STANDARD

When talking about ethical codes, it is important first to distinguish between a professional ethical standard and a legal standard. Law and ethics play different roles and to use each effectively these differing roles must be understood.

Ethical Standard

An ethical code for a profession sets forth conduct that a profession considers essential in upholding the integrity of the profession. Such a code is based on a commitment by those in the profession to public service and personal accountability. While voluntarily assumed, the code has very practical benefits for the profession itself as well as for the public served by the profession.

As a rule, standards set forth in a professional ethical code are more demanding than what the law may require because they are concerned with public perception as well as reality.

Such codes often have no enforcement mechanism; they depend on self-education and peer pressure for their promulgation. Even in those instances where a profession undertakes to police its own code, enforcement cannot be effective without a consistent and voluntary commitment from a sizable portion of the profession to conscientiously adhere to the code.

Key phrases often used to describe a professional code of ethics are "voluntarily assumed," "more demanding standards," and "self-enforced."

Legal Standard

A legal standard is quite different from a professional ethical standard. The purpose of the law is to require conduct that permits us to live in society without undue harassment. We accept adherence to the law, if legally enacted, as a civic responsibility. The law is not something we can choose to ignore.

The law does not seek to make us honorable, only bearable. Thus, as a rule, the law sets a less demanding standard than that required by an ethical code.

The law, however, has clout; it wields the power of governmental authority. If one falls below the legal standard, there is possible exposure to civil or criminal liability. This potential liability usually encourages adherence to the law.

Key phrases used to describe the law are "imposed by society," "less demanding standards," and "enforceable."

ETHICAL CODES PROMULGATED BY THE MUSEUM PROFESSION

With a clearer understanding of what distinguishes a professional ethical code, it is instructive to review how the museum profession in this country has approached the challenge of encouraging ethical behavior. So far the profession has promulgated a number of ethical codes and it favors codes that do not have enforcement mechanisms. The three major codes within the profession are:

- "Code of Ethics for Museums," the code promulgated by the American Association of Museums (AAM), ratified in 1994. The AAM is by far the largest professional organization serving the museum community.
- "Professional Practices in Art Museums," the code promulgated by the Association of Art Museum Directors (AAMD), ratified in 1992.
- "Statement of Professional Ethics," the code promulgated by the American Association for State and Local History (AASLH), ratified in 1992.

Of these codes, only the AAMD code addresses enforcement. It warns that a member or the member's institution can be punished if found guilty of violating the code. Punishment can be the suspension or expulsion of the member from the organization or, for the member's institution, the refusal of other museums in the organization to lend objects to the offending institution. Instances of such punishment appear to be rare.

The AASLH code has no enforcement procedure; nor does that of the AAM. The AAM, however, had a protracted debate on the issue of enforcement during the last revision of its code. In the early 1990s, when the latest revision of the AAM code was being drafted, there was a recommendation that the code contain a provision stating that any museum that was a member of the AAM would have five years in which to adopt a code of ethics for its own institution and that this code had to conform to the principles enunciated in the AAM code. A member institution not adopting such a code within this time frame would be subject to expulsion from the organization. After considerable consultation and debate, this provision was dropped from the final version of the code that was approved in 1994. However, this final version of the code does state that the AAM's Board of Directors recommends that member museums adopt their own institutional codes that follow the principles set forth in the AAM code. This, again, is merely a recommendation, not a requirement.

As of now, therefore, in this country most museums and museum personnel are not subject to any professional ethical code that has an enforcement mechanism. This means that

- Actual implementation of ethical codes within the profession depends almost entirely on self-education and peer pressure.
- If there is to be more emphasis on ethical behavior it is up to individual museums to write their own institutional codes, and write them so they are enforceable. In other words, in order to insist on ethical behavior a museum needs to make adherence to its code a condition of employment. A serious violation of the code would then make the individual subject to dismissal, a consequence that encourages adherence to the code.

EFFECTIVE USE OF ETHICAL CODES

It is fair to say that over the past few decades the museum community has spent more time debating and writing ethical codes than aggressively promoting their use. This impression is based on the observation that when apparent violations of codes make the news, there is rarely evidence of serious professional concern. Rather, there is silence on the part of the profession, or perhaps a few professionals point out that the individuals or museums in question did not break any law. In other words, the only important standard is the legal standard. This indication that museums and their personnel pay only token attention to ethical codes means they are neglecting to use another useful source for guiding them in making sound decisions about the management of their collections.

Ethical codes, if made an integral part of a museum's decision-making process, clearly offer another layer of positive guidance. A closer look at what such codes cover demonstrates this. As mentioned earlier, professional ethical codes are concerned with maintaining the integrity of a profession and they represent a consensus of those in the profession as to what standards should be maintained to justify public confidence in the profession. In the writing of such a code, the legal standard applicable to a profession is taken as a "given," the minimum society expects from those in the profession. But merely staying within the law does not always produce conduct that inspires confidence. Situations can arise in which the actions of those involved may be legal but nevertheless place in question their integrity. Situations can arise in which actions look to be illegal but cannot be litigated for lack of admissible evidence. These situations, when they occur, affect the integrity of the profession and thus an ethical code, building from the mandatory legal base, addresses ways to avoid such compromising situations.

Also, because legal standards are often written in broad language (for example, refer back to the three legal duties imposed on those who manage trust organizations), members of a profession may need help in applying these standards to their professional activities. An ethical code, utilizing past experience within the profession, usually spells out situations that should be avoided or should be approached with caution because of possible serious legal consequences.

In other words, a professional code of ethics offers very practical guidance on how to avoid even the appearance of irregularity when engaging in professional activity. In the museum field, these codes complement and illuminate the basic legal principles, covered earlier in this article, that form the foundation of prudent museum management. This is emphasized in the introduction to the AAM's "Code of Ethics for Museums":

> As nonprofit institutions, museums comply with applicable local, state, and federal laws and international conventions, as well as with the specific legal standards governing trust responsibilities. This Code of Ethics for Museums takes this compliance as given. But legal standards are a minimum. Museums and those responsible for them must do more than avoid legal liability, they must take affirmative steps to maintain their integrity so as to warrant public confidence. They must act not only legally but also ethically. This Code of Ethics for Museums, therefore, outlines ethical standards that frequently exceed legal minimums.

Conclusion

For museum personnel who want to use the law in a positive way, the first step should be mastery of the basic legal principles that undergird museum management. The second step is becoming very familiar with the ethical codes used in the profession. Together, these steps provide a solid base as well as clear direction for making professional decisions that are in accord with both the letter and the spirit of the law.

Hypothetical Situation

Let us take a serious situation that frequently confronts museums and consider whether the legal and ethical guides just described actually assist in arriving at well thought-out solutions. The situation concerns museums that grow without benefit of professional guidance and then must confront the challenge of bringing order and direction to their activities.

Our hypothetical museum was incorporated as a nonprofit organization thirty years ago in the state of X by a group of citizens interested in preserving the history of their community. The museum has always been supported and operated by enthusiastic volunteers, with some help, when funds permit, from part-time employees. The organization has now grown to a point where problems are becoming obvious. Collecting has never been disciplined, with the museum accepting most every object offered that has an association with the community. Little storage space is now left in the historic building the museum acquired years ago as its headquarters. Collection records are inconsistent, because over the years each person charged with recording collection information developed his or her own system. Exhibits are rarely changed because of the effort and expense involved. Money has always been a problem and will become an even greater one if the board of the museum decides that a professionally trained staff is necessary if the museum is to have a viable future. The museum has been fortunate in obtaining a small grant for the purpose of hiring a consultant to work with the board as it determines what decisions need to be made in the near future and what information should be considered by the board as it makes these decisions. Fortunately, the museum retains a highly qualified consultant.

At the board's first meeting with the consultant, the consultant presents the outline below to the board as the sequence he plans to follow in discussing issues that may need to be considered as the board establishes its plan of action.

CONSULTANT'S OUTLINE

1. *The issue of mission:* Here the consultant explains that for a nonprofit organization the issue of mission is critical, because the sole purpose of a nonprofit is to carry out its particular mission. Accordingly, the organization's mission statement should be very clear and constantly kept in mind as board decisions are made. The museum's board at some point will have to determine whether the organization has a good mission statement or must adopt a new one. To do this, the board must first review carefully the charter of the museum (its articles of incorporation), its bylaws, and the history of earlier board decisions that might relate to

mission. From this the board can determine whether the organization has an articulated mission statement (other than what might appear in the charter of the museum) and, if so, what it is. Later, after the board has much more information available to it, any existing mission statement should be reviewed to determine whether modification or clarification is necessary. The consultant reminds members of the board that they will need an understanding of the basic principles of trust law and of the duties of nonprofit trustees as they review the matter of mission.

2. *The issue of beneficiaries:* This issue is closely related to mission. A mission statement should state clearly and succinctly not only the purpose of the museum but also the segment of the public served by the museum (its beneficiaries).

   Clarification of who the beneficiaries are involves a review of documents pertinent to mission and an understanding of trust principles and the duties of nonprofit trustees.

3. *The issue of collecting focus:* A museum must collect within its mission statement and it should collect only what it can reasonably maintain, document, and make available to the public. (The consultant reminds the board of its trust responsibility to always be guided by what is best for the trust's beneficiaries. Collections that cannot be maintained properly, lack good documentation, or cannot be made available to interested persons are of little use to a museum's beneficiaries.) In light of this, the consultant explains that the board needs to examine current collecting practices and determine what, if any, changes need to be made. To do this, the board should assess the status of the museum's existing collection so that its strengths and weaknesses are known. It should also gather information on the strengths and weaknesses of museum collections in the area that can be easily accessed by the beneficiaries of its museum. Information on area museums will be important when the board actually has to decide whether its museum should more carefully focus its collecting in the future.

4. *The issue of deaccessioning collection objects:* If the determination is made that the museum has collected too broadly and that its beneficiaries will be better served by more focused collecting, the issue of deaccessioning—the permanent removal of objects from the museum's collection—will have to be faced. The consultant reminds the board that deaccessioning can raise many legal and ethical issues if it is not done properly. He points out, however, that professional codes of ethics and

a number of professional publications give excellent guidance on the subject. He stresses that the basic test in all deaccession activity is whether the board is very conscious of its trust responsibilities as it makes its decisions.

5. *The issue of funding:* The future of the museum cannot be discussed intelligently without considering also the question of funding. The consultant warns the board that here it will have to face some very difficult choices. The purpose of the museum is to carry out its educational mission, and this purpose can be skewed if fund-raising activities are allowed to take center stage. The consultant comments that when they discuss the issue of funding in more detail he hopes board members will reflect on how their duties of care, loyalty, and obedience might impact their options in selecting appropriate ways to raise money.
6. *The issue of staff:* Here the consultant points out that once the board has informed itself generally on the matters addressed in numbers 1–5, it will be able to address more intelligently the issue of hiring a professional director. After its self-education sessions the board will be better able to determine what qualifications should be sought in a director, and once that individual is in place the board will have the background to work effectively with the new director.

From the above it should be clear that without clear knowledge of the basic legal principles that undergird trust responsibilities and without familiarity with professional ethical codes the trustees of our hypothetical museum would have no road map for resolving their critical problems. In effect, the practical steps they need to take become quite evident once basic legal and ethical principles have been applied.

Notes

1. Hereafter the term "museum" will be used to mean any nonprofit or governmental entity that collects and/or exhibits objects for educational or aesthetic purposes.

2. Those who govern museums may be called trustees, directors, regents, etc. For simplicity's sake, and because it resonates to the duties involved, the term "trustees" is used in this article to mean those individuals charged with governing a museum. It should also be noted that when a museum is a part of a larger organization, such as a university, those managing the museum must deal with the

board governing the university or other organization in order to clarify the limits of their authority. Ideally this is done before problems arise. When a museum is a part of a government entity, those charged with managing the museum must follow appropriate lines of authority to clarify the scope of their powers. As a rule, university- and government-controlled museums tend to adopt the standards and practices promulgated by the museum profession.

3. Every museum has a purpose as set forth in its charter or other enabling document. From this purpose the museum draws up its mission statement. Essential knowledge for a trustee is a good understanding of the mission statement.

4. Most information comes from staff, but trustees should seek outside advice if they are not satisfied with the information staff provides.

CHAPTER 6

Collections Management

HYPOTHETICAL CASES, ACQUISITIONS, DEACCESSIONS, AND LOANS

Ildiko Pogany DeAngelis

In the first chapter of this presentation on legal and ethical issues of particular concern to museums, the author focused on the broad legal and ethical principles that should guide decision making in such organizations. These principles are found in trust law and in the ethical codes promulgated by the museum profession, and they impact all aspects of museum governance. In this second portion of this presentation, I will narrow the application of these principles to the collection-based work of museums: essentially the tasks of acquiring, lending, and disposing of collection objects.

The core work of museums is the development, care, and utilization of collections of tangible objects for aesthetic and educational purposes. If we apply the broad legal and ethical principles earlier discussed to this core work, certain conclusions become quite obvious. These are:

- How a museum goes about its core work should be a matter of written policy.

- While professional staff may propose such policy, the governing board of a museum has the power and duty to establish, and oversee the effectiveness of, such policy.
- Such policy must be in accord with the mission of the museum and must demonstrate due attention by the governing board to its duties of "care, loyalty, and obedience."

Today most museums in this country, in response to these obvious conclusions, have devised what are generally called "collection management policies." A collection management policy is a fairly detailed written statement that explains how a particular museum acquires objects, how it cares for and uses such objects, and when and how it may dispose of such objects. The policy serves as a guide to staff and as a source of information for the public. The very process of drafting such a policy reinforces the importance of the document because it impresses upon all concerned that the acquisition and management of collection objects are becoming increasingly complex activities. Accordingly, to avoid making serious mistakes in these areas, it is essential for a museum to articulate its philosophy and standards regarding the development and management of its collections.

Considerable material is available on the subject of how a museum writes and implements a collection management policy, a topic that goes far beyond the scope of this discussion. Rather, the purpose of this chapter is to illustrate why a collection management policy is so important to a museum. This is done by examining a series of hypothetical situations and considering how a well-drafted collection management policy would enable the museum to respond to the issues raised in an orderly and effective manner. This approach helps both museum people who have not yet been involved in drafting a collection management policy as well as those who want to assess the effectiveness of such policies already in place in their organizations.

Descriptions of the hypothetical situations follow. These situations pose collecting problems that should be familiar to most museums. To illustrate the process used in working with the hypotheticals, an analysis of the first hypothetical—concerning Museum X—follows the descriptions of all four hypotheticals. A bibliography to enable the reader to answer the remaining hypotheticals follows this analysis.

Hypotheticals

1. Museum X has been offered a collection of thirty artifacts from a donor who is a personal friend of several members of the museum's board of trustees. Upon inspection by the museum staff, it appears that sixteen of the works are not of museum quality and not the kind of objects usually accepted into the permanent collections. The board members express hesitation in telling the donor that over half of the works are not suitable, because the donor fancies himself to be a connoisseur and is convinced that his collection is first rate. The remaining fourteen works, which are of possible interest, lack sufficient provenance records. The board members worry that if museum staff probe the donor for further information on the works' provenance (how, when, where and from whom did the donor acquire the works, the history of past ownership, source, etc.) it would be akin to "looking a gift horse in the mouth" and the donor might be insulted. The board hopes that the donor will give a major gift of cash to the museum in the near future and everyone wants to "stay on the donor's good side." A board meeting is called and you, as the collections manager, are asked to advise the board on what to do. The proposal under discussion is to accept the entire collection of thirty artifacts and to later sell the unwanted works quietly to raise more cash. One of the board members, an art dealer, assures everyone that he could sell these unwanted objects anonymously through his contacts on the West Coast. Under this proposal, the remaining fourteen unprovenanced works would be added to the permanent collections.
2. Mr. John Smith, husband of the recently deceased artist Jill Smith, wishing to donate her papers and other effects to the museum, has approached Museum Y. The proposed gift includes her sketchbook and personal letters received from friends and professional acquaintances (including other artists, gallery owners, critics, and her students). The material offered also includes Jill Smith's personal diary, home movies of the Smith family, a copy of a video biography featuring an interview with Jill Smith and filmed by a graduate student from ABC College, a photo album of Jill's paintings, and several typed manuscripts by Jill Smith on art-related subjects. Museum Y is anxious to accept these materials. The sketchbook would be a welcome addition to the museum's

prints and drawings collection. The rest would be ideal for the museum's archive collection on local artists. The curator has announced that she is planning a retrospective exhibition of Jill Smith that will examine her work in context of her life and times. A virtual tour of the entire exhibit is planned for the museum's web site. You have been put in charge of this proposed acquisition. What steps should you take prior to accepting the gift from John Smith?

3. Museum Z is cleaning its storage facility and finds a group of antique silverware that no longer meets the museum's collecting goals. The accession records indicate that the silverware was a bequest in 1920 from Mrs. Jones to the museum subject to the following provision in the will:

    > I give my prized collection of silver to Museum Z provided that Museum Z agrees to permanently display my entire collection together as a unit in a special exhibition case bearing my name and dedicated by Museum Z for this sole purpose.

    The museum records show no evidence that the silver was ever on display. The curator of decorative arts proposes to deaccession the silver and to sell it at public auction. The proceeds would be used to purchase items needed for the collections and to buy additional storage units to house them. Is this proposal in keeping with legal and ethical standards?

4. In 1939 Mr. Avery Adams loaned a group of antique firearms to Museum A. The loan is evidenced by a copy of a letter from the then director indicating his appreciation for the loan. No time period was set for the loan. Many years later (in the 1950s) the museum's registrar sent a letter to Mr. Adams that was returned and marked "undeliverable." From 1939 to the present, the firearms were on display and labeled as a loan from Mr. Avery Adams. Last month, a man claiming to be Mr. Adams's grandson contacted the museum, demanding return of his deceased grandfather's gun collection. The firearms have appreciated in value significantly since 1939 and indeed the collection has become the centerpiece of a permanent exhibition that would be gutted if the guns were removed from display. The museum had also spent considerable funds on conserving the guns over the years. What are the museum's options? Would your answer be different if no museum records exist of how the firearms were acquired by the museum (no evidence that they were on loan)?

Analysis of Hypothetical #1

A first step in the analysis of Museum X's situation would be to identify the legal and ethical issues raised. They are as follows:

1. What are the legal/ethical ramifications of the proposal to accept the collection (including objects not of museum quality) and later sell unwanted objects to raise money for the museum?

Accepting objects for resale is not per se illegal or unethical. However, before the gift is accepted, full disclosure to the donor of the museum's plans to resell the object is required by both legal and ethical principles. Under applicable tax law, resale of a donated object by a museum is considered an "unrelated use" by the IRS and results in a less favorable tax deduction for the donor. Rather than being able to deduct the full fair market value of the object, as usually is done for objects donated to a museum, the donor's deduction in an unrelated use situation is limited generally to the value of the object at the time the donor acquired it. Therefore to make an informed decision, the donor needs to be apprised of the museum's intended "unrelated use" before the gift is completed.[1] The key issue is the intended use of the object by the museum at the time of acquisition. It is not appropriate to accept a gift on the pretext that it will be added to the collections and then to hold it for a few years until it "cools" to avoid unfavorable tax consequences for the donor. A museum that routinely accessions objects that it intends to resell or exchange is opening itself up to charges of collusion. This does not mean, however, that an object accepted in good faith may not be removed from the collections if experience or changed circumstances later indicate that such action is prudent and appropriate. The key term here is "good faith."

In addition, most donors expect that objects given to a museum will be preserved and made available to the public. A museum that routinely accepts all gifts and subsequently disposes of unwanted objects soon loses the confidence of the public. Ethical codes of the profession routinely limit accessioning to objects that meet the museum's mission and that the museum intends to keep for the foreseeable future. Standards that guide decision making on whether an object should be added to a collection should be determined in advance and include consideration of the museum's collecting goals, whether proper care can be given to the object, provenance, and condition. A hoped-for cash donation by a donor is not a proper consideration for accepting an inappropriate object for the collection. Collecting without focus and overcollecting may constitute a breach of the fiduciary obligations of care and loyalty.

Objects not formally accessioned into the permanent collections, but rather added to the museum's study or school collections, still qualify for the favorable "related use" tax treatment. In the eyes of the law, the objects are still used by the museum in pursuit of its tax-exempt purpose. However, it is advisable that the museum, in good faith, explain to the donor how the object will be used to avoid possible misunderstanding. To maintain donor confidence in the institution, forthrightness is always the best policy.

For a fuller explanation of "unrelated use" and citations to applicable laws and ethical codes, see Marie C. Malaro, *Legal Primer on Managing Museum Collections,* 2d ed. (Washington D.C.: Smithsonian Institution Press, 1998), 60, 208–09, 372–73.

2. Many of the objects in the offered collection lack provenance records and the board is reluctant to ask the donor for additional information. What legal/ethical questions might this raise?

If the donor is not queried about the provenance of the collection offered to the museum based on the fear of offending a personal friend of the trustees, the loyalty of the trustees to the museum and its beneficiaries (the public it serves) may be questioned.

Due care requires that museums make decisions on adequate information regarding the matter at issue. As explained by Professor Malaro in chapter 5, what is "adequate" information depends upon the importance of the matter and the resources of the organization. If a large art museum were weighing the acquisition of a very costly antiquity of doubtful provenance, its board would expect extensive background material on the proposal, as compared with what the board of a small historical society might look for when deciding whether to accept the portrait of a local hero. The test is one of reasonableness—what information would reasonable people in like circumstances expect. Neglecting to gather necessary facts may be a breach of the duty of care.

In any acquisition, a museum must assure itself that it is obtaining "clean" title (legal rights) to the object.[2] It should never be assumed that the person offering the gift is the true owner. Precautions are required. Unless such precautions are taken, the museum may find itself in the unenviable position of having to deal with a claimant seeking the collection's return. For example, under U.S. law a thief cannot pass good title. Even if the work is resold to an innocent purchaser, the original owner is entitled to return of his property. The current holder may assert technical defenses based on the premise that the owner's rights were lost due to the passage of time. In such cases, both the conduct of the owner in searching for the stolen property as well as the diligence of the holder in acquiring the property will be examined and weighed by the court. The best advice in the acquisition of any object is to question provenance, take advantage of art-loss registers, make reasonable efforts to get additional information from third-party sources (the amount of effort will depend on the nature of the objects at issue),[3] maintain good records of the entire search process, and make the acquisition public.

In addition to the consideration of theft, objects may have been improperly removed from their countries of origin, illegally imported into the United States, or subject to specialized legislation due to the nature of the object or its origin. Diligent inquiry at the time of acquisition will assist in bringing to light any such potential problems and also help identify ethical concerns.

In some cases, an object may be legally in the United States, yet its acquisition may be ethically improper. Although U.S. law may not formally recognize the export controls of other countries, the acquisition of such objects exported illegally from their countries of origin violates ethical principles established by many major museums based on principles set by the American Association of Museums and the International Council of Museums. Ethical codes set higher standards than the law to ensure the integrity of the profession necessary to maintain public confidence.

Once a work is acquired, its provenance should be open to public inspection, while confidentiality of selected information is maintained (such as home addresses and telephone numbers of donors). Transparency and accountability are expected from museums supported by the public.

For a more detailed discussion of acquisition issues, see Malaro, *Legal Primer,* 58–135.

3. Are there legal/ethical problems with the offer of the board member, who is an antique dealer, to sell the unwanted objects anonymously through his contacts?

Both the law and ethics stress the importance of avoiding conflicts of interest and even the appearance of conflicts of interest. A board member who is in the business of buying and selling the kinds of objects collected by the museum sets up a very difficult conflict-of-interest management problem. Facts routinely considered by the board for purchasing, deaccessioning, or even exhibiting might be viewed as valuable "insider" information with great potential of misuse for personal gain. Yet, someone with current market expertise may be able to offer extremely useful advice in certain board deliberations. In selecting board members and how the board will manage conflict issues, decision makers should be guided primarily by the need to maintain public confidence. No board member should participate or vote in any matter in which he or she has a potential financial interest. In such cases, avoiding the appearance of impropriety is essential. Even if such a board member is excluded from the deliberations, the board should weigh very carefully both the real conflict and the appearance of conflict in making its decision.

With respect to disposal of objects by a museum, the duty of care requires that the decision be made on reasonable facts with the best interests of the institution in mind. Assuming that a sound decision has been made to dispose of an object, the method used should also involve due consideration, especially if sale is considered. Again, the nature of the object will influence what may be most prudent. Generally, to avoid accusations of favoritism, museums prefer public auctions to private sales. A private sale may also raise the issue of whether the best price had been obtained for the beneficiaries of the museum (the public it serves).

Finally, with any sale, the museum, as seller, warrants to the buyer that the title to the object is clean and free from any encumbrance. By selling objects without known provenance, the museum is courting trouble. If the buyer is required sometime later to return the work to the victim of a theft, the buyer could sue the museum for damages based on a breach of warranty. In such a case, the measure of damages is not simply the amount the museum received as the purchase price, but the value of the work at the time of the return to the rightful owner (this might reflect the subsequent appreciation in its market value).

The legal and ethical issues raised by the failure to apprise the donor of the resale are considered above, under question 1.

For more information on the legal and ethical issues involved in deaccession and disposal of collection objects, see Malaro, *Legal Primer,* 216–33;

Stephen Weil, ed., *A Deaccession Reader* (Washington D.C.: American Association of Museums, 1997); and Marie C. Malaro, *Museum Governance: Law, Ethics, and Policy* (Washington D.C.: Smithsonian Institution Press, 1994), 50–59.

4. What are the problems facing the new collection manager, who has been asked to advise the board? Is her situation affected by whether the museum has a collection management policy? If there were a collection management policy, what provisions would the collection manager hope to find in the policy?

The collection manager is in an unenviable position. She has information that she is obligated to pass on to the board. Board education can be a politically difficult but essential duty of museum professionals. If the museum already has a collection management policy, her job may be easier if that policy is clear and offers effective guidance. Once such a policy is in place, a board that ignores the policy is violating standards that it set forth as reasonable and necessary. If there is no collection management policy, the collection manager has to impress on the board that the failure to establish policy regarding the core work of the museum is itself a violation of the duty of care. In either case, the board is leaving itself open to valid criticism and potential liability.

If a collection management policy is in place, it should set reasonable standards for acquisition, disposal, lending, care, access, insurance, and record keeping. It should be written with the needs of the particular museum in mind. The policy should clearly define areas of responsibility and delegate authority for final decisions to either an individual or a defined group. It should set standards for acquisitions (for example, an object is accepted into the permanent collections only if it meets the mission of the museum, it is accompanied by adequate provenance information to assure that clean and complete legal title is received by the museum, and its acquisition will not violate applicable ethical codes). The policy should clearly specify the limited circumstances under which objects not intended for the collections may be accepted for other purposes. The process of how acquisition decisions are made also should be evident. Proposals for acquisitions should be initiated and justified by professional staff. The level of authority needed for the final decision should be set keeping in mind the nature of the object (often meaning its value or special care needs) and whether there are any complicating factors, such as donor-imposed restrictions or copyright considerations. Written records of the entire process should also be required.

The task of writing or revising a collections management policy is not easy. But it provides a unique opportunity to educate the board and staff on their roles and on important basic principles that should govern how a museum should manage the unique and often irreplaceable assets, its collections, for the benefit of the public.

For further guidance, see Malaro *Legal Primer,* 10–19 ("What Is Required of a Board Member"), 45–57 ("Collections Management Policies"); Malaro, *Museum Governance,* 43–59.

5. How does the presence, or absence, of a good collection management policy affect the handling of legal issues?

Without a collection management policy that incorporates important legal principles, museums and their board members are vulnerable to legal liability. Ignorance of the law is no excuse, as the old adage states. Even if a legal issue is identified, museums without a policy must quickly find legal counsel to advise them on a case-by-case basis. Not only is this inefficient and costly, but it also leaves the museum board and staff unsure whether all necessary legal principles have been considered for the activity in general. A central goal of a collection management policy is to practice preventative law, to provide a clear map by which to avoid mistakes.

As explained above, a board may demonstrate due care by establishing policy and exercising oversight in its implementation. Collection management policy is an important tool for risk management for the institution and for individual members of the board.

6. How does the presence, or absence, of a good collection management policy affect the handling of ethical issues?

As noted above, ethics set professional standards higher than those required by the law. The purpose of such standards is to maintain the public confidence essential for the operation of any museum. Ethical policies issued by professional organizations are often general principles that need to be clarified and implemented in detail through specific guidelines individually tailored to the needs of a particular museum. For example, the ethical issues for acquisitions by a zoo are different from those for an art museum or a small historic house. The drafting of a collection management policy allows frank discussion between board member and staff of what ethical principles need to be considered and how they should be best implemented. Without such a policy, museums may soon find themselves in troubled ethical waters without a compass (knowledge of the broad ethical principles) or oars (specific guidelines).[4]

At minimum, the following professional ethical codes should be consulted by any museum drafting a collections management policy: American Association of Museums, "Code of Ethics for Museums" (1994); International Council of Museums, "Code of Professional Ethics" (Paris, 1986; reprinted in 1990); American Association for State and Local History, "Statement of Professional Ethics" (Nashville, Tenn., 1992); Association of Art Museum Directors, "Professional Practices in Art Museums" (New York, 1992), under revision, summer 2000. Codes of ethics of academic disciplines and other professional organizations compiled in J. Weisz, ed., *Codes of Ethics and Practice of Interest to Museums* (Washington, D.C.: American Association of Museums, 2000), should also be consulted.

Answers to Hypotheticals #2–4

To answer the remaining hypotheticals, #2–4, consult especially:

DeAngelis, Ildiko P. "Old Loans." In *The New Museum Registration Methods,* ed. R. Buck and J. Gilmore, 281–87. Washington D.C.: American Association of Museums, 1998.

Malaro, Marie. *Legal Primer in Managing Museum Collections.* Washington D.C.: Smithsonian Institution Press, 1998 (esp. chapter 4, "Acquisition of Objects"; chapter 7, "Unclaimed Loans"; and chapter 10, "Objects Found in Collections").

Malaro, Marie. *Museum Governance: Law, Ethics, and Policy.* Washington D.C.: Smithsonian Institution Press, 1994, 79–107.

Steiner, Christine, ed. *A Museum Guide to Copyright and Trademark.* Washington D.C.: American Association of Museums, 1999.

Weil, Stephen E., ed. *A Deaccession Reader.* Washington D.C.: American Association of Museums, 1997.

Notes

1. The "unrelated use" principle has an exception that applies to a group of objects accepted with the knowledge that the collection will need to be culled and a portion removed and sold. Provided that "unrelated use" applies only to an "insubstantial portion," the entire group or collection is still considered "related." As to what is "insubstantial," the IRS gives no clear guidance. In case of Museum X, sixteen out of thirty objects (the majority) would not appear to qualify.

2. In addition to clean title, the museum should be concerned with the completeness of title: Are there any restrictions imposed by the donor that limit the museum's ability to use the object? Are there any copyright, trademark, rights to privacy, or publicity issues involved?

3. The offered collection is described as containing "artifacts," a term defined to mean "objects showing human workmanship or modification." The legal and ethical considerations vary according to whether the collection is composed, for example, of Native American artifacts, early American silverware, or Holocaust era artwork.

4. In addition to the collection management policy, a museum should establish a self-enforced code of ethics for both staff and volunteers to address ethical standards not specifically addressed by the collection management policy.

PART THREE: WORKING WITH PATRONS

CHAPTER 7

Legal Issues Involved in the Privacy Rights of Patrons in "Public" Libraries and Archives

Tomas A. Lipinski

In recent years the issue of patron privacy in public libraries and archives (those funded with public monies) has attracted national attention through two seemingly unrelated incidents. First, President Ronald Reagan issued Executive Order 12333[1] in 1981. The executive order addressed "United States Intelligence Activities" in light of the mounting threat of terrorism. As a result, federal investigatory agencies like the Federal Bureau of Investigation (FBI) expanded surveillance activities in various institutional settings, such as the library. One program targeted public libraries in specific and was known as the Library Awareness Program.[2] Why the library? It was believed that many unsavory characters hatched their schemes in public libraries, where information concerning bombs, weapons and such were freely available.

A second incident has a somewhat tangential library-privacy connection. Privacy in video rental records became an issue during the Robert Bork Senate confirmation hearings in 1987. Judge Bork was a nominee to the U.S. Supreme Court. During the hearings, a record of his family's video rental history was published in a number of major newspapers. Many members of Congress were outraged at the ease with which such private information could be made available. Legislation was introduced in Congress to remedy the problem[3] and eventually the Video Privacy Protection Act of 1988 was passed.[4] What is of significance to the present discussion is that an earlier version of the legislation contained a provision for the federal (national) protection (confidentiality) of library (circulation) records.[5] While this language was eventually eliminated from the final version of the bill, various state forces mobilized to secure some type of formal protection (by statute, regulation or attorney general opinion) for public library records.[6]

Today, the legal basis for the protection of public library patron privacy is a creature of state statutory law. Moreover, the protection offered in a number of states expands protection beyond simple circulation or registration records. On the other hand, this patchwork approach means that protection varies from state to state and is often inadequate. However, in spite of this, several generalizations can be made. In addition, recent precedent may suggest the possible expansion of state library confidentiality provisions.

Protecting the Privacy of Library Patrons under State Laws

State confidentiality statutes have several common elements: institution, coverage, action and exception. The institution indicates what types of libraries or archives (more accurately, the library in an archive) are covered by the law. Most statutes cover only public libraries, i.e., those funded with public resources. Some state statutes indicate the specific type of "public" library covered by the statute, from traditional public to school to academic.[7] Most states, like Wisconsin, merely state that any library funded in whole or in part by public funds is subject to the provisions of the statute. Extending application is subject to interpretation by either courts or administrators. For example, the Wisconsin statute protecting the confidentiality of library records (Wisconsin Statutes § 43.30) does not apply to school libraries per se. However, there is an indication from the Wisconsin Department of Public Instruction that the state statute would protect the privacy of K–12 students in public school settings against parental and administration inquiries.[8] Expansion of a statute's scope can also occur by judicial interpretation. For example, a New York court recently indicated that the state's library privacy statute (containing language similar to Wisconsin statute 43.30) would protect a child's circulation record against parental curiosity in a traditional public (open to all members of the public) library setting.[9] In contrast, at least one state specifically excludes records of minors from protection in public library and school library settings, i.e., parental access is allowed.[10] Furthermore, the balance between the privacy of school library patrons (minor students) or minors in a traditional public library versus the authority of parents to direct the upbringing of their child is undergoing development in the courts. For example, the constitutional privacy right of minors against parental intrusion extends to health-related matters.[11] This may also suggest an expansion of the privacy rights of minors. On the one hand, since schools traditionally act in loco parentis, it could be argued that schoolchildren have no secrets from those in positions of authority in the school, such as the school media professional. This would be the case at least in those jurisdictions where the statute exempts the records of minors from protection. Librarians may, however, wish to protect the privacy of all patrons, including minors.

Could a parent request a list of school library material used or checked out by their child, or information on what web sites the child routinely visits? Perhaps there is no legal basis for a refusal; however, a right of privacy based upon ethical concerns might suggest otherwise. However a recent case in New Hampshire required that names and other identifying information from public school Internet logs be redacted prior to release to curious parents.[12] Granting borrowing privileges only to those children whose parents have agreed to honor their child's privacy is one option. What of protection for the college level student? Once the age of majority is reached it would seem difficult to find a legal basis for a parent's right to examine library records of their college-age son or daughter. This would be the case regardless of who bears the financial burden of the tuition commitment. As a practical matter, parents of college-age students might desire or believe it is their right to have such access, especially when those parents are financially supporting the education of their son or daughter.

Another problem is that confidentiality statutes apply only to publicly funded libraries, not to those libraries or libraries within archives that do not receive public monies, such as those that reside within private institutions—private institutions that are nonetheless open to the public, or have a large number of quasipublic patrons, such as a private university's faculty and students or its local community at large. Thus a large number of library and archive settings, while still fraught with problems of patron privacy, provide no legal recourse, as the library or archive is not covered by applicable state statute.[13] This underscores the need for an approved confidentiality policy to be in place and followed by all staff.

A second factor of concern in applying state library confidentiality statutes is coverage. The statute may focus on a particular type of record to the exclusion of others. A statute may for example, limit protection only to registration or circulation records[14] or it may include other types of records, such as notes from a reference interview,[15] or it may include any type of communication.[16] The statute may at the same time protect the confidentiality of the person—the library patron—not the underlying information. These are two quite different focuses. Consider the Wisconsin statute as an example. Section 43.30 indicates that, with certain exceptions, "records of any library which is in whole or part supported by public funds, including the records of a public library system, indicating the identity of any individual who borrows or uses the library's documents or other materials, resources, or services may not be disclosed."[17] The focus is not upon the person and his or her confidentiality, but upon the release of records "indicating the identity of" persons who use the library. In other words, records that do not identify a particular patron could be disclosed. The proscription also does not target the materials or services the particular patron uses; again the focus is upon prohibiting the release of the identity of the patron. So if a third party asked a librarian what the person sitting over by the third table was reading, the librarian, while not compelled to do so, could reveal what he or she observed the individual reading without violating the Wisconsin statute. This is so because the revealed observation is not a record containing identifiable information ("indicating the identity of any individual"); arguably it is not even a record. A similar result occurs if a third party asked to see the reference inquiry log for the day (suppose the log indicates what questions were asked and the sources to which patrons were directed). The librarian again, while not compelled to do so, could reveal the content of the log without violating the Wisconsin statute, as the log contains no information that indicates the "identity of any individual." One could even argue that a log that listed a patron's library card number next to the reference sources used would also not violate the Wisconsin statute, as a library card number does nothing to identify a particular person. However, a list of patron registration numbers could well be used in conjunction with additional access to registration records—unauthorized access to registration records would clearly be a violation of the statute—to eventually determine the identity of the targeted readers.

However, different states' statutes protect different interests. For example, the Florida statute does not allow a person to make "known in any manner any information contained in such records," but it limits such records to "registration and circulation."[18] Such a statute would even prohibit a circulation aid from releasing registration or circulation information verbally (even though this release may not be "record"). While it would not prohibit the release of the simple log sheet, the Florida statute would prohibit release of the enhanced log entries (those with registration numbers), as this would be part of informational content of the registration record. Obviously, this may or may not be the level of confidentiality (or the lack thereof) that most libraries or archives would like to offer to their patrons. These problems underscore the value of having a confidentiality policy, approved by the appropriate governing authority, that protects the privacy of library and archive patrons to the extent desired, often beyond the coverage provided by statute.

The third factor, action, considers what the library or archive may not do (and which would trigger the proscription of the statute). In general, this involves some type of disclosure to third parties of the proscribed record. Consider a library that routinely prints circulation receipts that reveal name, library registration number and title of the circulated item, then distributes the receipt to patrons as a record of the transaction. Is a confidentiality statue like Wisconsin's violated? The answer is "no" because the information, while meeting the definition of library record was not "disclosed" to a third party. What if the patron leaves the receipt in one of the items he or she returns. When the item is checked out to another patron, the subsequent borrower of the item comes into possession of the previous patron's receipt, with name, registration number and a list of the recent items borrowed. Has the library or archive violated the statute? Again, the answer is "no" because it was the patron who left the receipt in the item upon return. This could be construed as a consensual response (most state statutes allow for release subject to patron consent; see discussion below).

While the library did not violate the privacy of the patron, sensitive information may nonetheless have been revealed.

Other library practices may also raise privacy concerns. Consider a library that uses some form of manual sign-out or sign-up whereby subsequent patrons can view the names of previous patron-users of a particular resource or type of resource. One state legislature has had the foresight to anticipate the problem this might cause and requires libraries in its state to "use an automated or Gaylord-type circulation system that does not identify a patron with circulated materials after materials are returned."[19] Arguably, this statute may still not prohibit the printing of circulation receipts, but would just require the use of a system that does not store that data. These examples demonstrate the problems with printed receipts generated as a result of the use of automated systems or traditional manual record systems.

A final consideration is the exceptions to confidentiality that a statute creates by definition. Exceptions fall typically into three categories: court order or warrant, internal or external library administration, and consent. Court order means some direction or command delivered by a court or judge; a warrant is a form of court order that authorizes someone to do something, such as directing a law enforcement officer to make an arrest, conduct a search or perform a seizure. A subpoena is a request to take some action in conjunction with a covet proceeding such as to bring documents (e.g., circulation records) to court. (As a practical matter, staff need to be aware of what to do when the subpoena is served; e.g., the library or archive may consider refusal of subpoena execution pending a court hearing to review the grounds for the subpoena. If so, staff must be instructed as to the proper response. Situations can rapidly become complicated, as the legal counsel representing both parties—law enforcement and the library—may be part of the same legal office; e.g., both may be city attorneys. Legal counsel might also be from two governmental authorities with overlapping jurisdiction, e.g., a county district attorney representing law enforcement versus the city attorney's office or county corporation counsel representing the library. Furthermore, these issues are not routine and the attorneys may not be familiar with the applicable library confidentiality statutes.) Even the issue of compliance with a court order may not be that apparent. Some states restrict the "court order [to those arising] in a criminal proceeding."[20] In addition, one state court has held that a discovery order in a civil proceeding is not sufficient to override the protection afforded by the statute, as the matter must involve an order in conjunction with a criminal case.[21] However, most states appear to allow release pursuant to any "court order"[22] or specifically include a "civil court."[23]

Exceptions for internal and external administration would allow the library to release patron information to third parties for internal reporting purposes (billing of online database usage, for example). This might arguably include the release of circulation information to a parent or guardian in conjunction with the processing of fines or overdue notices. Also included is release to third parties for the external provision of services such as interlibrary loan, i.e., name of patron and item requested released to another library or archive.

Consent of course implies consent by the patron. However, the matter is not as clear when considering family members or professional colleagues. Can one pick up items held on reserve for his or her spouse, or can a research assistant obtain an item on hold for a faculty member at the interlibrary loan desk? It would appear that while no record "indicating the identity" of the spouse or faculty is disclosed when the item is merely picked by a family member or colleague, it would also appear that under some circumstances the spirit of a library confidentiality statute is less than fulfilled. What of the situation where one patron asks the library or archive which patron has borrowed item X, or if the patron asks: "can you tell me if Professor A has borrowed item Y?" It would seem that this is precisely the sort of confidence the library or archive would like to maintain, yet in Wisconsin the statute may not prohibit this type of release. In the first instance, a verbal revelation may not be a record. Second, no name or other personally identifiable information is released. Again, states that prohibit partial disclosure or do not necessarily tie the prohibition to personally identifiable information (i.e., more than "identity" alone) may bring stronger opposition to disclosure.[24] As observed earlier, the lack of more extensive statutory protection does not compel disclosure, but places stronger emphasis on the adoption of individual library policy to fill in the gaps in the statutory scheme. Obviously, if faculty desire this type of sharing, and the library or archive would like to accommodate such mechanisms, then a simple strategy of recording collegial acknowledgment would have the effect of complying with the privacy concerns of the library or legislature as articulated in the statute. It would also satisfy the needs of library or archive patrons. This recorded consent would then allow a fellow faculty or research assistant to retrieve material from or for another faculty member. At least one statute provides for the release of reserve items to other family or household patrons. In the alternative, a patron may limit the release of reserve items.[25] This is an area where a library or archive confidentiality policy can provide the detail a state statute may lack. Enforcement, however, is only as good as the staff that implements a given statute or policy.[26] The final step after adoption is training of staff so that front-line employees are familiar with the policy and its application in the various scenarios discussed herein.

The Rights of Students in Educational Library and Archive Settings

For librarians and archivists at educational institutions, the Family Educational Rights and Privacy Act of 1974 (FERPA)[27] may create additional privacy concerns if student information is somehow posted on the institutional web site or otherwise made available to third parties. In general, FERPA covers the release of student records to third parties.[28] This might occur if the institution is creating a video yearbook of student-patrons or electronic library transactions logs are accessible to subsequent users (and the logs contain personally identifiable student information). FERPA may also be implicated when students interact with institutional computing facilities, as when students create individual web pages containing personal information on the school server. If the school's web yearbook or other student information consists of simple name and address, or if sporting event information includes weight and height, it might be considered "directory information" and exempt under FERPA. However, in order to qualify for the directory exemption under 20 U.S.C. §1232g(5) the "educational agency or institution making public directory information shall give public notice of the categories of information which it had designated as such information with respect to each student attending the institution or agency and shall allow a reasonable period of time after which notice has been given for a parent to inform the institution or agency that any or all of the information designated should not be released without the parent's prior consent."[29] In other words, the information could not be posted unless the parent (of a minor) or student (of majority age) specifically consents to its posting or release. In the design of privacy protection mechanisms this is known as a positive opt-out, i.e., notice of the impending disclosure is given to the data subject and will proceed unless objection by the data subject is forthcoming.[30]

While many parents may not object to such information being printed in a school playbill or sports program, parents or students may not desire to see personal information posted on the World Wide Web, even the sort of directory information allowed by the section 5 FERPA exception. Disclosures of other information are prohibited. The World Wide Web is a wonderful tool, but it is also becoming the leading communication medium for sexual or other predators for finding victims.[31] This reality suggests that educational institutions must take precaution when releasing student information into that medium. It is recommended that parental or student notice and permission are sought before any personal identifying information of students is posted on the institution's web page or otherwise published.

A general right of privacy or right of publicity may also be a concern when the library or archive contemplates the publication of a patron's photographs or other personal information in printed publications or on the institution's web page. (The right of publicity is most likely a nonissue in most educational settings, as it protects a person's right to benefit from a commercial exploitation of his or her image, likeness or persona. For example, in higher education, National Collegiate Athletic Association rules prohibit student athletes from profiting—receiving royalties—from representations of their athletic performances.)[32] It is not possible to review the law of privacy or the law of publicity here.[33] However, it is important to note that those circumstances where a library or archive would need to be concerned about the privacy and publicity rights of patrons through publications of photographs or other personal information in analog or print environments is likewise a concern in web or digital environments. Consider a library or archive that allows patrons to register in a virtual gallery, facilitates a discussion among common resource users (e.g., a local genealogy group), or institutes a virtual reference service whereby previous queries are briefly indexed and made accessible to subsequent patrons. Depending on the particular facts (the level of patron information revealed) in each case, an issue of patron privacy or publicity right might be present. Of course, obtaining consent before participation or posting is always advisable and may alleviate subsequent claims of invasion of privacy or misappropriation of publicity rights.

Traditionally, the right of privacy includes four possible grounds for action: intrusion into seclusion, disclosure of private facts, false light, and appropriation (or more accurately a misappropriation) of likeness. Like the right of publicity, the right of privacy is dictated by state law and thus varies from state to state, making a complete and accurate discussion impossible. However, several general comments can be made. For a cause of action for intrusion the information released must be of some matter that is entitled to be private. Furthermore, the intrusion must be offensive to the reasonable person. It appears unlikely that a library or archive would actively invade the seclusion of its patrons. However, the release of personal patron information may be the sort of disclosure contemplated in the second and third genus of privacy invasions. The public disclosure of private facts must be some embarrassing private fact that again would be objectionable to the reasonable person. False light would also include a public disclosure that would place someone in a false light with the public, and it would also need to offend the reasonable person. The difference between disclosure and false light is that, in the latter, the facts disclosed have to be false. A library or archive might display photographs of patrons engaged in the use of the library or archive for use in various library or archive promotions or publications. What if the photograph revealed some embarrassing private fact? The photograph might indicate the patron is reading a book on "coping with your sex-change operation." This might satisfy the elements of a disclosure claim and it might also violate a state library confidentiality statute that prohibits a wide range of disclosures.

Consider a library that publishes a photograph in its monthly newsletter that poses a prominent elected official next to children using the library. The caption reads, "early readers get off to good start at the library." This might raise a question of false light (that the elected official is a beginning reader), though accusations of false light typically involve some ill intent or motive. A classic example is *Uhl v. CBS, Inc.*, in which a public official and hunter was shown in a highly edited television documentary to be shooting geese that were merely standing instead of flying.[34] "Offensive publicity in this context tends to consist of linking an unrelated person with controversial issues (e.g., drug use, prostitution, certain sexual attitudes, gambling) through the unauthorized use of photographs, attributions of opinion, or use of a name on a petition or in a lawsuit."[35] To avoid any dispute, permission should be sought whenever the likeness of a patron is to be published or otherwise used in promotional material. Carol Mann Simpson suggests a release form (intended for use in school settings but easily adaptable for general use) that allows subjects to choose from among certain formats of persona: name, voice, likeness, quotes, written material and graphic or other art work that may be released upon consent.[36]

A claim of appropriation requires that one's name or likeness be used without permission for some advantage of the user. Traditionally, the appropriation is thought to require a commercial or monetary advantage, but the line between a right of privacy misappropriation (the fourth genus of privacy invasion) and a right of publicity is blurred in the case law.[37] "The right of appropriation should not be confused with the right to publicity, which permits a person to capitalize on the commercial exploitation of his name or likeness, and to prevent others from doing so without his consent. . . . It, unlike the right of appropriation, survives the death of its owners and is assignable."[38] In the library or archive photograph scenario, the appropriation must be of the likeness, i.e., it must identify the person. Using the likeness (photograph) of a patron on a promotional poster sold to raise funds for the library might rise to the level of a misappropriation claim. Selling reprints of the photograph of the star player of the school basketball team might also qualify. However, misappropriation traditionally results when someone is thrust unwillingly into the public eye involving some aspect of his or her reputation or integrity (as opposed to a right of publicity, in which the commercial value of the image or likeness is exploited).[39] A right of publicity cause of action might lie if a celebrity image is used in the promotional poster. This would not be the case when the library uses a patron image, as the library could have chosen any patron. The patron whose image was used without permission (appropriation) was not selected because of any inherent commercial value or appeal. In any case, taking precautions when posting the persona of students or patrons, i.e., seeking permission, will limit the liability of the library or archive in this area.

Electronic Tracking, Data Collection and Communication

Another area of concern arises when the library or archive site is collecting information from visitors. Again, this might be done through an online log feature, registration or other facilitation of information exchange among patrons or among patrons and other third parties. Recent federal law[40] regulates the collection of personal information from children where the "website or online service is operated for commercial purposes." Although a library or archive web site would not normally operate a web site or online service for a "commercial purpose," it may be wise for a library or archive web site to nonetheless protect or limit its information collection and use practices. One option would be to conform the library or archive information collection practices to that of the new law, the Children's Privacy Protection and Parental Empowerment Act of 1998 (CPPPEA). An essential feature of the new law is its requirement that a web site collecting information from children have privacy notices posted that indicate what information is collected, how it will be used, if it will be released to third parties and the protection provisions available to site visitors.

The law requires that, for children twelve and under, the parents of the child who is the subject of the information collection or use must receive notice and an opportunity to prevent the collection of personal information (an opt-in). There is also a prohibition against a web site making a child's participation in a web activity conditional on the collection of more information than is necessary to participate in the initial activity. The CPPPEA applies to a variety of Internet environments, including a web site, pen pal service, e-mail and online message board or chat room. Personal information includes "individually identifiable information," including first and last name, physical or virtual address, phone or social security number. Most if not all library and archive scenarios discussed herein would not be covered by the "commercial purposes" definition of the new law (a violation is deemed an "unfair trade practice" subject to Federal Trade Commission enforcement action). Likewise, the library or archive patron base would seldom entirely consist of minors, thus making the law not applicable to every patron collection. However, the law still provides a valuable lesson for those public institutions, like libraries or archives, collecting personal information from patrons.

These principles can be used to construct a fair information practice for data collection: notice, access and options. If the library or archive collects information from patrons through its web site, e.g., registration or membership information, it would be wise to at least have a privacy notice directed to site visitors as part of the organization's legal web page. In the alternative, a similar warning may be located at the place on the site where the information collection occurs. Including a notice and consent (opt-in) provision that mirrors the provisions of the CPPPEA[41] is advisable. Such provisions would be consistent with developing standards of fair information practices in web environments.[42] Likewise, the library or archive should take steps to ensure that patrons do not release their own personal information and reading preferences to third parties. The release of personal information collected by third parties raises not only legal but ethical considerations that are beyond the scope of this article. Are the educational or other eleemosynary activities of the library or archive (patron pen pal feature or patron contest) a disguised marketing device to collect personal information about a patron's likes and dislikes and other preferences in the name of education vis-à-vis corporate sponsorship of the event? Controversy has arisen in K–12 settings as a result of the corporate sponsorship of various learning activities, from reading programs to science experiments.[43] Such sponsorships are nothing more than a subterfuge for the collection of marketing data.

Does the library or archive sell or otherwise release its membership lists to third parties, including marketers, or share its membership lists with similar organizations? If the data is collected electronically, then CPPPEA and the developing principles referenced herein may apply. Regardless, the fair information practice discussed and referenced should be instituted and adhered to by library or archive when patron information is collected or accessible to third parties. Patrons should have access to the store of data collected to determine accuracy of the information and have the ability to correct errors. Patrons should receive notice regarding the collecting practices of the site and have the ability to control the uses the library or archive makes of the information thus collected. (Note: the fair information practices discussed with respect to collection, use and release of personal membership data apply equally to museums, libraries and archives.)

A related issue is whether or not the tracking (active interception) of individual staff or student use of web site activity would violate other federal or state privacy laws. Major federal legislation regulating the interception of electronic communication is the Electronic Communications Privacy Act (ECPA),[44] which applies to oral, wire, and electronic communications, including the digitized portion of voice or visual communications. In general, the interception of oral, wire, and electronic communications is prohibited. However, issues of access to and release of stored communications are less clear. The statute is written in such a way as to allow access to stored electronic communications, such as e-mail, once the message is sent and stored on the employer's e-mail system. First, it should be noted that the ECPA does allow the provider of a computer communications system to access stored communications, which would be the library or archive that runs its own web server and other computing facilities.[45] However, there is debate regarding this issue. As one author notes, "some bulletin board operators and computer service providers argue that they have the right to authorize themselves to access the stored communications of users and have been known to rely upon this section of the statute as a carte blanche to monitor" these communications.[46] Release to third parties, it is assumed, is prohibited.[47] The focus of the ECPA is on the interception of the communication. Therefore, a library or archive that provides its own computing facilities, as most do, would be able to access stored messages or view postings made or determine a list of web sites visited on a certain account, for example. Most organizations use these exceptions to the ECPA to monitor employee accounts. Moreover, case law tends to support this interpretation.[48] Another way for a library or archive administrator to legally intercept a communication is to obtain the consent of the parties.[49] This consent may be made part of a general web or institutional computer network acceptable use policy that staff and patrons may be required to sign (or click on, thus indicating assent) before system privileges are granted.

Conclusion

A variety of laws exist to protect the privacy of library and archive patrons. Traditional protection mechanisms protect the record of patron use of public library material and services. Developing practices suggest that the protection of personal information in digital or web environments will expand. Public institutions need to be vigilant to potential for abuse and must recognize the shortcomings of existing law. A careful review of the governing state statute in conjunction with the implementation of a supplementing privacy policy is recommended.

Notes

This publication is designed to provide accurate and authoritative information in regard to the subject matter covered. However, this information is NOT provided as a substitute for legal advice. If legal advice or expert assistance is required, the services of a competent legal professional should be sought.

1. Exec. Order No. 12,333, 46 C.F.R. 59941 (1981).

2. See Herbert N. Foerstel, *Surveillance in the Stacks: The FBI's Library Awareness Program* (New York: Greenwood, 1991); Ulrika Ekman Ault, *The FBI's Library Awareness Program: Is Big Brother Reading Over Your Shoulder?* 65 New York University Law Review 1532 (1990).

3. Robert Homan, Video Rental Privacy Bill Introduced, *Electronic Media*, May 16, 1988, at 16.

4. Pub. L. No. 100-618, § 2(a)(1), 102 Stat. 3195, codified at 18 U.S.C. §2710 (2000).

5. Video and Library Protection Act, H.R. 4947, 100th Cong., 2d Sess. (1988); Video and Library Protection Act, S. 2361, 100th Cong., 2nd Sess. (1988).

6. Two excellent summaries of the law, state by state, are found in, Shirley A. Wiegand, *Library Records: A Retention and Confidentiality Guide* (New York: Greenwood, 1994); Arlene Bielefield and Lawrence Cheeseman, *Maintaining the Privacy of Library Records: A Handbook and Guide* (New York: Neal-Schuman, 1994).

7. See, Arkansas Statutes Annotated § 13-2-703(a); 24 Pennsylvania Statutes § 4428.

8. Robert J. Paul, *Access: Statutes Outline Requirements Regarding School Library Circulation Records,* Education Forward, August 1991, at 17.

9. *In the matter of Quad/Graphics, Inc. v. Southern Adirondack Library System*, 174 Misc. 2d 291, 664 N.Y.S. 2d 225 (1997).

10. See Alabama Code §§ 36-12-10 and 36-12-40; Florida Statutes § 257.261, which gives parents of persons under age sixteen access to their child's records.

11. *Hodgson v. Minnesota*, 497 U.S. 417 (1990).

12. *James M. Knight v. School Administration Unit #16*, Docket No. 00-E-307 (Superior Court, New Hampshire, 2001). See "Exeter Internet Ruling, Complete Ruling," *Portsmouth Herald*, January 8, 2001 at http://www.seacoastonline.com/news/1 8specialhtm; See also, "Set Internet Log Retention Policy to Avoid Lawsuits by Parents," *School Superintendent Insider*, June 2001, at 4.

13. See Bruce M. Kennedy, *Confidentiality of Library Records: A Survey of Problems, Policies, and Laws,* 81 Law Library Journal 746 (1989).

14. See California Government Code § 6267 ("registration and circulation"); District of Columbia Code § 37-106.2 ("circulation records"); Florida Statutes § 257.261 ("registration and circulation").

15. See Arkansas Statutes Annotated § 13-2-703(a) ("reference queries").

16. See South Dakota Codified Laws § 14-2-51 ("any information").

17. Wisconsin Statutes § 43.30.

18. Florida Statutes § 257.261.

19. Arkansas Statutes Annotated § 13-2-703(a).

20. 24 Pennsylvania Statues § 4428.

21. *In the matter of Quad/Graphics, Inc. v. Southern Adirondack Library System,* 174 Misc. 2d 291, 664 N.Y.S. 2d 225 (1997).

22. See Arizona Revised Statutes § 41-1354; North Carolina General Statutes § 125-19.

23. Arkansas Statutes Annotated § 13-2-703(a).

24. The Arkansas statute prohibits disclosure of "documents or information in any format, . . . including . . . title reserve requests." Arkansas Statutes Annotated § 13-2-703(a). In Florida, libraries "may not make known in any manner any information contained in such [registration and circulation] records." Florida Statutes § 257.261

25. Minnesota Statutes § 13.40.

26. Bruce S. Johnson, *"A More Cooperative Clerk": The Confidentiality of Library Records,* 81 Law Library Journal 769 (1989).

27. Pub. L. No. 93-380, Title V, § 513(b)(2)(i), 88 Stat. 574, codified at 20 U.S.C. § 1232g (1998).

28. See John E. Theuman, *Validity, Construction, and Application of Family Educational Rights and Privacy Act of 1974 (FERPA) (20 USCS § 1232g),* 112 A.L.R. Fed. 1 (1997).

29. See *Oregon County R-IV School District v. Le Mon,* 739 S.W. 2d 553 (Mo. App. 1987), on disclosure permitted under FERPA and implementing regulations (34 C.F.R. § 99.37) if notice, parental opt-out and time limit within which to object to release is stated.

30. Tomas A. Lipinski, "Legislative Responses to the Abuse of Personal Information in the Consumer Marketplace," in *Ethics and Electronic Information in the Twenty-First Century,* ed. Lester J. Pourciau (West Lafayette, Ind.: Purdue University Press, 1999), 199–230. A negative opt-out is a mechanism whereby the default is to release the information and the data subject must take affirmative steps to prevent disclosure. It is the weakest form of privacy protection. The strongest form is an opt-in mechanism in which the party wishing to release the information must seek the permission of the data subject before that release can occur. Here the default is against release. A positive opt-out described in the text herein is a middle ground.

31. David Armagh, *A Safety Net for the Internet: Protecting Our Children,* 5 Juvenile Justice 9 (1997); Federal Trade Commission, *Staff Letter to Center for Media Education* (July 15, 1997), available at http://www.ftc.gov/os/1997/9707/cenmed.htm.

32. Vladimir P. Belo, *The Shirts off Their Backs: Colleges Getting Away with Violating the Right of Publicity,* 19 *Hastings Communications and Entertainment Journal* 133 (1996).

33. See James N. Talbot, *New Media: Intellectual Property, Entertainment and Technology Law* (New York: Clark Boardman Callaghan, 1997), chapter 8, "Right of Privacy"; chapter 9, "Right of Publicity."

34. *Uhl v. CBS, Inc.*, 476 F. Supp. 1134 (W.D. Pa. 1984).

35. Kent D. Stuckey, *Internet and Online Law*, § 5.02[10], at 5-12–5-13 (2000).

36. Carol Mann Simpson, *Copyright for Schools: A Practical Guide for Schools*, 112 (2d ed.), appendix F, "Release Form."(Worthington, Ohio: Linworth, 1997).

37. James N. Talbot, *New Media: Intellectual Property, Entertainment and Technology Law*, § 8:13, at p. 8-13 (1997).

38. Kent D. Stuckey, *Internet and Online Law*, § 5.02[10], at 5-12–5-13 (2000).

39. James N. Talbot, *New Media: Intellectual Property, Entertainment and Technology Law*, § 8:9, at p. 8-11 (1997).

40. Children's Privacy Protection and Parental Empowerment Act of 1998, Pub. L. No. 105-277, 112 Stat. 2681, Title XIII (1998).

41. The Federal Trade Commission (FTC) earlier had advocated that for children over age twelve parental notice be required, but that parents only be given the opportunity to restrict collection after the fact (an opt-out). Consistent with the new law, the FTC now suggests that, for children age twelve and under, actual notice to parents and consent be received before the collection is conducted (opt-in). See Federal Trade Commission, *Privacy Online: A Report to Congress* (1998), available at http://www.ftc.gov/reports/privacy3/.

42. National Telecommunications and Information Administration, *Privacy and the NII: Safeguarding Telecommunications Related Personal Information* (1995), available at http://www/ntia.doc.gov/ntiahome/policy/privwhitepaper.html; and National Information Infrastructure Task Force Working Group on Privacy, *Principles for Providing and Using Personal Information* (1995), available at http://www.iitf.nist.gov/ipc/ipc.ipc-pubs/niiprivprin_final.html.

43. See Nadya Labi, *Classrooms for Sale,* Time, April 19, 1999, at 44; Alex Molnar, *Giving Kids the Business: The Commercialization of America's Schools* (Boulder, Colo.: Westview, 1996); and Molnar, "The Commercial Transformation of American Public Education" (unpublished manuscript), available at www.uwm.edu/Dept/CASE/documents/1999phil.html; and other publications available from CASE (Center for the Analysis of Commercialism in Education) at www.uwm.edu/Dept/CASE/archives.html.

44. 18 U.S.C. § 2501 et seq. (1998).

45. 18 U.S.C. § 2701(C)(1).

46. Kent D. Stuckey, *Internet and Online Law,* § 5.03[1][iv], at 5-20.2 (2000).

47. 18 U.S.C. §§ 2511(3), 2702(a).

48. See e.g., *Smith v. Pillsbury Co.*, 914 F. Supp. 97 (E.D. Pa. 1996). In this case, an employee was terminated for transmitting inappropriate and unprofessional remarks over his employer's e-mail system. It was ruled that once the employee had communicated over the system, any reasonable expectation of privacy was lost. See also Jana Howard Carey and Thomas Strong, *Privacy Law Limits Electronic Monitoring in the Workplace,* Employment Testing–Law and Policy Reporter, January 1996, at 1.

49. 18 U.S.C. § 2511 (1998).

CHAPTER 8

Welcome to . . . The Legal Responsibility to Offer Accessible Electronic Information to Patrons with Disabilities

Mary Minow

> When blind people use the Internet and come across unfriendly sites, we aren't surfing, we are crawling. . . . Imagine hearing pages that say, "Welcome to . . . [image] This is the home of . . . [image]." "Link, link, link." It is like trying to use Netscape with your monitor off and your mouse unplugged. See how far you'll get.
>
> Blind user, using a text reader to interpret the Internet[1]

Introduction

SCENARIO: PATTY PATRON IN THE LIBRARY

Patty Patron, who has been visually impaired since birth, comes into the library. She uses a Kurzweil machine to read printed books aloud to her. Next she uses a CD-ROM with full-text magazine articles, and again listens to the contents. She hears about an interesting book on modern art and checks the online card catalog to see if the library owns it. It does. Since it is difficult for her to make the trip to the library, she is delighted to learn that the library has a web page, with access to both the magazine article collection and the online card catalog, that she can access on her home computer.

Is this a realistic scenario? What do patrons with disabilities encounter when they try to access electronic information in libraries, museums and archives today? Until recently, computers were generally easy for most people with disabilities to use. "Screen readers" could turn written text into the spoken word, using ever more sophisticated synthesized voices. Very few technology applications contained auditory features, so most people who were deaf or hard of hearing had no trouble using the technology.[2]

Ironically, however, as technology has grown more sophisticated, with graphics, streaming video, and audio, screen readers can no longer "read" these features, unless the features are accompanied by text explanations.

Today, libraries, museums and archives increasingly create electronic content through the digitization of collections and the creation of web pages. Some disabled patrons cannot readily come to the libraries and museums at all. Remote access can bring the library and museum world to them, but only if the sites are accessible.

ADOPTING UNIVERSAL DESIGN GUIDELINES FOR ELECTRONIC INFORMATION

Libraries, museums and archives face legal challenges by their users when they purchase or create electronic content that is not accessible. To ensure that their patrons are able to use their electronic resources, they should adopt universal design guidelines for electronic information.

Universal design is a term used in architecture and elsewhere that describes design features that increase accessibility for all. For example, ramps provide wheelchair users, baby strollers and utility carts ready entrance into buildings. Universal design generally makes minor additions to digital content that are not visible to most users. The cost of these changes, for the most part, is minimal, although it increases with the sophistication of multimedia.

As respected institutions with both a mission and a legal obligation to provide patrons equal access to their information services regardless of disability, libraries, museums and archives should be at the forefront in adopting universal design standards when purchasing and creating electronic information resources.

POLICY IMPLICATIONS AND LEGAL ARGUMENTS

This chapter explores disability laws and public access as they apply to libraries, museums and archives. It gives a legal framework of disability laws as applied to public and private libraries, museums and archives, showing that a fundamental policy goal is expanding access to people with disabilities, particularly in new facilities and services. It looks at recent legal developments relating to disability access and the Internet, and makes the argument that libraries, museums and archives need to adopt standards ensuring universal access to information technology to expand information access to patrons with disabilities.

It examines policy implications and legal arguments concerning library adoption of universal guidelines. Specifically, it looks at the legal distinctions between existing materials, newly acquired materials, and content created by libraries, museums and archives, such as digital projects and web pages. It reviews current arguments revolving around the notion that privately created web pages are public accommodations, subject to the Americans with Disabilities Act (ADA). Finally, it examines the impact of accessibility regulations on cost, innovation, and the First Amendment.

Background Facts and Legal Doctrines

It is estimated that 12 million visually impaired persons plus 39 million learning disabled persons in the United States cannot access printed materials because of their disabilities. In addition, 11.7 million physically disabled people cannot hold a book or turn a sheet of paper.[3]

According to the President's Committee on Employment of People with Disabilities, the number of people with disabilities can be expected to accelerate quickly in the coming decades as the population ages. The Committee estimates that some form of disability will affect approximately one out of five U.S. citizens in her lifetime.[4]

The Trace Research and Development Center at the University of Wisconsin at Madison, a leading research center in the area of access to computers by people with disabilities, notes that there is a tremendous variety in the specific causes, combinations and severity of disabilities. The Trace center examines disabilities by categorizing access issues into four groups: visual impairments, hearing impairments, physical impairments and cognitive/language impairments.[5]

According to a study by the Disability Statistics Center, Institute for Health and Aging (University of California, San Francisco), people with disabilities are perhaps the single segment of society with the most to gain from computer access, yet have among the lowest rates of use.[6] Many cannot afford Internet access, making library and museum access especially critical.

ACCESSIBILITY

> The online system certainly is an exciting development and I plan to exercise it posthaste. Methinks it'll be fun once again to "browse the stacks," so to speak.
>
> User comment in 1993 on the development of an online public access catalog for the Washington Talking Book and Braille Library[7]

Today, the presentation of electronic information is changing. Amid this change, are patrons with physical impairments, hearing impairments and cognitive/language impairments able to access the information they seek in libraries, museums and archives?

Information technology is generally considered "accessible" if it can be used in a variety of ways that do not depend on a single sense or ability. For example, a system that provides output only in audio format would not be accessible to people with hearing impairments, and a system that requires mouse actions to navigate would not be accessible to people who cannot use a mouse because of dexterity or visual impairments.[8]

Early electronic content, usually text-based, was accessible with assistive devices. Though it was not immediately recognized at the time, the online public access catalog was "a god-send for disabilities access, especially for blind and visually impaired users."[9] The explosion of online databases, online public library catalogs and CD-ROM products benefited the visually impaired by making information more accessible.[10]

According to Barbara Mates, a prominent speaker and writer on library services to persons with disabilities, adaptive technology allows people with disabilities independent access to text-based information. Encyclopedias on CD-ROM can be read with synthesized voices, automatically translated into Braille or displayed on a screen in large print.[11] Such devices help both people with visual impairments and some learning disabled people with dyslexia.[12]

The standard computer interface—keyboard, mouse and screen—presents many obstacles for people with a variety of mobility impairments. Today, many companies have addressed many of these problems with ingenuity. Mouse and keyboard simulators as well as special switches allow persons with some mobility limitations to use computers. Voice recognition programs can allow a user to perform online searches.[13]

How accessible is the electronic information in libraries, museums and archives today? To address this question, one would need to look at two levels of access. First, does the computer have adaptive devices, such as speakers, text-based browsers and magnification? Second, if it does, is the electronic information created with universal design standards making it accessible?

In higher education, studies on these issues show that most institutions have a designated person in the library to deal with disability cases.[14] However, a 1996 study found that only 9 percent of the surveyed academic libraries in Ohio provided Internet services in audio form to patrons with disabilities.[15]

According to the World Wide Web Consortium (W3C), "common accessibility problems on web sites include images without alternative text; lack of alternative text for image map hot spots; misleading use of structural elements on pages; uncaptioned audio or undescribed video; lack of alternative information for users who cannot access frames or scripts; tables that are difficult to decipher when linearized; and sites with poor color contrast.[16]

Formed at the Massachusetts Institute of Technology in 1994, the W3C has sought to establish Internet guidelines and protocols. In 1996, it spun off the Web Accessibility Initiative in conjunction with the White House. The project was set up to make the Internet more available to people with disabilities.[17]

On May 5, 1999, the W3C released the "Web Content Accessibility Guidelines 1.0." The fourteen guidelines are general principles of accessible design. Each guideline is associated with one or more checkpoints describing how to apply that guideline to particular features of web pages. An appendix to the guidelines, "List of Checkpoints for the Web Content Accessibility Guidelines 1.0," presents the checkpoints sorted by priority. Priority one is for checkpoints that a developer must satisfy, otherwise some groups of people will be unable to access information on a site; priority two is for checkpoints a developer should satisfy, or else it will be very difficult for some people to access information; priority three a developer may satisfy, otherwise some people will find it difficult to access information.[18]

On February 3, 2000, the W3C announced the release of the "Authoring Tool Accessibility Guidelines 1.0." These guidelines show developers how to design accessible authoring tools that produce accessible web content. The guidelines explain how developers can encourage and assist in the production of accessible web content through prompts, alerts, checking and repair functions in their tools. Many of these principles promote interoperability of the web in general.[19]

On March 31, 2000, the federal government published its proposed "Electronic and Information Technology Accessibility Standards," to be followed by all federal agencies.[20] The standards were developed by the Architectural and Transportation Barriers Compliance Board (the Access Board), which is responsible for accessibility guidelines in buildings and transportation, including the "ADA Accessibility Guidelines for Buildings and Facilities" (ADAAG).[21]

The standards include provisions based generally on priority level one checkpoints of the "Web Content Accessibility Guidelines 1.0." The standards are also based on other agency documents on web accessibility and additional recommendations of the Electronic and Information Technology Access Advisory Committee. The committee was appointed by the Access Board and was composed of representatives of the electronic and information technology industry, organizations representing the access needs of individuals with disabilities, and other persons affected by accessibility standards for electronic and information technology.[22] A summary paragraph is in appendix B of this chapter.

EQUAL INFORMATION ACCESS

Libraries, museums and archives value equity of access among their patrons, regardless of disability. In libraries, for example, two of the eight core values of the profession (currently in draft form) are "Assurance of equitable access to recorded knowledge, information and creative works" and "Respect for the individuality and diversity of all people."[23]

One of the American Library Association's most venerable documents is its "Library Bill of Rights," which ensures equal treatment to all library patrons. An interpretative document, "Questions and Answers: Access to Electronic Information, Services and Networks. An Interpretation of the Library Bill of Rights," includes the following question and answer:

> Q. Does our library have to make provisions for patrons with disabilities to access electronic information?
>
> A. Yes. The Americans with Disabilities Act and other federal and state laws forbid providers of public services, whether publicly or privately governed, from discriminating against individuals with disabilities. All library information services, including access to electronic information, should be accessible to patrons regardless of disability. Many methods are available and under development to make electronic information universally accessible, including adaptive devices, software, and human assistance. Libraries must consider such tools in trying to meet the needs of persons with disabilities in the design or provision of electronic information services.[24]

The American Association of Museums (AAM), founded in 1906, has grown to include more than 16,400 members, including more than 11,400 museum professionals, 3,000 museums, and 1,900 corporate members. The AAM offers an accessibility award to a facility that excels in the use of universal design principles. In 1999, the award was given to the Brookfield Zoo for its accessibility program, which is led by a full-time coordinator and is responsive to program participants and visitors' evaluations.[25]

The emphasis on equality of access should propel libraries, museums and archives to take a leadership position, even if there were no federal and state laws. A hard look at the laws should expedite such actions, even when resources are tight.

DISABILITY LAW

The disability rights movement gained significant momentum by the early 1970s, and Congress responded by passing several laws protecting people with disabilities. The evolution of disability rights laws demonstrates that access to information and communication is a civil right for people with disabilities, with an overriding goal of expanding access to facilities and services.

The Rehabilitation Act of 1973 was the first piece of legislation designed to ensure federal agencies, their contractors, and their financially assisted programs and activities would provide access to their employees and beneficiaries.[26]

The Architectural Barriers Act of 1968[27] and the Education for All Handicapped Children Act of 1975[28] mandated that schools be accessible to people with disabilities.

The Telecommunications for the Disabled Act of 1982, which stated that "making the benefits of the technological revolution in telecommunications available to all Americans, including those with disabilities, should be a priority for our national communications policy," was the first federal law to directly address the need for access to new technologies by individuals with disabilities.[29]

In 1987, the Civil Rights Restoration Act extended section 504 of the Rehabilitation Act's coverage to any institution in receipt of federal monies by any department within a postsecondary institution, including student financial aid.[30]

In 1990, President George H. Bush signed the Americans with Disabilities Act into law. It is the first federal accessibility law to apply to private companies as well as government contracts. Title II, which covers public libraries, museums and archives, has nearly identical provisions as section 504 of the Rehabilitation Act, but extends the law to all state and local government, regardless of federal funding.[31] Title III covers private entities, many of which are covered for the first time, and is both less stringent and more detailed than Title II.

The Telecommunications Act of 1996 required telecommunications services and equipment to be accessible, where readily achievable. Where this is not readily achievable, such services and equipment must be compatible with existing peripheral devices, where readily achievable.[32]

In 1998, the Assistive Technology Act was designed to support programs of grants to states to address the assistive technology needs of individuals with disabilities, and for other purposes.[33] A guide to disability rights laws is available through the Department of Justice.[34]

Recent actions of the Supreme Court show a deep shifting of power from the federal government to state governments, particularly with regard to whether an individual may sue a state government in federal court. The Court ruled in January 2000 that states were immune to suit under the federal law against age discrimination.[35] The previous June, the Court ruled that state employees could not sue states for violating the federal labor law governing minimum wages and hours.[36]

In an unusual turn of events in March 2000, two separate ADA cases were accepted for review by the Supreme Court and then immediately settled. In *Florida Dept. of Corrections v. Dickson*, the Eleventh Circuit upheld the constitutionality of the ADA by rejecting the state's claim of immunity from suit by a prison guard in 1998.[37] In *Alsbrook v. City of Maumelle, Arkansas*, the Eighth Circuit came to the opposite conclusion, holding that states cannot be sued under the ADA.[38] Both cases settled, the first perhaps for political reasons, and the second for fear of losing.[39]

Nevertheless, a Supreme Court examination of the issue of state immunity to the ADA seems inevitable. On April 17, 2000, the Court agreed to hear another case, *Garett v. Univ. of Alabama at Birmingham Bd. Of Trustees*.[40] The key question is whether the U.S. Congress had the authority to extend the ADA's disability nondiscrimination mandate to the states.

The lower courts are split on the issue. In the spring of 2000, two cases in the Seventh Circuit held that states are immune, *Georgeen Stevens v. Illinois Department of Transportation* and *Erickson v. Board of Governors*.[41] A district court in Pennsylvania, however, found that the Commonwealth of Pennsylvania was not entitled to Eleventh Amendment immunity.[42]

In *Dare v. State of California*, the Ninth Circuit decided that a disabled parking placard fee was a surcharge that violated the ADA. In response, Governor Gray Davis recently asked the Supreme Court to hear the case, explicitly asking the Court to rule that Eleventh Amendment immunity protects California.[43]

In addition to federal laws, most states and some cities have their own antidiscrimination laws covering people with disabilities. In California, many state provisions are stricter than the federal provisions. Under California law, no person may be denied the benefits of, or be unlawfully subjected to discrimination under, any program or activity either funded directly or assisted financially by the state.[44] Additionally, persons who are disabled are entitled to full and equal access to places of public accommodation.[45] Where differences exist between state and local law and the ADA, the more stringent requirement applies.[46]

Americans with Disabilities Act

In 1990, the Americans with Disabilities Act (ADA)[47] was enacted to provide a national mandate for the elimination of discrimination against individuals with disabilities. ADA gave the federal government a central role in enforcing standards, invoking the sweep of congressional authority, including the power to enforce the Fourteenth Amendment and to regulate commerce.[48]

Of the various issues arising under the ADA, employment discrimination has received the greatest scrutiny and press coverage. However, Titles II and III of the act have had a sweeping impact on the obligations of public and private entities. These titles require physical access as well as equal opportunity to use public and private service and programs.

Disability Access Obligations of Libraries, Museums and Archives

All libraries, museums and archives that are part of federal agencies are subject to the Rehabilitation Act of 1973, section 508. National security systems are exempted. On August 7, 1998, section 508 was amended by the Workforce Investment Act. This act requires federal departments or agencies to develop, procure, maintain and use accessible electronic and information technology. Federal libraries, museums and archives must ensure that their electronic and information technology allows federal employees with disabilities to have access to and use of information and data that is comparable to the access to and use of information and data by federal employees who are not individuals with disabilities, unless doing so would impose an undue burden on the department or agency.[49]

Section 508 also requires that individuals with disabilities, and who are members of the public seeking information or services from a federal department or agency, have access to and use of information and data that is comparable to that provided to the public who are not individuals with disabilities.[50]

Since August 7, 2000, individuals may file complaints against federal agencies. Remedies and procedures used under section 504 of the Rehabilitation Act will apply.

Title II and III libraries, museums and archives are not included in the reach of the new section 508 legislation requiring the accessibility of electronic information. However, existing disability laws are sufficient to show an equivalent obligation. Legally, public and private libraries, museums and archives have different burdens in terms of architectural access, but identical obligations in providing accessible electronic information. Generally, publicly funded libraries, museums and archives have a higher burden to ensure removal of architectural and communication barriers and must do so unless it would cause a *fundamental alteration* in services or an *undue burden.* Private libraries, museums and archives need only remove architectural and communication barriers if it is *readily achievable* to do so.

However, it is important to note that *both* public and private libraries, museums and archives must provide auxiliary aids and services and ensure effective communication to patrons with disabilities, unless it would cause a *fundamental alteration* or an *undue burden* to do so. Moreover, even if it would be a *fundamental alteration* or an *undue burden*, the library, museum or archive must provide an alternative aid or service to the extent possible.

The Department of Justice wrote in a 1997 letter that both public and private entities must furnish auxiliary aids and services to ensure effective communication:

> The Americans with Disabilities Act (ADA) requires State and local governments and places of public accommodation to furnish appropriate auxiliary aids and services where necessary to ensure effective communication with individuals with disabilities, unless doing so would result in a fundamental alteration to the program or service or is an undue burden. 28 C.F.R. 36.303; 28 C.F.R. 35.160. Auxiliary aids include taped texts, Brailled materials, large print materials, and other methods of making visually delivered material available to people with visual impairments.[51]

Public libraries, museums and archives are state or local governmental units. Private libraries, museums and archives are not, and must provide "public accommodations" in order to be regulated by the ADA.

When asked whether public libraries fell under Title II or Title III of the ADA, the Department of Justice, Civil Rights Division, replied:

> Generally speaking, the question of whether an entity is public or private is not difficult. For example, a municipal library, as a department of the township, would be a public entity covered by Title II. The question may be difficult, however, where an entity has both public and private features. A library operated

> by a private organization would not be a "public entity" merely because it is open to the public. In such cases, it is necessary to examine the relationship between the entity and the government unit. The factors to be considered include whether the library is operated with public funds; whether the library employees are considered government employees; whether the library receives significant assistance from the government by provision of property or equipment; and whether the library is governed by an independent board selected by the members of a private organization or is elected by the voters or appointed by elected officials.[52]

All public libraries, museums, and archives are covered under Title II of the ADA and section 504 of the Rehabilitation Act. Title II extends the protections of section 504 of the Rehabilitation Act of 1973 to all state and local government entities, regardless of whether they receive federal financial assistance. Most receive federal funding and thus were already covered by section 504.

In addition, the U.S. Department of Education interprets the Assistive Technology Act to require states receiving assistance under the act's state grant program to comply with section 508 of the Rehabilitation Act.

Title II libraries, museums and archives must remove architectural and communication barriers, and provide auxiliary aids and services, unless it would cause an undue burden or fundamental alteration in the nature of the program or service. Title II institutions must additionally provide *program access* in existing facilities, even when to do so is not readily achievable.

Title II libraries, museums and archives, as units of state or local government, must provide "program access" in existing facilities; i.e., for facil-

Table 8.1. Institutions Covered under the Americans with Disabilities Act

Title II: State and Local Government (public ownership)	Title III: Public Accommodations (private ownership)
Public libraries, museums, archives (city, county, special district)	Private school libraries, museums, archives
Public school libraries	Private academic libraries, museums, archives
Public academic libraries, museums, archives	Most private corporate libraries, museums, archives

ities that began construction prior to January 25, 1992, programs or activities, when viewed in their entirety, must be accessible to patrons with disabilities.[53] "Program access" in a library includes, for example, technical services, reference services, the children's room, stacks of books and reference materials, a computer cataloging system, a computer employment search system, and a computer magazine search system.[54]

Communication barriers include, for example, alarm warning signals that are not both visual (such as flashing exit signs) and audible (such as fifteen decibels above the prevailing sound level).[55]

New construction must follow strict guidelines designed to provide universal access: either the Uniform Federal Accessibility Standards or ADAAG.[56]

Title II libraries, museums and archives also have an affirmative obligation to ensure that communication with people with disabilities is *as effective as* communication with people without disabilities.[57] They must furnish appropriate auxiliary aids and services accordingly.[58] In determining what type of auxiliary aid or services is necessary, it is required to give primary consideration to the requests of the individual, and that choice should be honored unless another effective means of communication exists, or unless it is a fundamental alteration or undue burden.[59]

"Auxiliary aids and services" includes, for example, qualified interpreters or readers for hearing-impaired or visually impaired persons, the acquisition or modification of equipment or devices or other similar services.[60]

The regulations "strongly encourage" consultation with a disabled patron. The key is the *effectiveness* of the provided aid. If provision of an auxiliary aid or service would result in a fundamental alteration or undue burden, the library, museum or archive must provide an alternative aid or service that would *not* result in a fundamental alteration or undue burden to the extent that such an accommodation is possible.[61]

While Title II deals strictly with public entities, Title III prohibits discrimination on the basis of disability by private entities in places of public accommodation. This title covers private libraries, museums and archives that are open to the public, or to segments of the public.[62] Title III of the ADA is considerably more detailed than Title II, which references section 504 in many aspects.

A public accommodation under Title III generally is any private entity, regardless of size, that offers goods and services to the public.[63] The Code of Federal Regulations defines a public accommodation as "a facility, operated by a private entity, whose operations affect commerce and fall within at least one of the following categories: . . . museum, library, gallery, or other place of public display or collection."[64]

Commerce is broadly defined, and encompasses travel, trade, traffic, commerce, transportation and communication (a) among the several states; (b) between any foreign country or any territory or possession and any state; or (c) between points in the same state but through another state or foreign country. The term "commercial facilities" means facilities (a) that are intended for nonresidential use and (b) whose operations will affect commerce.[65] Recent U.S. Supreme Court decisions demonstrate that the requirement in 42 U.S.C. 12181(1) and (2)(B) that the activity touch and concern interstate commerce is taken seriously.[66]

Title III prohibits public accommodations from discriminating against people with disabilities by denying them the opportunity to benefit from goods or services, by giving them unequal goods or services or by giving them different or separate goods or services.[67] Title III states that it is discriminatory to deny participation, provide unequal benefits or provide separate benefits and that benefit should be provided in the most integrated setting appropriate to the needs of the individual.

Title III libraries, museums and archives must remove architectural and communication barriers in existing facilities, when such removals are *readily achievable*, i.e., accomplished without much difficulty or expense.[68] Removal of such barriers may include the installation of ramps, repositioning of shelves and telephones, and widening doors and doorways. However, "barrier removal measures that are not easily accomplished and are not able to be carried out without much difficulty or expense are not required, . . . even if they do not impose an undue burden or undue hardship."[69] Under this exception, however, the library must make its services available to the disabled through alternative methods, if such methods are readily achievable. For example, if a lecture room is not wheelchair accessible, seminars might be offered in an alternate location that is accessible.[70]

The "readily achievable" standard is much lower than the "undue burden" standard of Title II. Factors to be considered include the nature and cost of the action needed; the financial resources of, and the number of persons employed at, the facility; the effect of the action on the entity's expenses or resources; the impact of the action on the operation of the facility; and the size, nature, type and financial resources of the entity.[71]

Although only modest efforts are required in existing facilities, considerable efforts are expected for new construction and alterations, even in private facilities.[72] The ADA recognizes the retrofitting of existing facilities may be very costly, and a higher degree of accessibility is required for new facilities. The intent is that over time, with new construction and alterations (i.e., after January 26, 1992) complying with the ADAAG standards, facilities will become more and more accessible.[73] The act does not require alterations for accessibility to be made; rather it awaits the time when alterations or new construction is done. Only the portion of the facility actually being renovated must meet accessibility standards. There is no requirement to upgrade other access points at the same time, unless the area undergoing alteration contains a primary function of the facility, in which case the path of travel to the altered area must be made accessible.[74] The regulations for new construction contain an exemption for "structural impracticability." The requirement that new construction be accessible does not apply where an entity can demonstrate that it is structurally impracticable to meet the requirements of the regulation.

Title III requires public accommodations to modify policies, practices or procedures where such modification would afford equal opportunity to disabled persons, unless doing so would *fundamentally alter* the nature of the goods and services provided.[75] Title III also ensures that individuals with disabilities are not excluded, segregated, or treated differently because of the absence of auxiliary aids and services, unless these would create a *fundamental alteration* of the nature of goods or services or would result in an *undue burden.* Libraries, museums and archives are required to provide auxiliary aids and services for individuals with disabilities, unless it would constitute an undue burden.

Unlike the *readily achievable* standard, the *undue burden* and *fundamental alteration* standards are extremely difficult to meet. The ADA anticipates that providing auxiliary aids and services will generally not result in undue financial and administrative burdens. Like Title III libraries, museums and archives, Title II institutions may be excused if accommodations would incur an "undue" financial or administrative burden. When determining what constitutes an undue financial burden, available funds of not only the local site, but also the resources of any parent organization, e.g., the city, county or state, are taken into account. Undue burden is defined as significant difficulty or expense.[76]

Libraries, museums and archives are not required to fundamentally alter the nature of their programs or services. For example, a private library is not required "to alter its inventory to include accessible or special goods that are designed for, or facility used by, individuals with disabilities," but must make those materials available through interlibrary loan "at the request of an individual with disabilities, if, in the normal course of its operation, it makes special orders on request for unstocked goods, and if the accessible or special goods can be obtained from a supplier with whom the public accommodation customarily does business."[77]

Enforcement

Under Titles II and III, an individual may file an administrative complaint or file suit in court without exhausting administrative remedies.[78]

The U.S. Department of Education's Office for Civil Rights (OCR) is responsible for ensuring that all educational institutions and public libraries comply with the requirements of all federal civil rights laws, including section 504 and Title II of the ADA. The opinions of OCR are generally accorded considerable weight by the courts in interpreting the requirements of these laws. OCR has issued several opinions applying the requirements of section 504 and ADA regulations to situations involving access to information.[79]

Monetary damages are not recoverable in the private suits. The complaint or suit can only obtain injunctive relief: an order that facilities be made accessible, that auxiliary aids or services be provided or that alternative methods be provided. Monetary damages *are* recoverable in suits filed by the attorney general. The attorney general is authorized to bring a lawsuit where there is a pattern or practice of discrimination, or where an act of discrimination raises an issue of general public importance. Courts may order compensatory damages of up to $50,000 for the first violation and $100,000 for any subsequent violation to remedy discrimination if the Department of Justice prevails.[80]

In cases of joint ventures, leases or other relationships between government entities and public accommodations, the practical result of the relationship will usually be that the facility has to comply with the highest standard represented by both titles. Each entity is generally liable only for its failure to ensure compliance with the portion of the law that applies to it. If a state or local government contracts with a private entity, it must ensure that it operates in a manner that satisfies the government's Title II obligations.[81]

Heightened Obligations: New Acquisitions and Creating Digital Information

Just as different standards are imposed for existing and new buildings, electronic information is treated differently depending on when it was purchased and how much control the institution has in shaping its accessibility.[82]

OLDER MATERIALS

Print materials, one could argue, are not accessible to persons with visual impairments, therefore libraries, museums and archives need not provide access to electronic materials in accessible formats.

However, both private and public libraries, museums and archives must make print sources accessible through the provision of auxiliary aids and services. What are legally sufficient auxiliary aids and services? In 1991, a student filed a complaint against San Jose State University, claiming insufficient auxiliary aids in using the card catalog and retrieving books. OCR found that library staff assistance was sufficient. Staff assisted students with the catalog and with book retrieval, and offered a one-on-one term paper conference to help the student do research. The staff would write down citations and read information from abstracts and encyclopedias.[83]

In 1992, William McNett, chairman of the Bradford County Commissioners in Towanda, Pennsylvania, wrote to the Justice Department asking whether his county office would need to transfer real property deed record books into electronic format for an attorney who was missing an arm.[84] The Justice Department responded that providing full access by having staff assist in lifting and handling the record books was sufficient and "further modifications "would not be necessary to avoid discrimination."[85]

In 1993, at the University of Baltimore, a patron filed a complaint that the university failed to provide a Kurzweil text-reading machine. The university said that staff and volunteers were available to retrieve information from the library's online catalog, CD-ROMs and other resources. OCR found insufficient evidence to support a finding of violation of section 504 of the ADA, because students were provided with staff assistance and assistive devices such as Zoom Text (which magnifies computer screen text) and MasterTouch (a voice synthesizer), both compatible with the online catalog and other resources. The university also provided Braille and enlarged type overlays on some computers in the reference area of the library.[86]

In 1994, a student filed a complaint against Los Rios Community College District, in part because the library and written materials were not fully accessible. OCR noted that

> [t]he DOJ [Department of Justice] guidelines are clear that printed materials are within the meaning of "communication." In describing the auxiliary aids and services that are appropriate, the DOJ guidelines recognize the critical role that modern technology now plays in providing program access to persons with disabilities.[87]

In 1997 at San Jose State University, a patron filed a complaint that, among other things, he did not have access to microfiched newspapers in a manner as effective as other students. Reader services were deemed sufficient to provide access.[88]

A suggested approach to making print materials accessible is offered in new guidelines published in April 2000 by the California Community Colleges in "Guidelines for Producing Instructional and Other Printed Materials in Alternate Media for Persons with Disabilities."[89] Written in response to an OCR statewide review in March 1996 of the extent to which community colleges in California were meeting their Title II and section 504 obligations, the guidelines offer the following illustration as a recommended approach to handling requests for alternate media:

> A member of the public using the college library requests large print versions of several novels. An effort should be made to ascertain whether large print versions of these books are available from the publisher, and if so, they should be obtained. If not, they may be available on tape and this option should be offered to the patron. Failing this, the library would need to provide the equipment necessary for the individual to read books

> with the needed magnification. This could be accomplished either through the use of a CCTV or a scanner and computer with magnification software.[90]

Essentially, although staff assistance may be sufficient, a greater reliance on assistive devices is preferable for both the institution and the patron. As Sarah Hawthorne states:

> Since optical character recognition scanners and adaptive computer software programs don't charge an hourly wage to "stand around" the way human readers do, it is not an undue burden to expect that most public libraries will have on hand, during the hours that the library is open to nondisabled users, a method by which a blind user can access the same information provided to nondisabled users.[91]

An important remaining issue is the degree to which a library, museum or archive can require a user to learn new assistive devices, when the user is already proficient with a different one. Sarah Hawthorne suggests that if a library is using a program that is generally regarded as providing effective access by persons with that type of disability (e.g., blindness), the person with the disability may be required to learn the program selected by the institution. But if the library has installed a program that is generally regarded as providing inferior access for persons with disabilities, the person with a disability can make a strong argument that "primary consideration" should be given to his or her particular software request in order to ensure that he or she is provided communication that is "as effective as" that provided to nondisabled persons.[92]

NEW MATERIALS

As illustrated above, an increasing expectation on the part of OCR is that new technology and materials will be available to supplement staff assistance.

As libraries, museums and archives purchase new materials, they should make a concerted effort to avoid subscribing to commercial databases that present obstacles to patrons using adaptive computer equipment, or be prepared to make the materials accessible through librarian or volunteer readers.[93] As Barbara Mates succinctly puts it, "Who would pay to access a cardiology database written only with cuneiform? Why pay for databases that screen readers can't access?"[94]

Newly acquired materials within the control of the institution should be accessible. In a strongly worded opinion in 1997, OCR wrote:

> [Comparable to existing buildings and new construction], from the date of the enactment of Title II onwards, when making purchases and when designing its resources, a public entity is expected to take into account its legal obligation to provide communication to persons with disabilities that is "as effective as" communication provided to nondisabled persons. At a minimum, a public entity has a duty to solve barriers to information access that the public entity's purchasing choices create, particularly with regard to materials that with minimal thought and cost may be acquired in a manner facilitating provision in alternative formats. When a public institution selects software programs and/or hardware equipment that are not adaptable for access by persons with disabilities, the subsequent substantial expense of providing access is not generally regarded as an undue burden when such cost could have been significantly reduced by considering the issue of accessibility at the time of the initial selection.[95]

What about the Internet, which is an entire package, outside of the control of any one institution? OCR has "repeatedly held that the term 'communication' in this context means the transfer of information, including (but not limited to) the verbal presentation of a lecture, the printed text of a book, and the resources of the Internet."[96]

Back in the days when the Internet was referred to as the "information superhighway," a patron complained that San Jose State University failed to provide access to it. OCR noted that this "fundamental tool in post-secondary research" was made accessible at some institutions through personal readers. Even then, OCR expressed a strong preference for adaptive technology:

> In most cases, this approach [the use of personal readers to help visually impaired patrons access the information superhighway] should be reconsidered. One of the most important aims in choosing the appropriate auxiliary aid has been to foster independence and autonomy in the person with a disability. When reasonably priced technology is available that will

> enable the visually impaired computer user to access the computer, including the World Wide Web, during approximately the same number of hours with the same spontaneous flexibility that is enjoyed by other nondisabled computer users, there are many reasons why the objectives of Title II will most effectively and less expensively be achieved by obtaining the appropriate software programs.[97]

Since many web sites are not accessible, Hawthorne advises, "readers may be used to assist the blind individual in navigating through information that is not easily decipherable when relying exclusively on adaptive technology."[98]

Along with assistive devices, libraries, museums and archives should provide staff training and instruction to patrons. In 1993, two visually impaired patrons wrote the Chicago Public Library seeking access to the card catalog and other information resources. By 1997, the patrons filed a complaint with the Chicago Commission on Human Relations claiming a violation of the Chicago Human Rights Ordinance, a local ordinance prohibiting discrimination to people with disabilities. The patrons said they could not access the online catalog and other resources such as the *Chicago Tribune,* Infotrac Health Reference Center and Infotrac Periodicals Index. By this time, the library had acquired a speech synthesizer for use with CD-ROM and other computer information, but due to the lack of staff training and failure to provide instruction to patrons in alternative formats, the commission found "substantial evidence of disability discrimination."[99]

WEB PAGES AND DIGITIZED COLLECTIONS

If libraries, museums and archives are expected to ensure the accessibility of the electronic information they purchase, it logically flows that the expectation of accessibility is especially high concerning the digital material they create. Both public and private libraries, museums and archives should learn about and adopt universal accessibility guidelines, and apply them to their web pages, digital archives and digitized collections. Although Title II libraries, museums and archives are clearly covered by disability laws, a debate is raging concerning whether private institutions' web pages are "public accommodations," and therefore subject to the ADA. This debate is discussed below.

Policy and Legal Arguments for Accessibility Requirements

The Internet, and the World Wide Web in particular, is fast becoming a cyberspace alternative to the physical space in which services, commerce and other interaction takes place. It is critical that sites used *in commerce,* like public accommodations in the physical world, be considered subject to disability laws. This discussion is of particular interest to private libraries, museums and archives that are posting information to the web. It is likely that we will soon have guidance from the courts and or Congress, buttressing the 1996 letter from the Department of Justice referenced above, stating that both public services and public accommodations must make their web sites accessible.[100]

On November 4, 1999, the National Federation of the Blind (NFB) filed suit against America Online (AOL) under Title III in Massachusetts federal court. NFB claims that AOL is inaccessible to blind users. The complaint has four counts. Count one claims a violation of the ADA's communication barriers removal mandate. Count two claims a violation of the ADA's auxiliary aids and services mandate. Count three claims a violation of the ADA's reasonable modification mandate. Count four claims a violation of the ADA's full and equal enjoyment of services mandate.[101]

Specifically, AOL does not function in the standard way required for screen access programs to convert the information into synthesized speech or a refreshable Braille display. It uses unlabeled graphics, commands that rely only on mouse clicks, and custom controls painted on the screen (which in effect are more unlabeled graphics). According to the complaint, "[AOL] has failed to remove communications barriers, . . . thus denying the blind independent access to this service in violation of Title III of the ADA."[102]

Is AOL a public accommodation, subject to the ADA in the first place? AOL serves as an "online interactive community," encompassing electronic mail, bulletin boards, chat rooms and events. Arguably, AOL is a place of exhibition and entertainment, a place of public gathering, a service establishment, a place of public display, a place of education and a place of recreation.[103] The issue is currently under debate before Congress.

Despite the 1996 Department of Justice letter, the question of whether privately operated web sites are public accommodations is a matter of hot debate before Congress. On February 9, 2000, an oversight hearing on "The Applicability of the Americans with Disabilities Act (ADA) to Private Internet Sites" was held by the U.S. House of Representatives Committee on the Judiciary, Subcommittee on the Constitution.[104]

Some see public accommodation as requiring a physical forum, and argue for the inapplicability of the ADA to cyberspace. Others view public accommodations as independent of a physical forum and argue that the Internet satisfies all requirements. Elizabeth Dorminey argues that the Internet and other electronic communications systems are not "public accommodations," since they are not listed in the statute as set forth in 42 U.S.C. § 12181(7), claiming that inclusion of some assumes the intentional exclusion of others.[105] However, while it is true that 42 U.S.C. § 12181(7) gives a detailed list, this list is illustrative and not exhaustive. This section indicates that a public accommodation can be a place of exhibition and entertainment, a place of public gathering, a sales and rental establishment, a service establishment, a place of public display, a place of education or a place of recreation. Therefore, as Jonathan Bick points out, the ADA defines "public accommodation" in terms of entities rather than physical places. Specifically, 42 U.S.C. § 12181 states that if the operations of an entity affect certain types of commerce, then it may be considered a public accommodation.[106]

Marca Bristo, chair of the National Council on Disability, testified on February 17, 2000, before the U.S. House of Representatives Committee on the Judiciary's Subcommittee on the Constitution.[107] In her testimony, Bristo gave a concise analysis of four reported federal court decisions that are widely believed to offer guidance on which factors the courts will consider and how they will rule when the question of Internet coverage comes squarely before them. Two of the four, *Carparts Distribution Ctr., Inc. v. Automotive Wholesaler's Association of New Eng., Inc.*, and *Chabmer v. United of Omaha Life Ins. Co.*, strongly support the assertion that nonphysical places may be considered public accommodations.[108] The other two, *Parker v. Metropolitan Life Ins. Co.*, and *Ford v. Schering-Plough Corp.*, are often cited as contrary authority. They can be distinguished from the others because they concern insurance policies, which are treated under very specific provisions of the ADA.[109]

Accessibility Standards Impose No Undue Burden

In considering whether or not new and existing electronic data must be accessible in both private and public libraries, museums and archives, one must also examine whether or not the "Electronic and Information Technology Accessibility Standards" impose an undue burden. They do not.

Information can easily be represented in multiple formats at low cost. Tim Berners-Lee, inventor of the web and director of the W3C said, "the Web excels as a medium in which accessibility can be addressed. On the Web, a computer can automatically and cost-effectively represent the same information in a variety of ways according to the needs of users. Within the neutral forum of W3C, industry leaders, disability representatives, and others convened to develop accessibility solutions that are reasonable, practical, and effective. Web sites designed using very simple tools naturally tend to be accessible. Even sophisticated sites, designed with major effort, can be kept accessible with only a small proportion of that effort."[110]

The Department of Justice states that federal agencies, like the private sector, have "seized upon the Internet as a low-cost way of making its goods and services available to a wide audience." It states that making federal agencies' web sites accessible to persons with disabilities is "extremely easy and cost-effective."[111]

Moreover, tax credits are available to small businesses to offset expenses incurred in complying with the ADA and some argue these may be available for web site accessibility improvements.[112]

Finally, in a case in which applying standards would be cost prohibitive, it is unlikely that any private litigant would be able to compel a web site owner to provide access. Frivolous litigation is not likely, since monetary damages are not available to private litigants unless the attorney general joins the suit.

Some argue that the real costs when applying standards is the stifling of innovation. Although adherence to accessibility standards may slow innovations in some areas, it spurs innovation in others. Elizabeth K. Dorminey says innovation in information technology occurs at the speed of light, but notice and comment rule making move at a snail's pace. She also says that regulation slows rather than speeds innovation and creates a ceiling on compliance.[113] However, Peter Blanck and his colleagues have conducted a review of economic activity in the assistive technology market, using data derived from the U.S. Patent and Trademark Office. The preliminary findings illustrate that the ADA fosters future technological innovation and economic activity in the private Internet-based service economy, in many ways unanticipated at the time that the law was passed.[114]

Multiple methods of access benefit everyone.[115] Greater accessibility means greater compatibility with a wide range of emerging technology. In particular, a text-based alternative to graphics and multimedia allows greater compatibility with the exceptionally fast growing trend toward handheld wireless devices. According to Michael Mace, chief competitive officer for Palm Inc., today there are about 6.5 million devices with the Palm operating system worldwide. Cell phone sales were about 275 million worldwide last year. According to Scott Woefel, general manager of CNN.com, only about forty-one million cell phones are capable of getting news, sports and financial data today.[116] Explosive growth is a strong probability, and text-based information may be the best suited to work with handheld devices.

Further, it makes economic sense to deliver electronic information in as many formats as possible. Witness the explosion of access from mobile phones, palmtop devices, the living room television and the dashboard of the car—devices that require many of the same accessibility standards.[117] Voice-centric devices are expected to capture 72 percent of the wireless service market, up from 43 percent in 2000.[118]

Listening to web sites by telephone will become increasingly common. AirTrac, a two-year-old Chicago reseller of wireless airtime, is planning to sell subscriptions to Internet access by telephone. The system will be marketed primarily as a business service for "EveryWhere Office," with reduced rates for visually impaired customers. To use the system, callers dial a central phone number and give a voice password to log on. From there, they surf wherever they want or access e-mail.[119]

ACCESSIBILITY STANDARDS CAUSE NO FUNDAMENTAL ALTERATION

Following accessibility does not require the deletion of graphics or sounds. Standards rarely require parallel text sites. Accessibility features are often invisible to those who do not use them, e.g., on some screens <alt-text> tags are turned off, or only appear when a cursor hovers over an image. Other accessibility features are minimal, such as the insertion of a break between hyperlinks on a list. These additions and minor changes do not cause a fundamental alteration. Further, even if a situation that *could* cause a fundamental alteration, either a parallel site could satisfy the requirement or, if necessary, the requirement in the guidelines would not apply. Again, frivolous lawsuits discouraged, due to the lack of monetary damages.

Some may argue that accessibility is an admirable goal, but that standards are not agreed upon, and thus the adoption of any particular set of standards is not universal. However, federal agencies will soon be required to follow the proposed "Electronic and Information Technology Accessibility Standards." The standards will be incorporated into the federal acquisition regulations and federal agencies and departments will be required to purchase only accessible electronic and information technology, with exemptions for national security systems and for instances where compliance would impose an undue burden on an agency.[120]

The Department of Justice emphasizes that even though new section 508 standards "cannot—and do not pretend to—ensure that all [electronic information technology] will be universally accessible to all people with disabilities, reasonable accommodations will always be required in some instances. However, as agencies pay more attention to accessibility when procuring or developing their [electronic information technology], they will find it easier and easier to provide reasonable accommodations when requested to so."[121] It is worthwhile to note that between 1991 and 1996, the ADAAG was amended four times. It was designed to be revised over time to assure that it remains "consistent with technological developments and changes in model codes and national standards and continues to meet the needs of people with disabilities."[122]

THE FIRST AMENDMENT AND ACCESSIBILITY REGULATIONS

The First Amendment states that "Congress shall make no law . . . abridging the freedom of speech."

Dennis Hayes, inventor of the Hayes modem, testified before Congress that "[b]ecause I helped to make the Internet possible, it is especially ironic that I am not able to use much of its best content. A congenital, degenerative vision condition has reduced my eyesight over the past few years. . . . And on the Internet, that is a significant problem—many of the most important destinations are so poorly designed that they are difficult for even the average user to navigate, much less a vision-impaired user. This is a source of great frustration for disabled people, since they are among the most likely to benefit from the products and services offered on the Internet."[123]

Hayes's testimony turned at that point. He strenuously argued against government regulation of private web sites. He argued that regulation not only hampers innovation in a dynamic media, and is unable to address the broad variety of disabilities, but also poses serious constitutional problems. He testified, "It is all well and good to mandate the behavior of government services, but how does this Congress intend to tell individuals how they must design and present personal web pages? At what point would such legislation cross the First Amendment?"[124]

The First Amendment restricts government interference in the content of speech, and is particularly strong in its abhorrence of government-regulated private speech. Here it is useful to first distinguish the privately operated "public accommodations" web site from the home hobbyist site. The former affects commerce, including goods and services offered to people with and without disabilities. An individual may post a list of hobbies, such as favorite musical groups, in the latter. The two categories merge closer in cyberspace than in physical space, as personal sites may become popular sources of information for all. Nevertheless, the "commerce" test included in the ADA is instructive in distinguishing which sites are subject to regulation and which are not.

Narrowing this discussion to privately operated web sites that affect commerce (which would include virtually all private library, museum and archive sites), what are the First Amendment implications?

Charles Cooper, on behalf of the National Federation of the Blind, has articulated a thorough analysis of the intersection of the ADA and the First Amendment regarding private web sites. He notes that requiring that content be compatible with screen access software would not restrict the speech of providers in any way. Cooper analyzes the issue in two parts. First, he finds no reason to use heightened scrutiny, since the ADA is not specifically targeting speech on the basis of its content or its speakers. Second, even if a court was to apply heightened scrutiny, it would necessarily use a content-neutral analysis and find that the regulations only incidentally burden speech.[125] If all web sites were required by regulation to be written only in a text-based form, then freedom of information for those who wish to present pictures or nontext information would be in serious jeopardy. If pictures and graphics are banned, some expression would be completely excluded. The new car photograph on the web could not be shown, for example.

The ADA does not restrict editorial discretion over the material transmitted; it does not require display of any speech that is not the author's own. In fact, if application of the ADA violated the First Amendment, then a requirement of closed captioning for television programming would also be unconstitutional. The Telecommunications Act of 1996 required closed captioning of most television programming, effective January 1, 1998, and is to be phased in over an eight-year period.[126] A governmental requirement to add captioning to a speaker's content is not an alteration of that content or a restriction on the speech itself in any way. As Cooper testified, "such an incidental burden on speakers that merely expands the reach of their own freely chosen message has never been found to violate the Constitution."[127]

Conclusion

Disability legislation has increasingly expanded civil rights, including nondiscrimination in the provision of goods and services to people with disabilities. As more goods and services move from physical space to cyberspace, it is critical to apply disability laws to the digital arena. Federal agencies are required by a newly amended section 508 of the Rehabilitation Act to adopt "Electronic and Information Technology Accessibility Standards." Although nonfederal libraries, museums and archives are not subject to section 508, they are required to provide auxiliary aids to ensure effective communication to their patrons, unless to do so would impose an undue burden or a fundamental alteration in the nature of their services. Although existing print material may be made accessible with staff assistance, the Department of Justice OCR has put an increasing emphasis on assistive devices to promote independence. The federal accessibility standards will stimulate the market for accessible materials, and nonfederal libraries, museums and archives would do well to adopt the standards, particularly with respect to new purchases and self-created digital resources. Universal access standards in web site design bring a wider audience of patrons to sites, including the homebound and others who prefer to get their information on text-based mobile telephones and handheld devices. Privately operated web sites are likely to be considered public accommodations, subject to civil rights laws. The issue is currently under litigation and the subject of legislative hearings. Governmental regulation is not in conflict with the First Amendment, because content is not regulated, and the burden on speech is only incidental. It is especially appropriate for libraries, museums and archives to provide access to their resources. It fits a core value of equal access and is in step with the existing law.

Notes

1. *New York Times Cybertimes,* December 1, 1996, quoted in Cynthia Waddell, "Applying the ADA to the Internet: a Web Accessibility Standard" (paper presented at the American Bar Association national conference, Washington, D.C., on June 17, 1998). Available at http://www.isc.rit.edu/~easi/law/weblaw1.htm.

2. Department of Justice, "Information Technology and People with Disabilities: The Current State of Federal Accessibility," available under "Background," at http://www.usdoj.gov/crt/508/report/intro.htm.

3. Barbara T. Mates, *Adaptive Technology for the Internet: Making Electronic Resources Accessible to All* (Chicago: American Library Association, 2000), 1.

4. "The President's Committee on Employment of People with Disabilities," http://www50.pcepd.gov/pcepd/archives/pubs/ek97/facts.htm.

5. "Trace Research and Development Center," http://www.trace.wisc.edu/about/#whatis. For a brief introduction to the major disability groups and some specific barriers to accessibility, see http://www.trace.wisc.edu/docs/population/populat.htm.

6. H. Stephen Kaye, "Disabilities Statistics Center, Institute for Health and Aging, University of California, San Francisco, California" (March, 2000), http://www.dsc.ucsf.edu.

7. Charles Hamilton, "Developing an Accessible Online Public Access Catalog at the Washington Talking Book and Braille Library" (December 1993), http://www.rit.edu/~easi/itd/itdv02n1/hamilton.html. Also, a European Commission study on the technical and logistic practicalities of people with visual impairments using online public access catalogs (OPACs) was published in October 1998. Specific findings and recommendations included: (1) include a dust jacket, contents page and synopsis information as regular fields, as both visually impaired and other patrons increasingly rely on electronic catalogs; (2) do not relegate visually impaired

people to a special workstation in a hidden corner; building accessibility into regular OPACs is technically quite possible; (3) since staff is more comfortable troubleshooting the standard OPAC than special machines, incorporate accessibility as a standard part of OPACs; (4) insist on greater standardization of access technology. http://www.sbu.ac.uk/~litc/lt/1999/news1331.html.

8. Department of Education, "Q & A Title IV-Rehabilitation Act Amendments of 1998 Section 508: Electronic and Information Technology," http://www.usdoj.gov/crt/508/deptofed.html.

9. Steve Noble, "The Virtual Library: Collaborative Data Exchange and Electronic Text Delivery" (paper presented at the conference "Where Assistive Technology Meets the Information Age," at California State University, Northridge, March 18–22, 1997), http://www.rit.edu/~easi/itd/itdv04n1/article4.html.

10. David W. Wilhemus, "Law Libraries and the Americans with Disabilities Act: Making Law Libraries Accessible to the Visually Impaired." *Law Library Journal* 86 (spring 1994): 299, 306

11. Barbara T. Mates, "CD-ROM: A New Light for the Blind and Visually Impaired," *Computers in Libraries* 10, no. 3 (March 1990): 17, cited in David W. Wilhemus, "Law Libraries and the Americans with Disabilities Act: Making Law Libraries Accessible to the Visually Impaired," *Law Library Journal* 86 (spring 1994): 299, 306.

12. Barbara T. Mates, *Adaptive Technology for the Internet: Making Electronic Resources Accessible to All* (Chicago: American Library Association, 2000), 3.

13. See Barbara T. Mates, *Adaptive Technology for the Internet: Making Electronic Resources Accessible to All* (Chicago: American Library Association, 2000); Tom McNulty, ed. *Accessible Libraries on Campus: A Practical Guide for the Creation of Disability-Friendly Libraries* (Chicago: American Library Association, 1999); and Courtney Deines-Jones, "Opening New Worlds of Information: Library Technology and Internet Access for Patrons with Disabilities" (1995), http://www.ualberta.ca/dept/slis/cais/deines.htm, for specifics on items such as screen magnifiers, voice interfaces, and Braille displays. The author has used voice recognition programs for over five years, including the Dragon Dictate module, designed to search an online legal database service, Westlaw, in a private room at the Stanford Law School library.

14. Tom McNulty, "Disability in Higher Education: An Overview," in *Accessible Libraries on Campus: A Practical Guide for the Creation of Disability-Friendly Libraries,* ed. Tom McNulty (Chicago: American Library Association, 1999).

15. Scott A. Carpenter, "Accommodation to Persons with Disabilities: A Census of Ohio College and University Libraries," *Katharine Sharp Review,* no. 3 (summer 1996) http://edfu.lis.uiuc.edu/review/summer1996/carpenter.html.

16. W3 Consortium, http://www.w3.org/1999/05/WCAG-REC-fact#barriers.

17. For more, information see http://www.w3.org/.

18. W3C "Web Content Accessibility Guidelines" are available at http://www.w3.org/TR/1999/WAI-WEBCONTENT-19990505/.

19. For example, the guidelines specify the importance of producing and preserving valid markup. See http://www.w3.org/2000/02/ATAG-PressRelease.html.en.

20. 65 Fed. Reg. 63 (March 31, 2000), Proposed Rules.

21. 28 C.F.R 1, appendix A to part 36 (1999)

22. 65 Fed. Reg. 63 (March 31, 2000), Proposed Rules. The members, listed by institution, include representatives from the Web Accessibility Initiative.

23. American Library Association Core Values Task Force, "Core Values 4th Draft," (March 25, 2000), http://www.ala.org/congress/corevalues/draft4.html.

24. American Library Association, "Questions and Answers: Access to Electronic Information, Services and Networks," http://www.ala.org/alaorg/oif/oif_q&a.html.

25. American Association of Museums, ADA and Universal Design Program, "Brookfield Zoo Is Named Recipient of the 1999 Museum Accessibility Award," http://www.aam-us.org/access.htm.

26. U.S. Architectural and Transportation Barriers Compliance Board, "Electronic and Information Technology Accessibility Standards: Section 508 of the Rehabilitation Act Amendments of 1998 Economic Assessment," "appendix," http://www/access-board.gov/508.htm.

27. 42 U.S.C §§ 4151, 415 (2000).

28. 20 U.S.C §§ 1400, 1406 (1988), cited in David W. Wilhemus, "Law Libraries and the Americans with Disabilities Act: Making Law Libraries Accessible to the Visually Impaired," *Law Library Journal* 86 (spring 1994): 299, 305.

29. The Telecommunications for the Disabled Act of 1982, Pub. L. No. 97-410, codified as amended at 47 U.S.C. § 610 (1988). The policy language is from the House report accompanying the bill, H. Rep. No. 888, 97th Cong., 2d Sess. 5 (1982), as cited in U.S. Architectural and Transportation Barriers Compliance Board "Electronic and Information Technology Accessibility Standards: Section 508 of the Rehabilitation Act Amendments of 1998 Economic Assessment," appendix, http://www.access-board.gov/sec508/508-reg-assess.htm.

30. Civil Rights Restoration Act of 1987, 20 U.S.C. § 1687, 794; 29 § 705, 6107; 42 § 2000d-4a, 1688. On student financial aid as receipt of federal financial assistance, see *Grove City College v. Bell*, 465 U.S. 555, 104 S. Ct. 1211; 1984 U.S. LEXIS 158 (1984), cited in Tom McNulty, ed. *Accessible Libraries on Campus: A Practical Guide for the Creation of Disability-Friendly Libraries* (Chicago: American Library Association, 1999), v.

31. 42 U.S.C. § 12101 et seq. (2000) and 28 C.F.R. 35 (1999).

32. Telecommunications Act of 1996, § 255 of Pub. L. No. 104-104, codified at 47 U.S.C. § 255, cited in U.S. Architectural and Transportation Barriers Compliance Board, "Electronic and Information Technology Accessibility Standards: Section 508 of the Rehabilitation Act Amendments of 1998 Economic Assessment," appendix, http://www.access-board.gov/sec508/508-reg-assess.htm. Two provisions focus entirely on access by persons with disabilities. Section 255 requires

all manufacturers of telecommunications equipment and providers of telecommunications services to ensure that such are designed and developed to be accessible, if readily achievable. Section 713 requires the Federal Communications Commission to establish captioning guidelines for video programming, but allows exemptions when captioning would be economically burdensome. See Federal Communications Commission Disabilities Issues Task Force, "The Telecommunications Act of 1996: What Does It Mean for People with Disabilities?" http://www.fcc.gov/dtf/dtftele.html.

33. 29 U.S.C. § 3001 et seq. (2000).

34. Department of Justice, Civil Rights Division, Disability Rights Section, "A Guide to Disability Rights Laws" (September 1, 1998), http://www.usdoj.gov/crt/ada/cguide.htm.

35. *Kimel v. Florida Board of Regents,* 120 S. Ct. 631 (January 11, 2000).

36. *Alden v. Main,* 527 U.S. 706; 119 S. Ct. 2240 (June 23, 1999).

37. *Florida Dept. of Corrections v. Dickson,* No. 98-829. The guard, Wellington N. Dickson, sued under the ADA, claiming that the state had withheld a promotion because of his heart condition. The state unsuccessfully argued that it was constitutionally immune from suit and that Congress lacked the authority to pass the ADA as applicable to the states.

38. *Alsbrook v. City of Maumelle,* 184 F.3d 999 (8th Cir. Ark. 1998).

39. According to plaintiff's lawyer Gerald Houlihan of Miami, the settlement talks in the Florida case were initiated by the state. Tom D'Agostino, managing editor of LRP Publications, writes that the case was likely settled for political reasons: Jeb Bush, whose father counts the passage of the ADA as an important accomplishment of his presidency, and brother George W. Bush, a candidate for the presidency at the time, may have propelled the state's settlement. The Arkansas case, "a sort of mirror image," brought the plaintiff seeking Supreme Court review and then settling for a pittance, according to Arkansas assistant attorney general Dennis Hansen, who said, "The amount they asked for was less than the cost of printing the briefs and flying to Washington to argue the case." D'Agostino suggests that the plaintiff's settlement motivation was shaped by the "sheer weight of recent Supreme Court precedent on the state immunity issue" *after* the Arkansas case review was granted. Tom D'Agostino, "Settlements Raise Questions, Stall Supreme Court Review of ADA Cases," *Disability Compliance for Higher Education* 5 (April 5, 2000): 9.

40. *Garett v. Univ. of Alabama at Birmingham Bd. of Trustees,* 193 F. 3d 1214 (11th Cir. 1999), cert. granted, 2000 WL 122158 (April 17, 2000) (No. 99-1240) cited in Legal Aid Society of San Francisco April 2000 Talking Points: Constitutional Challenge to the ADA.

41. *Georgeen Stevens v. Illinois Department of Transportation,* No. 98-3550 (April 11, 2000); *Erickson v. Board of Governors,* No. 98-3614, 2000 WL 307121 (March 27, 2000). The Seventh Circuit issued two opinions barring state employees from suing their employers in federal court for ADA violations.

42. *Jones v. Commonwealth of Pa.*, 17 NDLR 125 (E.D. Pa. 2000) (No. CIV A 99-4212), reported in "State Defendant Was Not Immune from Suit on Title II Claim," *Disability Compliance Bulletin* (April 7, 2000).

43. *Dare v. State of California*, 191 F. 3d 1167 (9th Cir. 1999). As of May 2000, the Supreme Court had not yet decided whether it would hear the *Dare* case. Reported in Legal Aid Society of San Francisco April 2000 Talking Points: Constitutional Challenge to the ADA.

44. Cal. Gov. Code, Sec. 11135 et seq. (2000) prohibits discrimination on the basis of disability by entities that receive state funds.

45. Cal. Civ. Code, §§ 51, 54.1 (2000).

46. 42 U.S.C. § 12201(b) (2000).

47. The law, regulations, etc. are available on the web at http://www.usdoj.gov/crt/ada/publicat.htm. The Department of Justice ADA homepage is http://www.usdoj.gov/crt/ada/adahom1.htm.

48. 42 U.S.C. § 12101(b) (2000), http://www.usdoj.gov/crt/ada/pubs/ada.txt.

49. Department of Justice section 508 documents and instructions, http://www.usdoj.gov/crt/508/508docs.html. See also Janet Reno, "Memo for the Heads of all Federal Agencies" (April 2, 1999), http://www.usdoj.gov/crt/508/memohead.html.

50. 63 Fed. Reg. 45053, http://www.access.gpo.gov/su_docs/aces/aces140.html.

51. Letter from Deval L. Patrick, Assistant Attorney General, Civil Rights Division, to Rep. Tom Harkin (September 9, 1996), http://www.usdoj.gov/crt/foia/cltr204.txt.

52. Department of Justice Letter DJ# 182-06-00019, May 3, 1992, to Suffolk Cooperative Library System, New York, http://www.usdoj.gov/crt/foia/cltr011.txt.

53. 28 C.F.R. § 35.150 (1999).

54. Department of Education, Office of Civil Rights (OCR) Complaint No. 01-92-4005, Town of Seekonk (Public Library) Region I (July 2, 1992).

55. OCR Complaint No. 02-93-4100, Henrietta Public Library Region II (July 22, 1993).

56. 56 Fed. Reg. 35, 694; 56 Fed. Reg. 144 (July 26, 1991) and appendix A to part 37.

57. 28 C.F.R. § 35.160(a) (1999).

58. 28 C.F.R. § 35.160(b) (1999).

59. 28 C.F.R. § 35.160(b)(2) (1999).

60. The Department of Justice has provided an expanded list of suggested auxiliary aids and services at 28 C.F.R. § 36.303(b).

61. OCR says that if the library is using a widely used program, one that is generally regarded by experts as reliable for access by persons with the type of disability (e.g., blindness) the person possesses, the person with a disability may be required to learn the program selected by the library. But if the library has installed a program that is generally regarded by experts as providing cumbersome, inferior access, the person with a disability may rely upon the Title II provision requiring

that "primary consideration" be given to her request to purchase particular software. See OCR Complaint No. 09-97-2002 1997 NDLR (LRP) LEXIS 525; 11 NDLR (LRP) 71 California State University-Los Angeles Region IX (April 7, 1997).

62. 42 U.S.C. § 12181 (2000).

63. 28 C.F.R. § 36.104 (1999). Religious entities and certain private clubs are exempt.

64. 42 U.S.C. § 12181 (2000); 28 C.F.R. § 36.104 (1999).

65. 42 U.S.C. 12181(1) (2000) (commerce) and 42 U.S.C. 12181(2) (2000) (commercial facilities). What does it mean for a facility's operations to "affect commerce"? The phrase "affect commerce" is a constitutional law concept frequently used in federal statutes enacted pursuant to Congress's power to regulate interstate commerce. Some factors to examine in determining whether a facility's operation affects commerce are: (a) whether the facility is open to out-of-state visitors; (b) whether the products it exhibits or sells originated out of state or have traveled through other states; and (c) whether facilities of this kind, in the aggregate, would affect interstate commerce. Americans with Disabilities Act, Title III Technical Assistance Manual 1994 Supplement, http://www.usdoj.gov/crt/ada/taman3up.html.

66. See, e.g. *U.S. v. Lopez,* 514 U.S. 549, 115 S. Ct. 1624 (1995), which ruled that the Gun Free School Zones Act was unconstitutional because Congress lacks power to regulate activity not affecting interstate commerce.

67. 42 U.S.C. § 12182. Prohibition of discrimination by public accommodations ¶ (a) General rule. No individual shall be discriminated against on the basis of disability in the full and equal enjoyment of the goods, services, facilities, privileges, advantages, or accommodations of any place of public accommodation by any person who owns, leases (or leases to) or operates a place of public accommodation.

68. 42 U.S.C. Sec 12181(2000).

69. 56 Fed. Reg. 35569.

70. Burgdorf, R. L. "Equal Access to Public Accommodations," *Milbank Quarterly* 69, supp. 1/2 (1991), cited in Ralph B. Weston, "Law Libraries and the Americans with Disabilities Act: Service to Disabled Patrons," http://www.law.utexas.edu/staff/rweston/ada-htm.htm.

71. 42 U.S.C. § 12181(9) (2000).

72. 42 U.S.C. § 12183 (2000).

73. 28 C.F.R. §§ 36.401-36.608 (1999), and appendix A to part 36.

74. 42 U.S.C. § 12183 (2000).

75. 42 U.S.C. Sec 12182(b)(2)(A)(ii).

76. 28 C.F.R. § 36.104(a)(3) (1999). See also Sarah Hawthorne, Jeffrey Senge, and Norman Coombs, "The Law and Library Access for Patrons with Disabilities" (paper presented at the conference "Where Assistive Technology Meets the Information Age," at California State University, Northridge, March 18–22, 1997), http://www.rit.edu/~easi/itd/itdv04n1/article5.html.

77. 28 CFR 36.307 (2000).

78. Department of Justice, Civil Rights Division, Disability Rights Section, "A Guide to Disability Rights Laws" (September 1, 1998), http://www.usdoj.gov/crt/ada/cguide.htm.

79. Chancellor's Office, California Community Colleges, "Guidelines for Producing Instructional and Other Printed Materials in Alternate Media for Persons with Disabilities," part I A (April 2000), http://www.cccco.edu/cccco/ss/dsps/OCR/Amg4.doc.

80. The remedies are those set forth in section 505 of the Rehabilitation Act, 29 U.S.C. § 794a, 42 U.S.C. § 12188(2000). See also U.S. Department of Justice, "ADA Enforcement," http://www.usdoj.gov/crt/ada/enforce.htm.

81. Lisa Huggins, "You Can Get There from Here: Program Accessibility Requirements under the Americans with Disabilities Act," *Alabama Lawyer* 56 (November 1995): 363.

82. "The magnitude of the task public entities now face in developing systems for becoming accessible to individuals with disabilities, especially with respect to making printed materials accessible to persons with visual impairments, is comparable to the task previously undertaken in developing a process by which buildings were to be brought up to specific architectural standards for access. Buildings in existence at the time the new architectural standards were promulgated are governed by "program access" standards. However, buildings erected after the enactment of the new architectural standards are strictly held to the new standards undetermined that the builder is on-notice that such standards apply. One who builds in disregard of the standards is ordinarily liable for the subsequent high cost of retrofitting. OCR Complaint No. 09-97-2002 1997 NDLR (LRP) LEXIS 525; 11 NDLR (LRP) 71 California State University-Los Angeles Region IX (April 7,1997).

83. OCR Complaint No. 09-90-2160 1991 NDLR (LRP) LEXIS 957; 1 NDLR (LRP) 325 San Jose State University Region IX (February 21, 1991).

84. Letter from William T. McNett, Chairman, Bradford County Commissioners to Justice Department Civil Rights Division (February 21, 1992), http://www.usdoj.gov/crt/foia/tal167.txt.

85. 202-PL-00049, letter from Joan A. Magagna, Deputy Chief, Office on the Americans with Disabilities Act, to William T. McNett, Chairman, Bradford County Commissioners (August 31, 1992), http://www.usdoj.gov/crt/foia/tal167a.txt.

86. OCR Complaint No. 03-94-2087 NDLR (LRP) LEXIS 1356; 5 NDLR (LRP) 115 University of Baltimore Region III (December 23, 1993).

87. OCR Complaint No. 09-93-2214-I NDLR (LRP) LEXIS 1606; 5 NDLR (LRP) 423 Los Rios Community College Region IX (April 21, 1994).

88. The patron requested a reader to assist him, and complained that the university conditioned his access upon a showing of academic relevance. The library handled each request on a case-by-case basis depending on staff availability. OCR

found the primary mission of the university library was to support the curricula, and that it may allocate resources accordingly. OCR noted that in some cases there is a duty on the part of the library to reassess the number of reader hours needed (in this case two hours were allocated over a two-week period). OCR suggested that the patron may have requested further time if needed, and did not find sufficient evidence that such a request would have been denied, even though the student said he felt that further requests would be futile. OCR Complaint No. 09-96-2056 San Jose State University Region IX (February 7, 1997).

89. Chancellor's Office, California Community Colleges, "Guidelines for Producing Instructional and Other Printed Materials in Alternate Media for Persons with Disabilities," part I A (April 2000), http://www.cccco.edu/cccco/ss/dsps/OCR/Amg4.doc.

90. *Ibid.*

91. Sarah Hawthorne, Jeffrey Senge, and Norman Coombs, "The Law and Library Access for Patrons with Disabilities" (paper presented at the conference, "Where Assistive Technology Meets the Information Age," at California State University, Northridge, March 18–22, 1997), http://www.rit.edu/~easi/itd/itdv04n1/article5.html. The paper continues, "Some administrative responsibilities, not imposed on non-disabled persons, may be assigned to persons with disabilities. For example, a library may be concerned about leaving expensive adaptive technology unguarded in an open area so that there may be prerequisites to using the equipment, such as obtaining a key from the librarian."

92. *Ibid.*

93. OCR Complaint No. 10-91-2019 1992 NDLR (LRP) LEXIS 1129; 3 NDLR (LRP) 219 University of Oregon Region X (June 30, 1992). A university student requested independent access to the library's CD ROM system, which provided automated access to information similar to the *Readers' Guide to Periodical Literature.* He requested that the library add memory to its two Macintosh computers so that he could use a screen-reading program called Outspoken. The university's method for providing persons access to the library's CD-ROM was to have reference librarians act as readers and to conduct searches as requested.

It was the position of the library staff that the two Macintosh computers were a gift to the university, were placed in the library as a convenience for the students, and did not provide access to any library program. Therefore, the library was not responsible for paying for any upgrade. OCR found that the reference librarian service as readers was a sufficient auxiliary aid necessary to access the *Readers' Guide* program in compliance with section 504 at 34 C.F.R. 104.44 (d).

94. Barbara T. Mates, *Adaptive Technology for the Internet: Making Electronic Resources Accessible to All* (Chicago: American Library Association, 2000), 3.

95. OCR Complaint No. 09-97-2002 1997 NDLR (LRP) LEXIS 525; 11 NDLR (LRP) 71 California State University-Los Angeles Region IX (April 7, 1997).

96. *Ibid.*

97. OCR Complaint No. 09-93-2214-I Los Rios Community College Region IX (April 21, 1994).

98. Sarah Hawthorne, Jeffrey Senge, and Norman Coombs, "The Law and Library Access for Patrons with Disabilities" (paper presented at the conference, "Where Assistive Technology Meets the Information Age," at California State University, Northridge, March 18–22, 1997), http://www.rit.edu/~easi/itd/itdv04n1/article5.html.

99. The letter notes that a finding of "substantial evidence" is not a finding of liability, but a preliminary determination. Unofficial posting of the Chicago Commission on Human Relations Order CCHR No. 94-PA-8/84, concerning *Kelly Pierce and Elsie Haug v. City of Chicago, Chicago Public Library* (July 29, 1998), http://www.innotts.co.uk/blind-l/9901/0266.html.

100. Letter from Deval L. Patrick, assistant attorney general, Civil Rights Division, to Rep. Tom Harkin (September 9, 1996), http://www.usdoj.gov/crt/foia/cltr204.txt.

101. The complaint is currently available at http://www.libertyresources.org/news/aol_1.html.

102. *Ibid.*

103. Jonathan Bick, "Applying the Americans with Disabilities Act to the Internet," *New Jersey Law Journal* (March 27, 2000).

104. The testimony is available at http://www.house.gov/judiciary/con0209.htm.

105. Elizabeth K. Dorminey, "The Applicability of the Americans with Disabilities Act (ADA) to Private Sites," presented to the Subcommittee on the Constitution of the House Committee on the Judiciary (February 9, 2000), http://www.house.gov/judiciary/dorm0209.htm.

106. Jonathan Bick, "Applying the Americans with Disabilities Act to the Internet," *New Jersey Law Journal* (March 27, 2000).

107. Marca Bristo, "The Applicability of the Americans with Disabilities Act to Private Internet Sites," presented to the Subcommittee on the Constitution of the House Committee on the Judiciary (February 17, 2000), http://www.ncd.gov/newsroom/testimony/bristo_2-17-00.html.

108. The first supporting case, *Carparts Distribution Ctr., Inc. v. Automotive Wholesaler's Association of New Eng., Inc.*, 37 F.3d 12, 19 (1st Cir. 1994), states a broad interpretation of public accommodations consistent with legislative intent. On remand, the district court found that the defendants failed to demonstrate the absence of any genuine issue of material fact related to whether they were a "public accommodation" under Title III. *Carparts Distribution Ctr. v. Automotive Wholesalers Association of New England.* 987 F. Supp. 77, 81. *Chabmer v. United of Omaha Life Ins. Co.*, 994 F. Supp. 1185 (N.D.Calif. 1998) also supports coverage.

109. *Parker v. Metropolitan Life Ins. Co.*, 121 F. 3d 1006 (6th Cir. 1997) and *Ford v. Schering-Plough Corp.*, 145 F. 3d 601 (3d Cir. 1998) both emphasize the distinction between availability of services at a "place of public accommodation" and the content of those services. Both cases have been used to support the proposition that

requiring an information provider to make information accessible would constitute regulation of the content of its services. However, the ADA provisions regarding services, 42 U.S.C. § 12201(c), exempt insurance decisions from Title III to the extent that they involve actuarial practices.

110. Tim Berners-Lee, cited by Judy Brewer, testimony before the Subcommittee on the Constitution of the House Committee on the Judiciary (February 9, 2000), http://www.house.gov/judiciary/brew0209.htm.

111. Department of Justice, "Information Technology and People with Disabilities: The Current State of Federal Accessibility," http://www.usdoj.gov/crt/508/report.

112. Peter David Blanck, testimony before the Subcommittee on the Constitution of the House Committee on the Judiciary (February 9, 2000), http://www.house.gov/judiciary/blan0209.htm.

113. Elizabeth K. Dorminey, "The Applicability of the Americans with Disabilities Act (ADA) to Private Sites," presented to the Subcommittee on the Constitution of the House Committee on the Judiciary (February 9, 2000), http://www.house.gov/judiciary/dorm0209.htm.

114. Peter David Blanck, testimony before the Subcommittee on the Constitution of the House Committee on the Judiciary (February 9, 2000), http://www.house.gov/judiciary/blan0209.htm. Blanck cites Peter David Blanck, *The Americans with Disabilities Act and the Emerging Workforce* (Washington, D.C.: American Association on Mental Retardation, 1998) and Blanck, ed., *Employment, Disability, and the Americans with Disabilities Act* (Chicago: Northwestern University Press, forthcoming 2000).

115. Cynthia Waddell, "The Growing Digital Divide in Access for People with Disabilities: Overcoming Barriers to Participation in the Digital Economy" (paper presented at the conference, "Understanding the Digital Economy: Data, Tools and Research," at the Department of Commerce, Washington, D.C., May 25–26, 1999), http://www.aasa.dshs.wa.gov/access/waddell.htm.

116. Felicity Barringer, "Big News on Little Screens: Information is Going Portable in a Hand-Held World," *New York Times,* April 10, 2000, C21.

117. Judy Brewer, testimony before the Subcommittee on the Constitution of the House Committee on the Judiciary (February 9, 2000), http://www.house.gov/judiciary/brew0209.htm.

118. "Wireless: Wireless Users Lean toward Voice-Centric Devices," http://cyberatlas.internet.com/markets/wireless/articles (July 29, 2001).

119. Margaret O'Brien, "System Brings Internet to Visually Impaired," *Chicago Tribune,* April 3, 2000, section 2, p.4. Another free service, Quack.com, gives movie, sports, traffic and weather information and was launched April 10, 2000. "The race is on for voice portals," *San Jose Mercury News,* May 1, 2000, 10C.

120. U.S. Architectural and Transportation Barriers Compliance Board, "Electronic and Information Technology Accessibility Standards Section 508 of the Rehabilitation Act Amendments of 1998 Economic Assessment," 5, http://www.access-board.gov/sec508/508-reg-assess.htm.

121. Department of Justice, "Information Technology and People with Disabilities: The Current State of Federal Accessibility," from "Other Requirements of the Rehabilitation Act," http://www.usdoj.gov/crt/508/report/intro.htm.

122. "Status on Access Board Rulemaking Efforts" November 1996, distributed by Disability and Business Technical Assistance Centers, cited in Laura F. Rothstein, *Disabilities and the Law*, 2d ed. (St. Paul, Minn.: West Group, 1997), 394.

123. Dennis C. Hayes, testimony before the Subcommittee on the Constitution of the House Committee on the Judiciary (February 9, 2000), http://www.house.gov/judiciary/hay30209.htm.

124. *Ibid.*

125. For the full analysis, see Charles Cooper, testimony before the Subcommittee on the Constitution of the House Committee on the Judiciary (February 9, 2000), http://www.house.gov/judiciary/coop0209.htm.

126. Federal Communications Commission Fact Sheet June 1999, "Closed Captioning of Video Programming," http://www.fcc.gov/cib/dro/ccfactsh.html. See also the home page for the Federal Communications Commission, Disability Rights Office, http://www.fcc.gov/cib/dro/ for further information.

127. Charles Cooper, testimony before the Subcommittee of the Constitution of the House Committee on the Judiciary, (February 9, 2000), http://www.house.gov/judiciary/coop0209.htm. Cooper cites *Gottfried v. Federal Communications Commission*, 655 F. 2d 297, 312 N. 54 (D.C. Cir. 1981), rev'd in part on other grounds by *Community Television of Southern California v. Gottfried*, 459 U.S. 298 (1983).

Appendix A. Key Definitions from Title 42 of the United States Code

Note: Except where noted, the definitions given below are excerpted from Title 42 of the *United States Code.* Section numbers are given for each definition. The italicized terms at the beginning of each entry were added by the author.

Auxiliary aids and services § 12102 (1) . . . The term "auxiliary aids and services" includes

(A) qualified interpreters or other effective methods of making aurally delivered materials available to individuals with hearing impairments; (B) qualified readers, taped texts, or other effective methods of making visually delivered materials available to individuals with visual impairments; (C) acquisition or modification of equipment or devices; and (D) other similar services and actions.

Commerce § 12181(1). . . . The term "commerce" means travel, trade, traffic, commerce, transportation, or communication—

(A) among the several States; (B) between any foreign country or any territory or possession and any State; or (C) between points in the same State but through another State or foreign country. (2) Commercial facilities. The term "commercial facilities" means facilities—(A) that are intended for nonresidential use; and (B) whose operations will affect commerce.[1]

Recent U.S. Supreme Court decisions demonstrate that the requirement in 42 U.S.C. 12181(1) and (2)(B) that the activity touch and concern interstate commerce is taken seriously.[2]

Disability § 12102 (2) The term disability means with respect to an individual—(A) a physical or mental impairment that substantially limits one or more of the major life activities of such individual; (B) a record of such an impairment; or (C) being regarded as having such an impairment.

Discrimination § 12132 . . . Subject to the provisions of this title, no qualified individual with a disability shall, by reason of such disability, be excluded from participation in or be denied the benefits of the services, programs, or activities of a public entity, or be subjected to discrimination by any such entity.

Private entity § 12181(6) The term "private entity means any entity other than a public entity (as defined in Section 201(1) [42 U.S.C. 12131])

Public accommodation § 12181(7) The following private entities are considered public accommodations for purposes of [Title 42], if the operation

---

[1] 42 U.S.C. 12181(1) and (2) (2000). What does it mean for a facility's operations to "affect commerce"? The phrase "affect commerce" is a constitutional law concept frequently used in federal statutes enacted pursuant to Congress's power to regulate interstate commerce. Some factors to examine in determining whether a facility's operation affects commerce are: (a) whether the facility is open to out-of-state visitors; (b) whether the products it exhibits or sells originated out of state or have traveled through other states; and (c) whether facilities of this kind, in the aggregate, would affect interstate commerce. "Americans with Disabilities Act, Title III Technical Assistance Manual 1994 Supplement," http://www.usdoj.gov/crt/ada/taman3up.html.

[2] See, e.g. *U.S. v. Lopez,* 514 U.S. 549, 115 S. Ct. 1624 (1995) (striking down the Gun Free School Zones Act as unconstitutional because Congress lacks power to regulate activity that does not affect interstate commerce), cited in "Testimony and Statement for the Record of Elizabeth K. Dorminey, Wimberly, Lawson Steckel Nelson & Schneider, P.C., before the U.S. House of Representatives Committee on the Judiciary Subcommittee on the Constitution" (February 9, 2000), http://www.house.gov/judiciary/dorm0209.htm.

of such entities affect commerce— . . . a museum, library, gallery, or other place of public display or collection.

Public Entity § 12131(1) The term "public entity" means—(A) any State or local government; (B) any department, agency, special purpose district, or other instrumentality of a State or States or local government and (C) the National Railroad Passenger Corporation, and any commuter authority (as defined in Section 103(8) of the Rail Passenger Service Act [45 U.S.C. §502(8)]).

Qualified individual with a disability § 12131(2) The term "qualified individual with a disability" means an individual with a disability who, with or without reasonable modifications to rules, policies, or practices, the removal of architectural, communication, or transpiration barriers, or the provision of auxiliary aids and services, meets the essential eligibility requirements for the receipt of services of the participation in programs or activities proved by a public entity.

Readily achievable 42 U.S.C. § 12131(9) . . . The term "readily achievable" means easily accomplishable and able to be carried out without much difficulty or expense. In determining whether an action is readily achievable, factors to be considered include—

(A) the nature and cost of the action needed under this Act; (B) the overall financial resources of the facility or facilities involved in the action; the number of persons employed at such facility; the effect on expenses and resources, or the impact otherwise of such action upon the operation of the facility; (C) the overall financial resources of the covered entity; the overall size of the business of a covered entity with respect to the number of its employees; the number, type, and location of its facilities; and (D) the type of operation or operations of the covered entity, including the composition, structure, and functions of the workforce of such entity; the geographic separateness, administrative or fiscal relationship of the facility or facilities in question to the covered entity.

Undue burden 28 C.F.R. 36.104 The term "undue burden" means significant difficulty or expense. In determining whether an action would result in an undue burden, factors to be considered include—(1) The nature and cost of the action needed under this part; (2) The overall financial resources of the site or sites involved in the action; the number of persons employed at the site; the effect on expenses and resources; legitimate safety requirements that are necessary for same operation, including crime prevention measures; or the impact otherwise of the action upon the operation of the site; (3) The geographic separateness, and the administrative or fiscal relationship of the site or sites in question to any parent corporation or entity; (4) If applicable, the overall financial resources of any parent corporation or entity; the overall size of the parent corporation or entity with respect to the number of its employees; the number, type and location of its facilities, and (5) If applicable, the type of operation or operations of any parent corporation or entity, including the composition, structure, and functions of the workforce of the parent corporation or entity.

Appendix B. The Access Board's Web-Based Intranet and Internet Information and Applications (1194.22)

These provisions of the standards provide the requirements that must be followed by Federal agencies when producing web pages. These provisions apply unless doing so would impose an undue burden.

The key to compliance with these provisions is adherence to the provisions. Many agencies have purchased assistive software to test their pages. This will produce a better understanding of how these devices interact with different coding techniques. However, it always should be kept in mind that assistive technologies, such as screen readers, are complex programs and take extensive experience to master. For this reason, a novice user may obtain inaccurate results that can easily lead to frustration and a belief that the page does not comply with the standards. For example, all screen reading programs use special key combinations to read properly coded tables. If the novice user of assistive technology is not aware of these commands, the tables will never read appropriately no matter how well the tables have been formatted. A web site will be in compliance with the 508 standards if it meets paragraphs (a) through (p) of Section 1194.22. Please note that the tips and techniques discussed in the document for complying with particular sections are not necessarily the only ways of providing compliance with 508. In many cases, they are techniques developed by the Board, the Department of Education, and the Department of Justice that have been tested by users with a wide variety of screen reader software. With the evolution of technology, other techniques may become available or even preferable.

(a) Text Tags
(b) Multimedia Presentations
(c) Color
(d) Readability (style sheets)
(e) Serve-Side Image Maps
(f) Client-Side Image Maps
(g)&(h) Data Table
(i) Frames
(j) Flicker Rate
(k) Text-Only Alternative
(l) Scripts
(m) Applets and Plug-Ins
(n) Electronic Forms
(o) Navigation Links
(p) Time Delays

A text equivalent for every non-text element shall be provided (e.g., via "alt.", "longdesc", or in element content).

Equivalent alternatives for any multimedia presentation shall be synchronized with the presentation.

Web pages shall be designed so that all information conveyed with color is also available without color, for example from context or markup.

Documents shall be organized so they are readable without requiring an associated style sheet.

Redundant text links shall be provided for each active region of a server-side image map.

Client-side image maps shall be provided instead of server-side image maps except where the regions cannot be defined with an available geometric shape.

Row and column headers shall be identified for data tables.

Markup shall be used to associate data cells and header cells for data tables that have two or more logical levels of row and column headers.

Frames shall be titled with text that facilitates frame identification and navigation.

Pages shall be designed to avoid causing the screen to flicker with a frequency greater than 2 Hz and lower than 55 Hz.

A text-only page, with equivalent information or functionality, shall be provided to make a web site comply with the provisions of these standards, when compliance cannot be accomplished in any other way. The content of the text-only page shall be updated whenever the primary page changes.

When pages utilize scripting languages to display content, or to create interface elements, the information provided by the script shall be identified with functional text that can be read by assistive technology.

When a web page requires that an applet, plug-in or other application be present on the client system to interpret page content, the page must provide a link to a plug-in or applet that complies with §1194.21(a) through (l).

When electronic forms are designed to be completed on-line, the form shall allow people using assistive technology to access the information, field elements, and functionality required for completion and submission of the form, including all directions and cues.

A method shall be provided that permits users to skip repetitive navigation links.

When a timed response is required, the user shall be alerted and given sufficient time to indicate more time is required.

Source: Access Board (excerpts); complete text available at http://www.access-board.gov/sec508/guide/1194.22.htm.

Further Resources and Accessibility Tools

WEBSITES

EASI Equal Access to Software and Information, http://www.isc.rit.edu/~easi/law.html. This is especially good for legal documents links, including an important OCR decision concerning electronic information in libraries, OCR 09-92-2002, California State University–Los Angeles 1997, http://www.isc.rit.edu/~easi/law/csula.htm.

Trace R&D Center, University of Wisconsin, http://www.trace.wisc.edu.

University of Iowa College of Law—Law, Health Policy and Disability Center, http://www.its.uiowa.edu/law/index.htm.

Waddell, Cynthia. A well-known advocate for electronic accessibility for people with disabilities under the law. Several presentations, papers and links, all exceptionally useful, are at http://www.icdri.org/cynthia_waddell.htm.

World Wide Web Consortium Web Accessibility Initiative (http://www.w3.org/) includes February 2000 "Authoring Tool Accessibility Guidelines," May 1999 "Web Content Accessibility Guidelines" and much more, including international policies, http://www.w3.org/WAI/References/Policy#USA.

ACCESSIBILITY TOOLS

United States. General Services Administration. Center for IT Accommodation (CITA). Tools to make your web pages accessible, http://www.itpolicy.gsa.gov/cita/wpa.htm. Includes "Bobby," at the Center for Applied Special Technology (CAST), http://www.cast.org/bobby.

HTML Writers Guild (HWG) AWARE (Accessible Web Authoring Resources and Education), http://aware.hwg.org.

BOOKS

Mates, Barbara T. *Adaptive Technology for the Internet: Making Electronic Resources Accessible to All.* Chicago: American Library Association, 2000. This book gives excellent current information on available adaptive technology for library patron use, with electronic information resources. For example, large-print key tops for persons who are visually impaired; high contrast and simple fonts for OPACs and web pages; the ability to change font size, contrast and colors; white space to reduce distraction (7–9).

McNulty, Tom, ed. *Accessible Libraries on Campus: A Practical Guide for the Creation of Disability-Friendly Libraries.* Chicago: American Library Association, 1999.

Paciello, Mike. *WebABLE! Making Web Sites Accessible to People with Disabilities.* Foster City, Calif.: IDG Books, 1999.

CHAPTER 9

Seven Levels of Safety

PROTECTING PEOPLE IN PUBLIC BUILDINGS

Bruce A. Shuman

> I can hear nonlibrary folks now saying, "Problems? What kind of problems could those library workers have? They just sit around and read most of the time." If only the library world was as peaceful as outsiders envisioned it!
>
> Mark Willis

Libraries, archives, and museums, whatever they may represent to the public, are also workplaces for their employees, and given human nature, can be potentially dangerous places to visit or work. A recent study of violence in the workplace conducted by the National Institute for Occupational Safety and Health reveals that "workers most at risk to workplace violence are those who deal with the public, exchange money and deliver goods and services." Naturally, our staffs are included in this category. When people don't feel safe in public buildings, they tend to avoid them for fear of danger, assault, injury, or worse. Other types of workplaces have different levels of security, commensurate with their functions, features, and design, but most libraries, archives, and museums are public places, with little or no admission requirements, which sadly makes both employees and visitors vulnerable to violence.

Clearly, there is a need for security in our buildings, but how much and what kinds of security are desirable, feasible, and affordable are subjects open to debate. As a general rule for public buildings, more is better, but in most buildings open to the public, a high level of physical security is exchanged for reasonably barrier-free access. This chapter delineates seven levels of security in contemporary human workplaces, ranging from "perfect security" to "total vulnerability," with library and museum buildings placing quite low along the continuum. Because of the nature of such institutions, staff and the general public are vulnerable to occasional unpleasant surprises. Your staff, however, are not helpless just because all are free to enter and partake of your institution's services. A reasoned and coherent security policy, consisting of preparations and countermeasures to enhance building security, is vital. Preparation of staff for violent incidents in the workplace and rapid response and reaction to such incidents are extremely important, and should be included and discussed in a comprehensive security plan that provides remedies to the problem of personal vulnerability while maximizing security for all building occupants.

The Problem: The Public Building as a (Potentially) Dangerous Place

This chapter deals with physical aspects of security in public buildings, particularly with violence perpetrated by patrons, who enter the places we work in every day with agendas of their own. *Not* included in this discussion are other types of security problems common to libraries and other, similar facilities, such as (1) the preservation and retention of books and other materials; (2) electronic security, or protecting computer records and files against hackers and other cybercriminals trying to gain access to them out of motives ranging from prankishness to revenge; and (3) "inside jobs," in which perpetrators of violence are staff members. Our discussion focuses on protecting people in the building from aggressive or dangerous actions of visitors, which is part of the greater problem of security in a public setting.

Many members of any community share the notion of a library or archival building as a refuge, a safe haven, dusty and quiet, and full of books containing the dead thoughts of dead writers from a dead past, and in whose sedate halls one can let one's guard down and relax. It may be jarring therefore for the average citizen to entertain the notion of such a place as dangerous. Sure, we know that bad things occasionally happen in post offices or in online brokerages that cater to day traders, but the *library?* The *museum?* Give me a break! Thankfully, most people don't place our buildings on their lists of places to avoid for fear of being shot, stabbed, or assaulted, but the potential exists all the same, underscoring that in today's world it is always prudent to watch your back, wherever you go.

Strange and troubled people have always found library and museum buildings appealing and sometimes magnetic. The early-twentieth-century English author G. K. Chesterton wrote of his conviction that every London-area family with a madman among its number dropped him off in the sedate precincts of the British Museum for the day; otherwise, how could so many bizarre and eccentric people congregate in one spot every afternoon? Chesterton's observation of almost a century ago speaks to us across the years. Threatening (rather than merely annoying), mentally troubled, and occasionally violent people enter our workplaces every day, if for no other reason than it's so easy to get in. Once inside, they are free to demonstrate the dark side to human behavior. For evidence, consider the following recent news items:

- A librarian is murdered while working alone in a small-town library. The next day, a sixteen-year-old youth from a nearby town is arrested and charged with armed robbery, murder, and felony murder. His motive, he explains, was the desire to possess the staff member's expensive jewelry.
- A patron suddenly kills two reference librarians in a branch public library. The gunman, a homeless transient, is later described as a regular patron of the library. Witnesses say that he entered just before closing, carrying a handgun, and without warning opened fire on several employees, fatally wounding two librarians. The assailant is described as having no history of criminal behavior or mental illness, but it is subsequently revealed that he'd had a grudge against the county, and claimed he had suffered extreme emotional and mental distress after being falsely imprisoned for twenty-eight days when he was mistaken for a fugitive from another state.

- A man carrying a pistol and what he says is a bomb takes eighteen people hostage at a large downtown library. An alert off-duty deputy, who manages to sneak in among the hostages, subsequently shoots and kills the gunman. Luckily, no hostages are hurt, despite a tense five-and-one-half-hour standoff, but the bomb found on the dead man's person proves to be "live," and big enough to blow up the whole building.
- A library clerk working in a branch public library system is beaten to death by a young man who has been harassing several of the women on the library staff, making obscene phone calls, and exposing himself to female staff members. The victim had complained to police a week earlier that the man had been harassing her, but the police pointed out that, unless an actual crime was committed, they could do nothing.

Are these isolated incidents, taken out of context? Perhaps. Thankfully, violence in libraries and other public buildings is quite rare, but these news items underscore the fact that public gathering places are occasionally dangerous places to be, and may become settings for unpredictable behaviors and violent crime. Therefore, we need to do whatever possible to create a strengthened security posture that will serve to protect building occupants and reduce the risk of such incidents, promoting in the public a sense that they may visit and use our facilities in safety.

One effective and common antidote to permitting disturbed or dangerous people to act out their hostilities in our workplaces is hiring and training a force of resourceful and seemingly omnipresent guards. Such a remedy, however, is beyond the financial means of many smaller and poorer institutions. Consequently, alternative ways must be found to heighten our security posture, and instill in patrons and staff alike the feeling that they are reasonably protected against the threat of violence. Commercial public places, such as sports stadiums and office buildings, have a mix of police, guards, surveillance cameras, and alarm systems in place to deal with problem behavior, yet many institutional buildings do little to protect building occupants. Reasons for this may include naïveté, apathy, or misplaced trust in human nature, but the main culprit is frequently lack of funds: a budget that does not allow for remedies to help ensure public safety.

L'AFFAIRE KREIMER

When a person throws a punch or pulls a weapon, you know you've got a clear problem that calls for the summoning of the police. But while physical threats to personal safety are hard to miss or mistake, what about patrons who do not plan to harm others physically, but clearly enjoy making them afraid or nervous? Sometimes, intimidation, terror, and the threat of violence (as opposed to violence, itself) is the perpetrator's objective. Consider one Richard Kreimer, a frequent visitor to the Morris Free Library, Morristown, New Jersey, who a few years back was given to hanging out in the library all day, staring at women and shambling along behind young girls as they searched out books, his penetrating gaze causing them to recoil with terror, which was, doubtless, the whole idea.

Homeless by choice, Kreimer spent his nights in shelters, on the streets, or under bridges, but his days were spent at the library, where he displayed such a combination of an appalling lack of personal hygiene and objectionable, menacing behavior that library staff itched to throw him out of the building. One day, in fact, when the number of complaints had become voluminous, the decision was made to do just that, police were summoned, and Kreimer was forcibly ejected from the building. When the outraged Kreimer demanded reasons, the library director cited the aroma of his unwashed body and clothes, his unsettling staring, and his habit of following young females through the stacks, where he would stand very close to them (but careful never to touch them or say or do anything that could be defined as criminal behavior). The director added that Kreimer would be free to return when he had made appropriate changes in his personal hygiene and comportment.

Kreimer, an intelligent, educated man despite his appearance and demeanor, found a lawyer to take his case and sued both the police and the library, saying that, as a citizen, he had just as much right to be in the building as others did, and that his behavior was breaking no rules that he knew of. The staff thereupon feverishly consulted the city's laws and the library's existing rules of conduct, and discovered—to their chagrin—no provision prohibiting either smelling bad or staring. And at the time, "stalking" was not a punishable offense in New Jersey. Thus Kreimer's lawsuit won him (at least initially) sizable sums in compensatory and punitive damages.

The magistrate who found for Kreimer was careful to point out that he did so not out of sympathy, in the name of First Amendment freedoms, or to ensure equal justice under the law. He awarded damages, he said, because the library had failed to define in its rules of conduct the man's specific behaviors as transgressions meriting eviction. Kreimer was therefore entitled to enter and use the library freely, despite personal hygiene or motivations. Soon, Kreimer returned, victorious, still unwashed and malodorous, and this time looking for a little payback. So he picked up where he had left off, reeking, staring, and shambling after young girls. One can readily understand why the library staff and security personnel, after the judge's decision, silently prayed for Kreimer to go over the line and commit any kind of crime or misdemeanor—so that they could roust him again and this time make it stick, or even get him arrested and sent to a correctional institution. But Kreimer, shrewd for all his malice and strangeness, knew just how far he could—and couldn't—go, and he broke no law or existing rule after his triumphant return.

The story doesn't end there, thankfully. The initial judge's verdict in favor of Kreimer was reversed on appeal, the appeals court ruling that the rights of the many outweigh the rights of a single individual, and declaring the library correct to have thrown out a patron who caused many others to experience fear, intimidation, or discomfort, while at the same time passively acting as a deterrent to others to enter the building and partake of its facilities and services. Moreover, the financial award of the initial verdict was set aside.

Now just imagine . . . what if Kreimer or someone like him finds his way into *your* library, archive, or museum? What is needed is discussion and some consensual decisions on how staff will respond when confronted by a threatening and highly offensive person who conveniently (for him) doesn't happen to be breaking any established rules. Since such behavior is not deemed a police matter, administrators and staff are faced with an array of options, none ideal, and all controversial, but each of which may be worth considering. Here are just four:

1. Change the rules such that terrible smells and stalking behaviors are now forbidden and/or punishable.
2. Have someone suited to play "social worker," trying to "reach" the man, and getting him to see that his odor and behavior are disruptive and annoying, and convincing him to attempt to reform.
3. Turn the tables; get the guards to follow him around and make him acutely aware that he's being watched every second.
4. Ignore him, as best you can, and caution patrons to avoid him. Maybe he'll go off in search of new places to bother people.

None of these alternatives is especially likely to achieve the desired result, but doing nothing is not an option. Suggestion: have the staff role-play and discuss this scenario as a group, and then decide what to do should Kreimer or someone like him appear at your public building to torment its occupants.

Libraries and most museums are public places, which is at the same time the good news and the bad news. Freedom may be a wonderful thing, but security postures for gathering places vary widely, and different levels of building security carry corresponding price tags. Consider these seven levels of security in public places and determine where *your* building falls on this continuum.

LEVEL 1: PERFECT SECURITY

Perfect security is only an ideal. A public place with zero tolerance for problem behaviors, such that people in it are 100 percent safe is not a practical possibility. Where human safety is concerned, there is no such thing as perfect security, despite your best attempts to ensure it or strengthen it. There are, in fact, only varying degrees of *insecurity.* It's a fact: deal with it!

LEVEL 2: EXTREMELY GOOD SECURITY

It is now increasingly possible to transact library business (or even "visit" museums or archives) via the Internet, without leaving home. Powerful search engines and millions of web sites make it possible for one to locate and browse collections, view paintings, consult specific books and articles, compile data, and download or print desired information, all from the privacy—and safety—of home! When transacting such business from home, the chances of being assaulted, robbed, hit over the head, or even shouted at are virtually nil. And even better, you don't have to dress up (or even put on shoes!), or worry about driving hazards, inclement weather, parking problems, or the high cost of gasoline.

So, since physical exposure to other people is zero when you do research via the web, what keeps this level of security from being perfect? Communication is almost always a two-way street. Electronic access may protect your body from physical harm, but your computer's operating system and files are still at risk from wily and determined hackers. Once you open a channel via a modem between your computer and an Internet provider, and thence to the entire world, you risk having your private files and information read, stolen, altered, compromised, or subjected to viruses, with unpredictable and potentially unpleasant results. Ironically, the connection that enables you to interact with remote sites from home also makes it possible for you to give up your most private and personal information, often without even being aware of it.

LEVEL 3: VERY GOOD SECURITY

Military installations have (or at least should have) very good security, as do corporate entities with valuable secrets to protect. For instance, you can't just stroll into the Pentagon or the Texas Instruments Tech Center and take pictures or have a look around, unless you work there or take a scheduled tour. In such places, employees work in high-security areas with guards providing heightened safety for building occupants. Governmental agencies and corporations take important and costly steps to ensure that only authorized and accredited persons are admitted to secure facilities, and all visitors must identify themselves to the satisfaction of protectors to gain access to the people, machinery, and information within. Such high levels of security may be bolstered by new technologies such as password access, retinal scans, palm print and fingerprint analysis, and voice recognition. These barriers are generally effective in distinguishing legitimate, authorized staff and visitors from spies, criminals, and impostors, but no security technology can claim to be perfect. A clever criminal, intent on information piracy, may eventually succeed in breaching even the strongest electronic fortress walls. To get into such a workplace with a weapon and attack the people inside, however, he must work out how to fool, bypass, disable, or defeat any electronic countermeasures in place.

LEVEL 4: COMMENDABLE (GOOD) SECURITY

A particular commercial restaurant in the inner city has, as its principal security problem, keeping those inside safe inside, and those who belong outside, outside. Workers in this carry-out eatery labor in a bustling kitchen separated from a storefront waiting room by a thick wall of transparent Lucite. Customers enter the waiting room, shout their orders into speakers in the bulletproof wall, pay (in advance) through small pass-through windows, and watch the skillful cooks scurry about their ovens and burners in full sight but, importantly, not within reach. Customers may thus see the cooks at work, but harming—or even touching—them is impossible. When orders are ready, they are passed through a hatch in the Lucite. Larger orders are brought out to the waiting room by a huge man, rippling with muscle and sporting a "don't-mess-with-me" face, but that's the extent of personal contact or exposure for restaurant staff. Unless you want to try overpowering the big man, in order to rob or harm restaurant employees, you must find a way to bypass or circumvent that Lucite barrier; otherwise, pointing a handgun at the people in the kitchen and demanding the contents of the cash register will get you nowhere, except perhaps prison. The barrier is bulletproof, after all, and so when someone inside casually picks up the telephone and dials 911, if you're smart, you'll leave while you still can, knowing that the police are on their way.

LEVEL 5: SO-SO SECURITY

Frequent fliers spend a good chunk of their time commuting to other cities by air or waiting in airports for their flights. But just to get as far as the waiting area—let alone on the plane—you must submit to a routine security check of both your person and your carry-on baggage, while elsewhere in the terminal X-ray scanners (and sometimes trained dogs) check your luggage for dangerous or prohibited items. To pass from the ticketing arcade into the gate area, you're scanned by a device that detects metallic items, and persons found to have concealed handguns (or other metal weapons) on their persons are not only forbidden to enter the concourse, but subject to arrest. Unfortunately, the system is not perfect, because people still do occasionally find a way to defeat security countermeasures and get aboard airplanes with weapons. But metal detectors do weed out most of the desperate or deranged individuals who hope to skyjack or crash an airliner by shooting their way into the cockpit. True, there are holes in airport security, but at least the airlines are making a determined effort to cut back on crime aloft, leaving passengers and flight crews more secure. Even if airport security cannot absolutely guarantee travelers' safety, it does a reasonable job of deterring and reducing life-threatening incidents.

LEVEL 6: TOKEN SECURITY (BETTER THAN NOTHING)

Larger and wealthier libraries and museums may not have an array of crime-stopping technology at their disposal, but they employ security forces of paid guards who are tasked with monitoring entrances and exits, patrolling public rooms and stacks, and generally keeping the peace. Guards normally receive fairly extensive law enforcement training before assuming their duties. Building guards are not normally armed, but are trained and experienced in such skills as dealing with threatening behaviors, crowd control, isolating violent people, and rudimentary psychology.

But Guards, however well-intentioned, are sometimes elderly, slow, out of shape, poorly trained, inattentive, indifferent, or lazy, and thus likely to be of very little help when staff must deal with persons who threaten them or other building occupants. Sometimes, library guards may be observed spending most of their shifts reading newspapers or chatting up staff or patrons, and thus are inattentive to their duties. Just having someone around to summon police, however, *is* helpful, and having *any* kind of security presence in a public building may deter individuals intent on violence or other criminal activity. Frequent (but unscheduled) patrols by uniformed, serious-looking guards equipped with communications devices will go a long way toward deterring problem behaviors. Guards are much better than nothing when interposed between building occupants and potentially violent visitors.

LEVEL 7: TOTAL VULNERABILITY

People working in a level 6 milieu may count themselves luckier than some of their colleagues, because all too many library and museum staff work in level 7 buildings—and level 7 is as unsafe as it gets. Such institutions have no security whatsoever because they can't afford it or don't think they need it, leaving all building occupants vulnerable to crime and violence. Denied the protection of their first line of defense—vigilant security—staff working within such places can only deal with incidents as they arise.

Employees of such buildings—especially those working at public workstations—are naturally as much at risk as the members of the public.

It'd be really great if all bad guys, criminals, perverts, and psychopaths would wear sweatshirts identifying themselves as such. But how obvious are those who walk through the front doors who happen to suffer from full-blown psychosis or are bent on mayhem or mischief? Such visitors may look like normal people, but can, without warning, become dangerous to those around them. And while chances of such an occurrence are statistically negligible—even in large cities with high crime rates—the element of risk is always there.

Why Libraries?

Why does problem behavior occur in library buildings more often than it does in, say, high-rise office buildings, sports stadiums, or airport terminals? Perhaps it is the openness of access to library buildings together with the absence of admission fees that permits perpetrators to enter freely without explaining themselves and, once inside, do what they please. For some, it's that the library is often the only public building open evenings and weekends, seasonally heated and cooled, and containing free public restrooms, making it attractive to people who have no place else to go. Possibly, though, it's because many libraries are either undefended or poorly defended, meaning that would-be aggressors feel comfortable about starting confrontations. Whereas museums and archives almost always have guards on site, alert to various dangers, libraries all too often do not, which invites trouble.

How do violent incidents in public buildings become possible? For a start, there are no barriers to protect staff from personal interaction with the public, which is intentional, because easy interaction helps the library in meeting the community's informational and recreational needs. Barriers to personal contact in libraries are, in fact, either minimal or nonexistent. Even in high-crime areas, libraries do not choose to enact stringent security measures, because free and open places require free and open access. With no metal detector at the front door, moreover, people are free to bring any weapons they choose with them, concealed or in plain sight. Oh, sure, there is often a barrier, but this is usually only a detection gate through which you must pass as you exit the building, a way to keep books not properly checked out from leaving the library. That's the normal extent of much library security; any barrier you encounter affects your getting *out;* getting in is, by design, a piece of cake.

Security Measures

Some libraries employ a number of security solutions to reduce crime and create an aura of safety in their buildings. Such measures include having on-duty or off-duty police stationed inside the library, employing paid security guards to serve as unofficial "bouncers" and peacekeepers, technical solutions like security cameras, emergency telephones, and rationing keys to public restrooms. Still, a large proportion of library security efforts are aimed at keeping the books from walking away, and while protecting library property from theft and mutilation is commendable, personal safety is much *more* important for a simple reason: human lives are at stake. Books, videos, and even computers can be repaired or replaced; people cannot.

Now imagine that, for whatever reason, during your stint at a public desk, a patron produces a handgun and starts shooting. It doesn't really matter why or at whom. The salient fact is that the person has a gun and has gained access to the building with it unchallenged by any countermeasures. Here's the catch: the building's defenses tend to be reactive, rather than proactive. While we are entitled to require such things as shirts and shoes of our patrons, staff are not permitted to deny access to people because they are dressed a certain way, because they don't like their looks, or just on general suspicion. Public means public; we are not permitted to make such distinctions. In a very real sense, we can't holler until we're hurt.

Face it: public employees routinely work in such surroundings, vulnerable to approach or assault by anyone whose mind may be full of strange whispered voices or uncontrollable urges. They work in a combat zone, for which some believe they deserve customary hazard pay. And as bad as that sounds, it gets worse. Not only are such employees at risk from harm that could come to them from the actions of deranged or angry people in their midst, but so are their patrons, who innocently trust their hosts, and that they are safe from harm.

Are we (and our patrons) thus without protection and defenses against such actions? Security guards are hired to monitor the activities of visitors and prevent or interdict acts that are against the law, against the rules, violent, dangerous, illegal, or potentially harmful to other occupants of the building. But salaried security guards are often a luxury simply beyond the library's financial limits. As one smug member of a staff in the medium-sized city's downtown library told me, in explaining why there were no security guards in view, "We're all security officers, here." Yeah, right.

A pair of pertinent questions arise in this regard: How can public buildings bolster their security postures such that—even if they cannot erect sturdy barriers—they can create an ambiance in which both patrons and staff can feel reasonably secure? Is there necessarily a tradeoff between a heightened security posture and placing annoying barriers in the path of library visitors? To answer these questions in a way favorable to a reasonable level of personal security in your building, you're going to need a plan.

Solutions: A Workable Plan for Preventing Violence in Public Buildings

As violence—and the fear of violence—increasingly disrupt our workplaces and drain our resources, we must take steps to create a safer environment for staff and patrons. While no library or institution is immune to threat, prevention of most dangerous or frightening events is possible with careful planning and cooperation. Preparation and readiness are first lines of defense. There's a lot of truth in the old adage that an ounce of prevention is worth a pound of cure.

The importance of a continuous posture of defensive readiness is clear. It is easier and far better to prevent attacks than it is to diagnose what went wrong later and work out an appropriate subsequent response. But while we can't possibly anticipate and deter all attacks, good planning will help significantly in warding them off, in damage control subsequent to the event, and in figuring what to do to prevent any "next times." The actions listed below are thus offered as candidate basic ingredients of an integrated master plan for building safety and security. Not all may be applicable to an institution's specific circumstances, and some will simply be too costly to warrant serious consideration. But including some of these steps will help anticipate, prevent, contain, and resolve some of the more common types of violent incidents that may occur.

PREPARATION: BEFORE PROBLEMS OCCUR

Ways to help prevent violent incidents include:

- Designate a staff member as "building security officer," putting them in charge of public safety, and provide for an "officer of the day" whenever the building is open to the public.
- Maintain good relations with local police and try to encourage them to include the institution's premises on their "rounds," especially during evening and weekend hours.
- Monitor crime patterns in the community continuously and brief staff on what, in particular, to watch out for.
- Perform a building security audit, in which all existing defenses and deterrents are reviewed and evaluated. Analyze your present security posture and take remedial steps to upgrade it, including justifications for requested improvements.
- Create and promulgate a comprehensive building security policy and hold meetings to explain and discuss it with all staff members.
- The public must be aware that threats, violence, and verbal abuse will not be tolerated. Post rules of conduct and unacceptable behaviors in conspicuous public places, and have paper copies for handing out to patrons in case of questions.
- Where possible, purchase security equipment (e.g., surveillance cameras) to augment existing surveillance capabilities.
- Provide telephones and lists of emergency telephone numbers (e.g., police, paramedics, firefighters) at all desks. Consider silent assistance bells or intercoms.
- Hire trained security guards; train them well in procedures, crisis management, and crowd control. A uniformed guard should be at or around the front door to the building during normal hours of operation, and patrols of the building should be irregular and unpredictable.
- Emphasize to staff the need for security, and make them aware that "security is everybody's business." Encourage staff to be alert and observant at all times and make them aware that human behavior is difficult or impossible to predict.
- Where funds permit, have on-duty staff work in pairs or teams.
- Provide staff training in security precautions (e.g., calm-voiced assertiveness, avoidance of overreaction, careful observation, problem recogni-

tion, descriptions, communication skills, and interpretation of verbal clues and body language).

- Establish special code words (e.g., a distinctive surname), so that staff members can communicate danger or warning signals verbally or by telephone without alerting others present to problems.
- In frequent in-service workshops, provide group exercises (drills and simulations of confrontations) designed to reduce response time in emergencies.

ACTION: STAFF RESPONSE AND REACTION

Appropriate actions and things to remember when incidents arise include:

- Remember the most important goals: protect human lives and ensure nobody gets hurt.
- Attempt to isolate a problem patron from others in the room or area.
- A calm voice and a reasonable, pleasant manner may defuse tricky situations or at least buy time.
- Separate merely annoying problems from threatening or dangerous ones and act accordingly.
- Apply and enforce all rules fairly, firmly, and consistently.
- Treat homeless people as you would others, providing that they follow the rules.
- When responding to a crisis, rely on your conditioning from repeated drills and role-plays.
- Never be afraid to "bother" the police with a problem; that's what they're there for.

PSYCHOLOGICAL FACTORS

Some aspects of "good security" may seem to run contrary to the nature and mission of a public building, and thus be deemed undesirable. There is an unavoidable tradeoff between how much security is provided and how free of constraints building occupants are, or feel themselves to be. Ubiquitous guard presence and scanning surveillance cameras may reduce crime and promote the comforting sense of being protected, but the same security measures may also be perceived as intrusive impediments to the intellectual freedom that people expect from free institutions in a free society. From a staff point of view, a high degree of security (e.g., Lucite shields between employees and the untrustworthy public, password access) might protect employees from the potential actions of violent patrons, but it is important to think through what would be gained and what lost if such changes are brought about.

FISCAL REALITIES

Good building security normally entails the purchase of considerable equipment or a much larger payroll for guards. While it is possible to achieve consensus on the *desirability* of such measures, opinions vary considerably on which security measures are most effective and whether enhanced security is important enough to warrant the additional outlay of funds. In terms of costs, however, it is generally true that you get what you pay for; *good* security is expensive, and *very good* security is very expensive.

Marshaling arguments intended to convince the funding body (or community) that considerable additional spending for augmented security is well spent can be a daunting task in this era of taxpayer unrest, Internet access, and dwindling inner-city tax bases. Still, you have to try. Even if you win only a small concession in the form of upgrading public safety, you've accomplished something. You may fall well short of your idealized building security posture (as every public institution must), but *any* security beats none at all.

Select Bibliography on Building Security and Safety

Arterburn, Tom R. "Librarians: Caretakers or Crimefighters?" *American Libraries* 27 (August 1996): 32.

Brand, Marvine, ed. *Security for Libraries: People, Buildings, Collections.* Chicago: American Library Association, 1984.

Carparelli, Felicia. "Public Library or Psychiatric Ward? It's Time for Administrators to Deal Firmly with Problem Patrons." *American Libraries* 15 (April 1984): 212–15.

Chadbourne, Robert D. "The Problem Patron: How Much Problem, How Much Patron?" *Wilson Library Bulletin* 64 (June 1990): 59–60.

Chaney, Michael, and Alan F. MacDougall, eds. *Security and Crime Prevention in Libraries.* Brookfield, Vt.: Ashgate, 1992.

Comstock-Gay, Stuart. "Disruptive Behavior: Protecting People, Protecting Rights." *Wilson Library Bulletin* 69, no. 6 (February 1995): 33–35.

Danford, Robert, and Susan Cirillo. "Violence in the Library: Protecting Staff and Patrons." *Library Administration and Management* 11 (spring 1997): 64–88.

Davis, Patricia. "Libraries in Crisis: Safety and Security in Today's Library." *Texas Library Journal* 12 (summer 1995): 21–30.

Faulkner-Brown, Harry. "The Role of Architecture and Design in a Security Strategy." In *Security and Crime Prevention in Libraries,* ed. Chaney and MacDougall, 70–87.

"Has Workplace Violence Become Part of Your Job?" *Library Personnel Newsletter* 4 (September–October 1994): 3–4.

Houlgate, J., and M. Chaney. "*Planning and Management of a Crime Prevention Strategy.*" In *Security and Crime Prevention in Libraries,* ed. Chaney and MacDougall, 46–69.

Lewis, Janice S. "Workplace Violence." *RQ* 34 (spring 1995): 287–95.

Lincoln, Alan, and Carol Zall Lincoln. "Controlling Crime: A Security Checklist." *Library and Archival Security* 8, no. 1 (spring–summer 1986): 145–52.

McNeil, Beth, and Denise Johnson, eds. *Patron Behavior in Libraries.* Chicago: American Library Association, 1995.

Minor, Marianne. *Preventing Workplace Violence: Positive Management Strategies.* Menlo Park, Calif.: Crisp, 1995.

Nelson, James B. "Safety in the Public Library." *Show-Me Libraries* 44, no. 2 (winter–spring 1993): 368.

Owens, Sheryl. "Proactive Problem Patron Preparedness." *Library and Archival Security* 12, no. 2 (1994): 11–24.

Pease, B. G. "Workplace Violence in Libraries." *Library Management* 16, no. 7 (1995): 30–39.

Rubin, Rhea. "Anger in the Library." *Reference Librarian* 31 (1990): 39–50.

St. Lifer, Evan. "How Safe Are Our Libraries?" *Library Journal* 15 (August 1994): 35–39.

Salter, Charles, and Jeffrey L. Salter. *On the Frontlines: Coping with the Libraries' Problem Patrons.* Englewood, Colo.: Libraries Unlimited, 1988.

Shuman, Bruce A. "Problem Patrons in Libraries: A Review Article." *Library and Archival Security* 9, no. 2 (1989): 3–11.

Turner, Anne M. *It Comes with the Territory: Handling Problem Situations in Libraries.* Jefferson, N.C.: McFarland, 1993.

Winters, Sharon. "A Proactive Approach to Building Security." *Public Libraries* 33, no. 5 (September–October 1994): 151–56.

PART FOUR: ETHICAL CHALLENGES

CHAPTER 10

The Fight of the Century? Information Ethics versus E-Commerce

Marsha Woodbury

On Ethics and Identity

CYBER IMPOSTORS STEAL DIAMONDS, ROLEXES

Two Memphis men used the Internet to engineer an identity-theft scam that allowed them to use the credit cards of half a dozen top business executives and order more than $700,000 worth of expensive watches and jewelry. The two men, James R. Jackson and Derek Cunningham, face millions of dollars in fines and several decades worth of prison time if convicted on conspiracy and fraud charges. The case is being held in New York. Manhattan U.S. Attorney Mary Jo White says communications tools offered by the Internet are allowing criminals to engage in new schemes and strategies. Experts say identity theft can be carried out easily over the Internet. All scam artists need to do is pay a fee to an information broker to get an individual's Social Security number. Online databases also

> contain address information, while an individual's mother's maiden name can be found in obituaries or other public documents. (*USA Today*, May 8, 2000)

Today we can barely keep up with the online world, with viruses, copyright, patents, trademarks, fraud, cell phone etiquette, IPOs, and identity theft. The speed of change and my growing unease led me to adopt the presumptuous title of this chapter, "The Fight of the Century? Information Ethics vs. E-Commerce."

The title refers to the 1971 Frazier-Ali boxing match, which some writers called the best bout of the last century. As I see it, information ethics is taking a hammering from e-commerce, and unless we all become involved, the fight will be a first round knockout, over before it begins. But before tackling the new century, this chapter will focus on a few aspects of the past in order to highlight some of the current issues.

In the nineteenth and twentieth centuries, lynchings occurred so commonly in the United States that people bought and sent "lynching postcards." Today, we are offended by the idea of people mailing postcards showing a dead person hanging from a tree with a message saying, "I was here." Nevertheless, people did. They mailed the cards until 1908, when the U.S. Postal Service decided that such material ought not to be carried in the mail. After embarrassing racial incidents, several states were shamed into outlawing the sale of these postcards.[1] The efforts to stop mailing of materials that deeply offended a large part of the population correspond to the controversy today over community standards, online censorship, and cultural pollution.

Who could have foretold in 1900 that in the next century we would unleash the atomic bomb, put a man on the moon, or create the Palm Pilot? Women in the United States could not vote at the start of the century. They struggled so hard to get the vote, and voting seemed extremely important. Yet, a century later, people apparently do not value voting so highly, as there is now apathy, and less than half the population voted in the presidential election of 2000. Could anyone foresee the apathy at the time women fought so hard for the right? We cannot predict what is going to happen. However, some trends leap out at us, and we would have to be blind to miss them. We can foretell today that what happens with privacy and data mining and national ID cards and biometrics will change our sense of who we are as people. The big players in this revolution are the same people forming start-ups and dealing in e-commerce all over the globe. Our future is in their hands.

The Main Areas of Concern about Information

The following example contains critical information issues: privacy, accuracy, security/access, and ownership.[2]

If I speed down the highway and the police stop me, the resulting traffic ticket will contain true but potentially harmful information about me, for my driver's insurance policy premium may increase and friends and relatives may lose confidence in my driving judgment.

What would happen if I was also behind on child-support payments, and the computer put my name together with this infraction? Government officials might track me down and make me start paying my monthly contribution. If I were drinking alcohol, matters would get worse, for I might not be hired for certain jobs due to this evidence of drunk driving.

Now, what if I were not going too fast and never got a ticket, but someone mistyped some information, and my name went in the records for speeding or driving under the influence of alcohol? Moreover, what if a prospective employer used computers to learn everything it could about me and found out about the phantom ticket? Although I did not do anything wrong, I could forfeit a prospective job.

This scenario brings up key questions: What aspects of traffic tickets or any other piece of information should be private? How can we ensure the accuracy of information stored about us? Who can and should have access to that information? Who owns information about us?

Ethics

How do I know who I am? As we all do, I fill one role at work, another role at home, another at leisure, another in public. I change my behavior and lower or raise my defenses, depending on where I am. Finding out who I am is of enormous consequence, and this quest is shared by all of us.

We are, in essence, our moral and ethical selves. My ethical self should not vary from one situation to another. When I change my surroundings, I always bring *me* with me. Thus, if I am not consistent—if I behave one way at work and a different way elsewhere—then I am in danger of losing "me." My values are the integral part of me, and through my values I know myself.

This thought brings us to ethics. Ethics is moral decision making. When a mother grabs her child and flees a burning building, she does not have a spare second to contemplate her choice; she acts on instinct. That is not an ethical choice; it is a reaction.

Given time to think about what we are doing (provided that we do not have a gun pointing at our head), we usually try to select the most moral option among many. We may choose to ignore the niggling voices of our conscience, and do something we are not proud of. When I see what is happening online, I worry that some programmers and businesspeople appear to have no "niggling voice" in their ear, that their choices are not based on any ethical standard that I can recognize.

If ethics is about moral decision making, then what ethical guidelines do people have? Where did they learn them and how widespread are they? What laws are best to deal with information? Will we obey these laws? Who can enforce the laws? If an offshore gambling site breaks the mores of Minnesota, how does Minnesota preserve its mores?

A young Amherst graduate now living in New York spoke to me about his new job. He works in "Silicon Alley," creating the banner ads that rake in personal information about web surfers. I asked him if he worried about ethics, and he said "No." He added, "We need that advertising money to finance the Internet." In this fellow's mind, his work supported my use of the Internet, as though the Internet never existed until the browser came along. History began in 1995.

Shared values are the mortar of a society. Society has to have its mores and trust among its members. Part of our current problem is that traditional ethical values are situated in the physical world, where the ultimate measure of an action is how that action affects the people we live with. One constraint on physical behavior is that others can observe what we do, and the results of our moral decisions are "out there" for all to judge.

In the online world, we sit in front of a computer, away from the public eye, and we write "flaming" e-mail messages, creep into other people's servers, and do all sorts of things we would not do in a face-to-face situation.

My specialization is computer and information ethics, a field that deals with a more difficult ethical concept to grasp, that is, the sacredness of information itself. In the information age, one of our duties ought to be preserving the privacy, security, and integrity of information. We have to ensure access to it and maintain ownership of it, and the battle to do so is constant.

Check the course offerings in computer science departments around the country. Is ethics mentioned anywhere? Is it required as a single course? Is it supposedly integrated into all courses? Both the Association of Computing Machinery's "Curriculum 91" and the Computer Science Accreditation Board's standards recommend the inclusion of ethical issues in computer science curriculum. Why? If they did not demand that ethics be taught, it might not be.

Recently, as I searched the web for materials on programming, I clicked a link and suddenly a pornographic page popped up. I immediately hit the close button, only to have a new pornography site appear. Every time I clicked the window shut, another page popped up. I felt like Mickey Mouse in *Fantasia*, with the broomsticks proliferating. The entrepreneurs who ran the porn sites had literally hijacked me. What if I had been using a browser at work, and my boss monitored my web usage? I could be fired for accessing pornography on the job. Hijacking destroys that most important element in information ethics, trust in the reliability and accuracy of information.[3]

Pornography and gambling are leading the way in online commerce, and I cannot tell how soon others will follow. Do not imagine that page hijacking is something that only pornographers do. One example of "hijacking" involves trademarks. Trademarks such as Pepsi and Playboy are very highly valued by their owners. Companies spend years developing brand recognition and the good faith of the customer. A questionable practice of some companies is to embed in their web pages, invisible to the visitor, the names of very popular products and sites. Calvin Designer Label Company incorporated the words "Playboy" and "Playmate" into the invisible coding on its adult-oriented web sites. Likewise, National Envirotech Group, a pipeline-reconstruction company, embedded the names of a larger competitor, Insituform Technologies Inc.

This trick diverted traffic from Playboy and Insituform to their competitors. Such practices also diminish the value of search engines as a way for people to find accurate information about companies. Diverting people on the Internet is like slapping a sign on a freeway that says "Shell," and when you pull up in front, you are at Exxon.

To maintain trust and a common morality, we protect information, as we would guard jewels. The danger with counterfeit money is a devaluing of all currency; the same concept applies to the integrity of information.

E-Commerce

Silicon Valleys exist across our country, from New York to Austin to Palo Alto. What is happening in these places? Who are the business people who work there? What are their values? Do they use moral reasoning to arrive at decisions? What are their priorities?

Recently, an author said that he was struck, while doing a recent series of interviews with e-commerce CEOs, on the "low quality of the dot com CEOs when compared with the traditionalists." He characterized the dot com CEOs as "lacking in depth, experience and common business sense, driven primarily by jealousy and greed in a race to go public as quickly as possible and rake in those stock options. 'Hey, why get rich slowly with a lot of work when I can get rich quickly with not much work?' is the general thinking."[4]

That author predicted a stock market "shakeout," which occurred soon after. He wrote that the dot coms would fail, and take with them "a sinful amount of venture and day trader capital." The toll on human capital would be even worse: "An entire generation of business leaders will be corrupted. They will have great skills in designing obtuse ad campaigns, doing barter deals, negotiating with investment banks and venture capitalists, and doing secondary road shows. But this generation will have no skills in marshaling sales forces, hiring executive teams, working out fair business contracts with customers, and building employee morale and culture that is sustainable beyond a two-year period."[5]

Not long ago, a company called RealNetworks released software called RealJukebox that let people listen to CDs and digital music while working on a computer. People simply downloaded the software from the Internet and installed it on their hard drives. RealJukebox sent back the unique ID number generated by each installation of the RealNetworks software on each PC, together with the names of all the CDs played, the number of songs recorded on the hard disk, the brand of MP3 player owned, and the music genre listened to most. The unique ID number could be mapped to a person's e-mail address via the registration database.[6]

Information stored on my hard disk in cookies is hard to control as well. Either I go to the inconvenience of approving all cookies, install cookie cutter software, or live with ongoing monitoring. In sum, I am a deer in the woods, trying to hide from hunters, yet wearing a global positioning system chip clipped onto my ear.

The Internet is making identity theft one of the signature crimes of the digital era. Identity theft is the pilfering of people's personal information for use in obtaining credit cards, loans, and other goods. Any visitor to cyberspace can find web sites selling all kinds of personal information and, with that information in hand, acquire credit, make purchases, and even secure residences in someone else's name.

The Social Security Administration reported that it received more than 30,000 complaints about the misuse of Social Security numbers in 1999, most of which had to do with identity theft. That was up from about 11,000 complaints in 1998 and 7,868 in 1997.[7]

How is identity theft tied to the Internet? The evidence is clear. For example, GeoCities, a Web portal that claims nearly 20 million visitors a month, sold information solicited during its registration process, despite an explicit online assurance it would not do so. The data included income, education, marital status, occupation, and personal interests. In January 2000, the Federal Trade Commission charged eight California businesses with billing consumers for unordered and fictitious Internet services, using their credit card account numbers.[8]

Identity theft, as any victim can attest, can destroy a personal credit rating and lead to very expensive litigation that may take years or perhaps decades to fully correct. The victim cannot rent an apartment, obtain credit, or even hook up to phone service. Identity theft and related computer crimes supported over the Internet may become an unparalleled destabilizing force for the twenty-first century.[9]

Practices of E-Commerce Companies

> There is one and only one social responsibility of business—to use its resources and engage in activities designed to increase its profits so long as it stays within the rules of the game, which is to say, engages in open and free competition without deception or fraud.
>
> Milton Friedman[10]

I can buy Viagra online because regulators cannot keep up with the proliferating web sites. As soon as one site closes down, another takes its place. Who are the doctors prescribing drugs online? Who facilitates their work?

Recently, Amazon.com entered the spotlight for featuring books posing as editorial picks. In fact, publishers paid for books to be featured on Amazon.com's home page. While product placements are commonplace, the issue is one of ethics. The readers thought that Amazon selected the books on merit.[11]

People need to be aware of exactly what they are revealing and to whom when giving out information, however inadvertently. Online services know not only their members' social security and credit card numbers, but may also hold entire profiles on people, including what bulletin boards they join—discussion groups for cancer survivors, for instance, a potential danger for a job applicant. Here is an email message that I recently received:

> Date: Sat, 29 Jan 2000 23:30:00 PDT
>
> From: "Customer Service at itn.net" <amex-efares@itn.net>
>
> Subject: An important announcement from Internet Travel Network
>
> Sender: "Customer Service at itn.net" <amex-efares@itn.net>
>
> To: Internet.Travel.Network.Subscribers@ml-sc-0.itn.net
>
> Reply-To: "Customer Service at itn.net" <amex-efares-reply @itn.net>
>
> This is a special post only email. Please do not reply.
>
> Dear Internet Travel Network subscriber:
>
> We are pleased to announce that ITN.net has combined forces with American Express Travel and Entertainment to bring you a new and enhanced online travel site. The creation of this powerful site provides new capabilities and benefits for all of your travel needs. By typing in the URL, www.itn.net, you'll be able to continue to make all of your travel plans online.
>
> What you gain with our new relationship with American Express is continued access to ITN's airline booking system which provides competitive airfares and schedule information. . . .
>
> To make this transition as easy as possible, your profile and password information will be transferred to the new reservation system. Past booking information will continue to be available. Now you'll get to explore these travel services from one of the world's largest travel agencies, American Express.

> We look forward to welcoming you to the new American Express Travel Home Page.
>
> Sincerely,
>
> Gadi Maier
> President & CEO
> GetThere.com

This message told of a recent merger of two travel firms, ITN and American Express. My files automatically went to American Express, and I had no power to stop them. ITN evidently owned my information and used it as an asset in the business merger.

A few years ago, such an occurrence would have seemed less threatening. After all, banks and stockbrokerages merged all the time and transferred personal records. However, today, with massive and easily searchable databases, the transfer of data about us without our consent is frightening. Yet that was the company's main asset, its customer database, with my name and travel preferences.

Some companies also gather data merely for the purpose of selling it. Few protections against these practices have been established, though some have been proposed in Congress. I attended a Washington hearing between the top government administrators and business representatives, and the overwhelming message from the capital was that self-regulation is going to be our only choice in the ethical handling of our information by e-commerce businesses.

Privacy of Information

> You already have zero privacy—get over it.
>
> Scott McNealy, chairman and chief executive of Sun Microsystems[12]

The sometimes embarrassing aspect of combining computer technology with credit card use is that I cannot even hide from myself, let alone from the rest of the world. The Visa card readout from my bank account tells me more than I want to know. Formerly, when we dealt in cash and checks, we had little idea how we spent our money. With credit cards and electronic money, the bank not so kindly itemizes my expenses for me so I can see where I spend my money—hotels, travel, meals, and entertainment—not a pretty sight.

Privacy is not mentioned in the U.S. Constitution. Justice Louis Brandeis argued in an 1890 *Harvard Law Review* article that people have the right to keep parts of themselves private. Later, in a famous dissent in a privacy case, he wrote, "Subtler and more far-reaching means of invading privacy have become available. . . . Ways may some day be developed by which Government, without removing papers from secret drawers, can reproduce them in court, and by which it will be enabled to expose to a jury the most intimate occurrences of the home.[13]

In Europe, privacy protection laws are much stricter than in the United States. It is illegal to combine the health care database with the tax database, for example. In the United States, such strictures do not apply as firmly.

In my textbook on computer and information ethics, I use the following scenario created by Glenn Brookshear to make students think about privacy:

> Today there are websites that provide roadmaps of most cities. These sites assist in finding particular addresses and provide zooming capabilities for viewing the layout of small neighborhoods. Starting with this reality, consider the following fictitious sequence. Suppose these map sites were enhanced with satellite photographs with similar zooming capabilities. Suppose these zooming capabilities were increased to give a more detailed image of individual buildings and surrounding landscape. Suppose these images were enhanced to include real-time video. Suppose these video images were enhanced with infrared technology. At your own home 24-hours-a-day. At what point in this progression were your privacy rights first violated?[14]

Marketers say that consumers give out their information "willingly" in exchange for services, but cookies from banner ads are invasive. A friend of mine wrote in an e-mail message:

> I was looking at www.cnn.com this morning when I got a cookie alert. It said something like, "To increase your viewing experience we would like to install a small file 'cookie' on your system."

> Upon clicking on "more info," [I found that] the cookie was from a banner ad, for Nicorette [a product to help you stop smoking].
>
> Seems like the phrase should have said, "To provide info to the advertiser. . . ."[15]

Likewise, when we open e-mail containing a web page, another cookie could be left on our drive, and this time, because it arrives through e-mail, our exact e-mail address could be linked to data about sites that we previously visited.

Prominent companies are associated with privacy invasion. After a lawsuit, the Chase Manhattan Bank and the Internet company InfoBeat will no longer be sharing customer data with telemarketers. Chase had violated its own privacy policy when it divulged personal and financial information about as many as 18 million credit card and mortgage holders across the country, while InfoBeat inadvertently provided customer e-mail addresses to advertisers because of a software problem that has since been corrected.[16]

For years, people in many countries have worried about national databases and national identity (ID) cards. In one very public case, a New Hampshire company began planning to create a national identity database for the U.S. government. The company would have begun by putting driver's license and other personal data into one giant database.[17] The company officials believed their system could be used to combat terrorism, immigration abuses, and other identity crimes, and the company received $1.5 million in federal funding and technical assistance from the Secret Service. This piqued the interest of foreign governments, who inquired about whether technology could be used to verify the identities of voters.[18]

Privacy advocates complained loudly about the plans to scan in license photos, and states stopped their plans to sell the information. However, the company intends to offer a revamped version of its system that will gather photos and personal information from one customer at a time at retailers, banks, and other participating companies. By collecting photographs individually, the company hopes to head off complaints that it is violating drivers' privacy by gathering the images without their consent.[19] Just as supermarkets gather data about our shopping habits, slowly this company will compile data linked to a picture, eventually building a huge database capable of identifying all of us.

As for government information, recall that government agencies are publicly owned, and are required by law to give open access to the information they hold. The government cannot copyright information. With the data produced by global positioning systems, a geographic information system, businesses can create entirely new data out of old information, and that may then indirectly reveal information that is supposed to be private.

The Future

A computer scientist summed up the battle this way:

> In this age of information, we, the professionals who are entrusted with this data, are increasingly being looked at as people who are no better than a drug dealer who stalks out an elementary school looking for future clients. We possess something much more powerful than drugs, though, we have at our control the information stores that control the world and most of the people who inhabit it.[20]

Professionals design and build everything electronic, from our databases, web sites, and critical software to the microchips in our cars and microwaves. Unlike civil engineers or architects, these professionals do not have to pass any tests to be licensed. And they do not have to read or sign off on a code of ethics. All they have to do is start programming.

Recently, I discovered classmates.com. This web site allows me to locate old friends from the Ukiah High School class of 1964. If I want to e-mail them, I pay $25 for that privilege for the coming two years. I did not hesitate to join, to give them my e-mail address, Visa card number, and all the information that anyone needs to track me down. The site owners will be instantly rich, even though the site could disappear in three months. I have no guarantee, no assurance whatsoever. What they sold me was irresistible: the chance to find old friends. Compare $25 with the effort it would take to locate these people—it is a bargain. Or is it?

After several million of us have suffered identity theft, people will call for a technological fix. We can imagine being forced to accept national IDs, implanted chips, and retinal scans. How else can we trust that people are who they say they are? Yet, does a match on a retinal scan really tell us anything? Someone could switch the master database, so the scan is linked to another identity. Information is only as good as the integrity of the database underneath it.

As far as the national identity card issue goes, the government will not lead the way, but business will. The brave new world envisioned by the Hewlett-Packard Company gives me pause. They predicted that in the future, a doctor will pick up a context-aware badge when entering a hospital. The badge will recognize the doctor through biometrics (fingerprint, iris, face or voice recognition). A global positioning system device in the badge will locate the doctor. The badge will know what is going on around the physician because of the servers embedded throughout the facility, and everyone else will be wearing context-aware badges, too.

When the doctor enters a room, the system will recognize the doctor, it will confirm that he or she is seeing the right patient, and the relevant charts will automatically come up on a computer screen. If an unauthorized person approaches the screen, the screen will go blank.

Is that so far away from where we are now? The technology is in the hands of people acquiring instant wealth, and whose children expect to be rich by the age of twenty-five. Reports from Silicon Valley are worrisome.

Is privacy going to be lost to technology? What can we do about it? Here are some self-help suggestions:

- Be informed. Push hard for open access to stored information about you.
- Use encryption.
- Support legislation to protect privacy. Right now, the money in government is bolstering enforcement of copyright and patent protections while leaving e-commerce privacy abuse to "self-regulation."
- Use an anonymous server to send e-mail or access Internet sites when you want privacy.
- Prevent widespread distribution of Usenet, private listserv postings, and chat group discussions by using passwords, domain name filtering, Internet address filtering, or a firewall to prevent access by unauthorized users.[21]
- Use cookie cutter software to select the cookies you want stored on your hard drive.

The activists today work for a better future, one in which information is treated with respect. A century ago, we had radicals fighting for equal rights for women. After public protest, the government stepped in and stopped the mailing of lynching postcards. Today we have organizations like the Computer Professionals for Social Responsibility, Electronic Privacy Information Center, and the American Library Association espousing information ethics.

Most Internet activists realize that key technologies and policies affecting our future will come from the field of telecommunications. Nevertheless, this sensitivity is relatively recent. When Congress passed the Telecommunications Act of 1996, few computer and information professionals knew about little more than the Communications Decency Act. However, after realizing the key decisions that will determine the future of the Internet, e-commerce, and information ethics, these same programmers and librarians are arguing section 251(b) with telecommunication carriers and discussing what is intrastate versus what is interstate with the Federal Communications Commission.

The Internet is both dependent on traditional telecommunications and, in some ways, a competitor to them. Those interested in Internet policy can follow telecommunications debates, both national and international. We can keep an eye on who has the right to regulate e-commerce and telecommunications issues, and we can make our voices heard.[22]

Until that time comes, fasten your seatbelts. We are in for quite a ride.

Notes

1. Jace Clayton, "'Without Sanctuary': A Display of Lynching Photography" (June 5, 2001), http://www.africana.com/DailyArticles/index_20000323.htm.

2. Richard O. Mason, "Four Ethical Issues of the Information Age," *Management Information Systems Quarterly* 10, no 1 (1986), http://www.misq.org/archivist/vol/no10/issue1/vol10no1mason.html.

3. If you want to learn more about this practice, read the Federal Trade Commission complaint at http://techlawjournal.com/courts/ftcvpereira/19990914com.htm.

4. George Forrester, "My View: Hollow.Com" (April 2000), http://www.forrester.com/ER/Marketing/0,1503,183,FF.html.

5. *Ibid.*

6. Jonathan Weinberg, "Hardware-Based ID, Trusted Systems, and Rights Management," *Stanford Law Review* 52 (2000), 1251, http://www.law.wayne.edu/weinberg/trusted.1201.PDF.

7. Timothy O'Brien, "Aided by Internet, Identity Theft Soars," *New York Times on the Web,* April 3, 2000, http://www.nytimes.com/library/tech/00/04/biztech/articles/03theft.html, August 22, 2001.

8. *Ibid.*

9. Hal Berghel, "Identity Theft, Social Security Numbers, and the Web," *Communications of the ACM* 43, no 2 (2000): 17–21.

10. Milton Friedman, "The Social Responsibility of Business to Increase Its Profits," in *Ethics, Leadership, and the Bottom Line,* eds. Charles Nelson and Robert Caveny (Croton-on-Hudson, N.Y.: North River, 1991), 245.

11. The Better Business Bureau is a useful source of information about e-commerce practices, at http://www.bbb.org/.

12. John Markoff, "A Growing Compatibility Issue in the Digital Age: Computers and Their Users' Privacy," *New York Times on the Web,* March 2, 1999, http://www.sci.tamucc.edu/~physweb/ethics/IntelChip.html.

13. *Olmstead* v. *United States,* 277 U.S. 438, 473–74 (1928) (J. Brandeis, dissenting).

14. J. Glenn Brookshear, *Computer Science: An Overview,* 6th ed. (Reading, Mass. Addison-Wesley, 2000), 534.

15. Steve Teicher, personal communication, February 2000.

16. *New York Times,* January 26, 2000, http://www.nytimes.com/aponline/f/AP-Internet-Privacy.html.

17. Declan McCullagh, "Smile for the US Secret Service," *Wired News,* September 7, 1999, http://www.wired.com/news/news/politics/story/21607.html.

18. Robert O'Harrow Jr., "Firm Changes Plan to Acquire Photos: Drivers' Pictures Ignited Privacy Furor," *Washington Post,* November 12, 1999, E03.

19. *Ibid.*

20. Robert Stinnett, "Ethics in the Age of Information" (June 5, 2001), http://www.theultimateos.com/editorials/oct99/ethics.asp August 22, 2001.

21. Susan E. Gindin, "Lost and Found in Cyberspace: Informational Privacy in the Age of the Internet," *San Diego Law Review* 34 (1997), 1153.

22. Andy Oram, "Key Policy Issues to Watch in Telecom" (2000), http://webreview.com/wr/pub/2000/01/14/platform/index.html.

CHAPTER 11

Information Ethics

ITS DEMARCATION AND APPLICATION

Johannes J. Britz

We are currently living in the so-called information age, an era in which economic activities are primarily information based: an age of informationalization. The rise of the information age is mainly due to technological developments. The main characteristics of the new era are a rise in the number of knowledge workers, a world in which communication has become more open, and internationalization evident in the transborder flow of data.

This paradigm shift brings new ethical and juridical problems that are mainly related to issues such as the right of access to information; the right of privacy, which is threatened by the emphasis on the free flow of information; the protection of the economic interest of the owners of intellectual property; and issues pertaining to the quality of information and the acceptance of responsibility thereof by information professionals.

Against this background, this chapter investigates the ethical questions facing the information professional working in libraries, archives and museums. The article is divided into three parts. The first part focuses on ethics, the ethical decision-making process and the demarcation and defining of information ethics. The second part discusses the ethical principles and norms applicable to the ethical decision-making process. Part three explains and illustrates how the ethical decision-making process can be applied by information professionals to the ethical issues pertaining to users' right to privacy.

What Is Ethics?

Ethics is a branch of philosophy that deals with human conduct and character. As an academic discipline it is divided into descriptive ethics, metaethics, and normative ethics. Descriptive ethics focuses more on the description of the ethical behavior of people without any normative prescriptions. Metaethics focuses on issues such as the origin of ethics and definitions of moral concepts such as "good." Prescriptive ethics investigates ethical problems from a normative perspective. The main aims are making value judgments and formulating ethical guidelines for individuals, professions and society.

In practical terms, normative ethics, the subject of this chapter, boils down to questions such as: Is the action I took fair? What would be the right thing to do? Answers to these questions are not always obvious, and differences of opinion on these answers may arise.

THE ETHICAL DECISION-MAKING PROCESS

The Subject of the Ethical Action

The subject of the ethical decision-making process is the autonomous human being who can be held responsible for his or her actions. This is based on the assumption that an autonomous human being has the freedom of choice and therefore can be held responsible and accountable for, among other things, his or her ethical choices and actions.

The Different Elements in the Decision-Making Process

The process of ethical decision making consists primarily of the identification and assessment of the ethical problem, the choice to act and the action itself. This assessment process is based on ethical norms and principles such as truth, honesty, justice and respect for human life. These norms and principles are not static, but are interpreted and applied within specific contexts.

The Three Schools of Thought

Ethical decision making is furthermore exercised from a specific perspective. Such perspectives are sometimes referred to as specific philosophical schools of thought. The two main schools of thoughts are the deontological (from the Greek word *deon,* which means duty) and the teleological (from the Greek word *teleos,* which means consequence). The deontologists emphasize the compulsory character of an ethical action. Thus, the norm sets an unconditional claim, e.g., "you are not allowed to make an illegal copy of a document." The focus is therefore on the duty to obey the imperative of a norm—regardless of considerations of goodness, including the actual consequences of an action or even the motive for the action. The consequentialist, on the other hand, will judge an ethical action, and define "good," in terms of the result/outcome. According to this approach, the stealing of intellectual property might be justified if the end result is the education of poor communities. There is, however, a third school of thought—so-called rule-utilitarianism—that emphasizes the importance of both the result of the ethical act and the appropriate norm for the given situation. This approach seems to be more balanced in the process of ethical decision making because it takes into account the following variables:

- the situation
- the different role players
- the motive for action
- the decision to act
- the result of the action
- the appropriate norms and principles.

The Interest of the Individual versus the Interest of the Community

Ethical decision making must also be clear on whether it will give preference to the interest of the individual or that of the society. Three basic approaches can be followed. In the first paradigm, the importance of the individual is deemphasized and the interests of the community are regarded as more important. This school of thought is supported mainly by the "communitarians" (Van den Hoven 1997, 34). In its most extreme manifestation, this paradigm can, for example, lead to the complete negation of an individual's freedom to be private. The second approach, of which the American Library Association is a good example, emphasizes the rights of the individual and regards these rights to be of more importance than the interests of the community. This approach, supported by the "liberalists," could lead to an absolutism of the rights of individuals at the expense of the interests of the community.

It can therefore be argued that both aforementioned approaches—in their extreme manifestations—might fail to provide proper solutions to the "individual versus community" problem. Another approach seeks a balance between the communitarian and liberalist approaches (Britz 1999, 302). According to this approach, the individual's rights, as a primary principle, will be fully acknowledged and protected, while the community's interests (with regard to crime prevention, a stable order and a fair contribution of all to the maintenance of public goods) are also taken into consideration.

THE DEMARCATION OF INFORMATION ETHICS

Information Ethics As a Broad Concept

"Information ethics" applies to a broad range of situations, because everyone uses information, be it at work, for entertainment or in any other context. As such, every person has an ethical responsibility in the use thereof.

Furthermore, information ethics, as a form of professional ethics, is applicable to a variety of occupations, such as the medical profession, for example, in the ethical issues pertaining to the handling of patients' records; computer scientists (computer ethics), journalists (media ethics); and information professionals, such as information managers, archivists and librarians.

The Demarcation of Information Ethics

Because the boundaries between these professional fields are sometimes not clear, it is important to identify and demarcate the core elements of information ethics as it pertains to information professionals such as librarians, archivists and museum professionals. This can be done by narrowing the scope of information ethics to the professional activities of the above-mentioned information professionals. Information ethics can therefore be defined as professional ethics that deals with ethical issues in all areas of the professional gathering, organizing, value adding, storage, retrieval, distribution and management of information products and services on behalf of a third party. Capurro (1985, 122), in line with this definition, formulates information ethics as "the ethics of knowing, . . . an ethics of individual and collective responsibility towards knowledge, its production, communication and use."

Information professionals are mainly involved in publicly available information sources. In this context the following seven key role players can be identified: authors, publishers, database producers, database vendors, information professionals, information services/organizations and the end users (Froehlich 1992, 292). All these role players must be taken into consideration in the ethical decision-making process.

THE ETHICAL FRAMEWORK OF THE INFORMATION PROFESSIONAL

For a better understanding of the ethical issues and responsibilities of the information professional, an ethical framework should be formulated. Within this framework, it is possible to further demarcate and contextualize information ethics.

Power and Dependency

The processing of information on behalf of a third party implies two ethics-laden concepts. The first is *dependency* and the second, ensuing from the first, is *power*. Users of information products and services are, to a certain extent, dependent on the information professional for the information they need. The level of dependency might vary, depending on the specific information need and the category of information. This form of dependency implies power in the hands of those who possess the needed information—in other words, the information professional. As such, the information professional must handle this "information power" with an ethical sensitivity and responsibility. The information professional must not misuse this power, neither to his or her own benefit or to the disadvantage of the user.

The Exclusion of the Generation and Use of Information

In the demarcation of information ethics, it has been indicated that ethical questions relating to the generation and end use of information is not the focus of the information professional. Thus, the information professional working in a archive cannot be held morally responsible for the content of the information that is gathered, nor for the consequences of the use thereof.

However, there are exceptions. An information professional might be held ethically responsible where he or she was professionally involved in the generation of new information, for example, the interpretation of information for decision making. This aspect will be dealt with in more detail under the subheading "Continuum-Based Activities," below.

The fact that the information professional's ethical responsibilities do not primarily focus on the generation of information poses interesting ethical questions. For example, can libraries, archives and museums be totally "ethical-neutral" in their acquisition policies? And closely linked to this question, to what extent must the values and norms of the society being served be taken into consideration?

The Use of Information Technology

Technology is regarded as instrumental and supportive in the professional activities of the information professional. The ethical issues involved in the use of information technology must therefore be seen from this perspective. Ethical problems pertaining to the creation of hardware and software, as well as the individual use of information technology (hacking, cracking, reading of other people's e-mail, etc.) are therefore not specifically applicable to the field of information ethics. However, when the use of information technology in the execution of professional activities threatens, for example, the privacy of clients or enhances the illegal copying of documents, it becomes an ethical issue for the information professional.

Socioethical Issues

Information ethics is furthermore not restricted to the professional relationship between the user and an information professional. Libraries, museums and archives do not operate in a social vacuum; they have a socioethical responsibility toward society. It can be argued that it is the social obligation of information professionals to get involved in social issues such as information poverty, information illiteracy, and government policy regarding the (non)distribution and (non)management of information as a national asset.

Continuum-Based Activities

The activities of the information professional can be represented on three continuums, namely, content, intellectual and diagnostic continuums. These continuums can be used to illustrate that the ethical responsibility of information professionals can vary, depending on the kind of activities they are involved in. The higher the professional activities lie on the respective continuums, the higher the ethical intensity and, by implication, the ethical responsibility of the information professional.

The following illustrate the increase of ethical responsibilities on the different continuums:

- *Metacontent continuum.* The word "metacontent" refers to the metainformation about an information product—in other words the bibliographic descriptors (author, title, key words, etc.) that are used in the description and classification of information products. The ethical issue at stake on the metacontent continuum pertains to the question of the level of accuracy of the descriptors that are assigned to represent the document in the classification system. In cases where the assignment comprises only author and title information, the ethical responsibility is limited to aspects such as the correct spelling of names. However, with the adding of key words and abstracts (activities that are higher on the metacontent continuum) to describe the document, the ethical responsibility will increase. Among others, the following ethics-related questions then come into play: Do the descriptors correctly represent the document in the retrieval system? Which concepts must be used to describe politically and culturally sensitive documents and artifacts? These ethical questions not only are relevant to the information professional (in terms of the choice of descriptors that must be made), but they also have a bearing on the classification and cataloging system used. For example, what must be the correct ethical action in a case where the classification system does not make provision for the assignment of classification numbers for, say, the Babgatla people living in South Africa?

- *Intellectual continuum.* This continuum pertains to the level of intellectual input in the content of documents by the information professional. Intellectual input in this context refers to those activities by information professionals that are aimed at changing the content itself: translations, interpretations (e.g., executive summaries) and the altering of the format of the content (e.g., the change from a textual format to graphics). The ethical responsibility on this continuum relates to the quality/correctness of these activities, as well as the outcome/use of the information to which value has been added. If there is no intellectual input in the content, the ethical responsibilities will be limited to those ethical issues raised at the discussion of the metacontent continuum. The more the intellectual input (higher on the intellectual continuum), for example, the translation of a document, the more the ethical responsibility, because the information professional can now be held (ethically) responsible for the correctness of the content that has been changed. The following question can even be raised: To what extent is the information professional responsible for use of the information to which value has been added?
- *Diagnostic continuum.* The diagnostic continuum refers to the reference interview between the information professional and the user. Apart from the ethical responsibility to conduct a thorough interview, there can be, depending on the situation, a corresponding growing ethical responsibility and the kind of information that is gained from the reference interview. For example, an information professional will have a limited ethical responsibility toward a client who just asks for a book with the title *Suicide or Not?* than when the information professional is aware (via information gained from the interview) that the user who wants the book is very depressed and possibly suicidal. In the first case, the responsibility of the information professional is only to supply the requested material, whereas in the second example the information professional may be faced with the dilemma of whether or not to get involved in the personal life of the client. It is interesting to note that the American Library Association's code of ethics states clearly that librarians must distinguish clearly in their actions and statements between their personal philosophies and attitudes and those of an institute or professional body (Zipkowitz 1996, 118).

THE MAIN ETHICAL ISSUES CONFRONTING THE INFORMATION PROFESSIONAL

Apart from the abovementioned ethical issues, the information professional is confronted with the following main categories of ethical problems:

- the right of access to information
- the right to intellectual property
- the quality of information
- the right to privacy

Each of these ethical issues will be discussed briefly.

Access to Information

The right of access to information has become one of the most important ethical issues in the information era. This is mainly due to the fact that there is a growing realization by most democratic societies that access to information is a basic, instrumental human right that must be legally protected. Public information services (e.g., libraries, archives) are furthermore perceived as one of the primarily social institutions that must protect and promote this basic right.

This right of access to information is, however, a complicated issue. It is in the first place a restricted human right. A person has a right of access only to information needed to satisfy other basic human rights. A person cannot claim the right of access to trade secrets or other people's private information. It is therefore within the right of an archive to restrict the right of access to some private collections of individuals. Second, although access to information can be seen as a basic human right, it does not imply the free access thereof. In certain cases it can be justifiable to charge a fee for access to information. Third, access to information cannot be equated with accessibility. For example, providing access to information on the Internet does not necessarily imply accessibility. For example, in South Africa only 10 percent of the population have access to the Internet. A closed collection policy by a library or archive can be seen as another example in which access to information does not imply accessibility. Fourth, the inequality between people codetermines the right of access to information.

Although all people are of the equal value, they cannot always be treated equally with regard to access to information. For example, children can be denied access to certain categories of information to which an adult might have access. However, inequalities between people do not justify any negative discrimination based on color, race, gender, or religion.

With regard to the right of access to information, the information professional is therefore confronted with ethical questions such as,

- Can there be any form of censorship?
- On which grounds can people be denied access to information?
- Is it justifiable to have a closed collection?
- Will the digitization of information enhance its accessibility?
- In which cases can it be justified to ask a fee for access to information?

Intellectual Property

Information professionals are also confronted with the issue of the intellectual property rights of authors and distributors of information products. These rights must be respected and protected by information professionals. Apart from the ethical issues, there are also economic and legal concerns surrounding these rights.

One of the main problem areas is the clash between intellectual property rights and other information-related rights, such as the right of access to information and the right to intellectual freedom. Woodward (1990, 10) defines intellectual freedom as "the [right of access] to the intellectual efforts of others and a right to distribute one's own intellectual efforts." It implies not only freedom of expression, but also access to other people's intellectual products. The assumption here is that knowledge is a common good, and must remain accessible for the benefit of society. Therefore, a question arises: must a higher value be put on the strict protection of ownership of intellectual property or on the right of access to these intellectual products? This is also sometimes referred to as the dilemma of "the right to know versus the right to own."

Other practical issues pertaining to intellectual property are questions such as,

- Is it ethically correct to install more photocopy machines in libraries, museums or archives than are needed? Will such a situation encourage users to infringe on copyright?

- What is the appropriate way to inform users on copyright legislation?
- What must be done in cases in which the application of copyright (e.g., payment for information) excludes poor communities from access to information?

The Quality of Information

The third ethical issue concerns the quality of information products and services that are rendered by information professionals. It deals with matters such as the completeness, accuracy, reliability and currency of information products and service (Taylor 1986, 50). Capurro (1985, 115) uses the concept of "completeness" rather than "quality," while Mason prefers "accuracy" (1986, 46). Quality issues are especially relevant because people base their decisions on, form their opinions on and organize their lives around information. The following malpractices regarding the quality of information can occur: the misrepresentation by information professionals regarding the work they can perform, search biases—for example the inclination to favor certain search techniques or databases (Froehlich 1992, 301)—and the misrepresentation of information itself. It is therefore appropriate to ask:

- What verification measures exist to ensure the quality of information?
- Who has to bear the responsibility for ensuring the quality of existing information?
- In which circumstances can the information professional be held morally and legally responsible for decisions that stem from incorrect information?
- How can the competency of information professionals be verified?
- Are artifacts exhibited in museums or personal-related documents displayed in an archive presented in such a way that there is no loss of meaning or human dignity? To put it another way, how can "contextual integrity"—the presentation of information so that the context necessary for understanding it is not lost—be maintained?

The Right to Privacy

The right to privacy has indeed become one of the most important ethical issues for information professionals. This is mainly due to the increased use of information technology. The right to privacy raises ethical questions such as:

- Who has a right of access to a person's private information?
- Which private and personal information of a user can be collected?
- Can private and personal documents of people be displayed to the public?
- Under which circumstances must a person's private information be made public (the problem of individual freedom versus social responsibility)?

Solutions to these and related ethical problems pertaining to privacy will be dealt with in detail in the last part of the chapter.

Applicable Ethical Principles and Norms for the Information Professional

It has been illustrated that the assessment process for an ethical problem (as part of ethical decision making) is based on norms and principles interpreted and applied within specific situations. In this part of the chapter, six basic principles are identified and discussed, as are the norms of justice, truth and freedom.

BASIC PRINCIPLES

Just as there is no general agreement on which ethical theory and approaches are the correct ones, there is no universal agreement on ethical principles, which are based on ethical theory. According to Kluge (1994, 339), the following fundamental principles have to some extent found universal acceptance and can be applied to information ethics:

- *The principle of human autonomy and respect for a person.* This implies that every human being has a fundamental right to self-determination, the right to choose and the right to freedom. These rights are only limited when they infringe on the rights of other people. According to this principle, every person has a right of access to information needed to exercise other basic human rights.
- *The principle of impossibility.* This principle implies that under certain conditions rights and obligations cannot be exercised. For example, the right of access to information might be overruled in cases in which it is impossible to make such information available. For example, it is im-

possible to translate all government information in South Africa into the eleven official languages.

- *The principle of relevant difference.* This principle acknowledges that rights and duties are exercised and fulfilled in specific contexts. It does not occur in isolation. The information professional's context is therefore one of a professional client relationship, which requires that the information professional, among other things, acknowledge the autonomy of and respect the client, and ensure the integrity and quality of the information as well as the confidentiality of personal-related information. Provision must, however, be made for possible overriding duties and rights—for example, when there are grounds to believe that serious harm is likely to result to another person. This might require the disclosure of a user's personal information.
- *Principle of best action.* This principle entails an obligation by information professionals to handle all information in the best possible manner. This "best action" pertains to, among other things, the formulation of the search strategy, the treatment of the client's privacy, the search process (databases used, etc.) and the quality of the information.
- *Principle of priority.* According to this principle, rights may be prioritized. Depending on the context, the process of prioritization can be executed by the client or the information professional. For example, a family of a dead person can waive the right to privacy regarding personal documents, when it can be of benefit to research. Emergencies can also provide reason to prioritize rights.
- *Principle of equality and justice.* This principle entails that all persons must be treated as equals. This implies that everyone, irrespective of color, age or gender, must be treated equally as information users. Negative discrimination is ethically indefensible. Although all information users are of equal value, this does not imply equality. Inequality relates to age, occupations and ownership of information. Restrictions on access to certain categories of information in an organization can be justified on this principle. For example, the managing director of a company might have the right of access to more information in the company than the junior assistant.

APPLICABLE ETHICAL NORMS

Apart from these basic principles the following ethical norms can be distinguished: justice, freedom and truth.

Justice

The Greek philosopher Aristotle defined justice as an act of giving a person what he deserves *(suum cuique tribere)* and justice is seen by many philosophers as the highest norm *(summum bonum)*. Aristotle's definition is still widely used today. According to the *Oxford Wordfinder* (1993), justice as a norm implies the fair treatment of a person or the exercise of authority in the maintenance of rights.

Based on Aristotle's definition of justice, the following four categories of justice can be distinguished: commutative justice, distributive justice, contributive justice and retributive justice. All four categories of justice are applicable to information ethics.

Commutative justice calls for fundamental fairness in all agreements and exchanges between individuals or social groups. In its economic application, it calls for equality in transactions (National Conference of Catholic Bishops 1986, 54).

In terms of handling information products and services, commutative justice underscores the importance of the relationship between buyers and sellers of information (information providers and information users), as well as the application of copyright laws in ways that secure the economic interests of authors and publishers. This exchange relationship must be guided by fairness, especially in matters of payments (including royalties). Commutative justice is also applicable to the competency of information professionals and the quality of the information products and services that are rendered. If an information professional presents himself or herself as competent, then, based on the principle of fair exchange, the responsibility to render high-quality service is implied.

In its broad sense, distributive justice concerns the fair allocation of the benefits of a particular society (i.e., income, wealth, power and status) to its members (National Conference of Catholic Bishops 1986, 54).

Distributive justice pertains to the fair distribution of information to people, in order to satisfy basic needs. This form of justice is of specific social relevance. For example, it can be argued that public libraries (as social institutions) have a responsibility to ensure the fair distribution of basic information that people need to exercise their basic human rights. From an occupational perspective, it can also be argued that companies have an obligation to determine the information needs of their employees, and to implement mechanisms ensuring the effective distribution of all information that is needed to exercise their duties. For the information professional, this would imply the responsibility to provide the information user, in the best possible manner, with the information that is needed.

Contributive justice implies that an individual has an obligation to be active in society, and that society itself has a duty to facilitate participation and productivity without impairing individual freedom and dignity (National Conference of Catholic Bishops 1986, 54).

With regard to the flow and access of information, contributive justice can serve to maximize the use of information for productivity. This form of justice also implies that the generators and distributors of knowledge have an ethical responsibility to add value to and maintain the accessibility of information that benefits society. Based on the viewpoint that contributive justice implies society's responsibility to facilitate participation and enhance productivity, it can be argued that society, and more specifically information services, has a responsibility to create an information environment that will stimulate creativity and productivity. This implies the responsibility to make accessible the best information products and services available. It therefore presupposes the implementation of channels for the effective and equal distribution of information, the quality of its control and enabling people to create information products in order to benefit society. To enhance and stimulate the generation of new knowledge, the responsibility to enhance productivity further implies the effective application of a legal framework to ensure the fair protection of economic interests of both authors and publishers.

Retributive justice, also known as punishable justice, refers to the fair and just punishment of the guilty. With regard to the use and handling of information, this form of justice provides an important guideline for the protection of intellectual property, the misuse of information and the acceptance of responsibility regarding the handling of information.

The application of justice as an ethical norm is dependent on a few variables, namely, the right of participation, marginalization, and subsidiarity. These variables, and their relevance to the information professional, are as follows:

- Participatory justice implies that everyone must have equal opportunity to access information in order to participate in the different socioeconomic and political processes (Bedford-Strohm 1991, 277). Participatory justice is therefore an important principle in terms of the accessibility of information and the uplifting of information-poor societies. It can therefore be argued that information professionals, working in the environment of developing nations, have an obligation to make information products and services accessible to communities. This can be done for example, by means of translations into the native language or, in the case of illiteracy, the presentation of information in pictorial formats.

- Marginalization implies the active exclusion of people from society and can, for example, be the suppression of free expression or the purposeful exclusion from or hampering of access to collective information needed for development. Marginalization may also refer to information powerhouses that, by restricting information based on proprietary grounds, can deny individuals access.
- Subsidization, by contrast, is a positive force that fosters equal social opportunities and participation. This force implies that individuals and institutions such as libraries, archives and museums have the responsibility to involve themselves in the creation of equal opportunities; this is what the (U.S.) National Conference of Catholic Bishops in 1986 called "institutional pluralism." Based on this principle, it can be argued that the information infrastructure of a country does have a responsibility to subsidize the distribution of information beneficial to its citizenry.

APPLICABLE ETHICAL NORMS: FREEDOM

Freedom is another norm that is of relevance to the information professional and specifically applicable to the rights of access to information and to privacy.

In philosophical terms, there are two types of freedom: formal freedom and material freedom. Formal freedom is a person's freedom to choose, while material freedom pertains to the content of a person's choices. Material freedom is further subdivided into two categories: "freedom from" and "freedom to." "Freedom from" emphasizes the negative aspect of freedom, for example, an individual's right of "freedom from" restriction of access to information (censorship). This form of freedom implies, therefore, certain restrictions on access to and use of information. "Freedom to," on the other hand, is the positive expression of material freedom. An example of "freedom to" is the freedom of expression.

However, of specific relevance to the information professional is the link that exists between the exercising of the freedom to make a choice and the availability of the correct information to enable such a choice. It can be argued that an individual, to be able to exercise the basic right of freedom of choice, has a basic right of access to all necessary, relevant and correct information.

The relationship between freedom and responsibility also has important implications with regard to access to information. This relationship can be described as the acceptance of responsibility for the choices made. Freedom can therefore be defined within the framework of responsibility and accountability. Thus, it behooves information mediators to exercise particular responsibility in the ways they disseminate information, because of the impact information has on the choices people make and the perceptions they form.

This right to freedom has furthermore both an individual and a social dimension. The individual's right to privacy finds expression within the framework of a specific social context. The freedom to choose privacy is abridged only by the freedom of other individuals in a society or organization. Government and other institutions can, within limits, restrain this freedom when it is necessary to gather and use personal information, for example, when the government collects census data or when an institution needs information for staff-management purposes.

APPLICABLE ETHICAL NORMS: TRUTH

Truth is another important ethical norm and virtue for any information professional. The *Oxford English Dictionary* defines truth as "conformity with facts, agreement with reality." Truth acts as a normative guideline in the areas of the correct and accurate processing and provision of information as well as the quality of information. It is therefore applicable when information professionals are confronted with issues such as:

- the option to buy fewer but better-quality information products,
- the ensuring of the contextual integrity of information products and
- the acceptance of responsibility when inaccurate information has been provided.

As a virtue it is applicable to the following cases:

- not discussing users' queries with other people (trustworthiness),
- not overcharging a user when the information professional is at fault in the provision of inaccurate information (honesty) and
- not presenting oneself as an expert in a field in which one is not knowledgeable (openness).

A Practical Application of the Ethical Decision-Making Process: Users' Right to Privacy

This part of the chapter explains and illustrates how the ethical decision-making process can be applied by information professionals to the ethical issues pertaining to the handling of a user's private and personal information. The focus is primarily on the formulation of general ethical guidelines and not on an ethical decision-making process in a specific situation.

DEFINING PRIVACY

For an information professional to be able to formulate guidelines regarding the right of privacy of its users, it is important, first, to establish what is meant by privacy and determine the categories of information that privacy has a bearing on.

In its broadest sense, privacy is defined as the right to be left alone, the right of control over one's private life as well as freedom from judgment. In legal terms, privacy is described as an individual condition of life characterized by exclusion from publicity (Britz 1999, 297).

Different categories of private information can further be distinguished, namely private communications (e.g., reference interviews), information that relates to the privacy of a person's body (medical information), other personal information such as a person's age or address and information with regard to a person's possessions (e.g., the number of books borrowed by a person).

ETHICAL RELEVANCE FOR LIBRARIES, ARCHIVES AND MUSEUMS

The next step would be to determine the ethical relevance regarding the handling of private and personal information of users by information professionals. Two such levels can be distinguished. First, information professionals are confronted with all four categories of personal and private information in their professional activities. For example, the information gained from a reference interview can relate to all four categories of private information.

Second, increasing use is made of technology in the processing of private and personal information of users. Technology makes it much easier to copy, distribute and merge private information. These possibilities pose serious ethical concerns for information professionals.

THE MAIN ETHICAL ISSUES

The next appropriate step would be to identify the main ethical issues at hand. These issues can be summarized as follows:

- Deciding which categories of personal and private information the information professional is entitled to gather. For example, is it appropriate for libraries to request a user's Social Security number when the user is applying for membership in a library? The question is furthermore of importance for archivists when they are confronted with the question of whether or not to collect private and personal documents of people.
- The confidential treatment of such information. This issue refers specifically to information gained during the reference interview. The main ethical questions in this area are: Can personal details, obtained from the reference interview, be used for purposes other than those for which it was specifically gathered? Is it ethically correct to reuse a search strategy formulated in consultation with one user for another user? Is it appropriate to discuss the nature of a specific query with a third party? (Froehlich 1994, 418). For archivists, the main ethical issue pertains to the question of whether or not to exhibit private and personal documents in public.

- The accuracy of information. This issue is of specific importance when an information professional is working with personal information that can have a direct influence on the life of a person or the way in which a person might be perceived. An example is the exhibiting of personal-related artifacts in a museum without the correct "context of understanding."
- The purposes for which various categories of information may be used. The question here is whether an information professional may use any of the four categories of private information for any reason other than the original one given for gathering the information. Is it, for example, appropriate for an archivist to use personal documents of individuals for research purposes without the consent of the person (or family) to whom the information pertains?
- The rights of a person in regard to the use and distribution of that person's personal and private information. This ethical problem relates to the abovementioned aspects and boils down to the question of user consent. Related questions are: Does a user have the right to verify any personal and private information that is being held by a library, archive or museum? If so, what are the person's rights regarding the correction (and verifying of corrections) of this information?
- The gaining of access to and use of a person's private and personal information without the person being aware of it. This is a growing concern because technology opens new possibilities here, for example, in the merging of different personal files of individuals into one central database.

After the identification of the main ethical issues pertaining to privacy, the information professional has to formulate ethical guidelines to ensure the appropriate handling of users' personal and private information. First, the approach that will be followed must be clarified. Then the appropriate norms and principles must be identified, interpreted and applied to the ethical issues at hand. It is then possible, based on these norms and principles, to formulate ethical guidelines.

THE APPROACH TO FOLLOW

Three different approaches to finding solutions to ethical problems have been identified. Each approach will have a different outcome. The communitarian approach, for example, emphasizes the rights and interest of society, therefore, individual rights, such as privacy, are not a high priority. The libertarian follows the opposite approach.

The third approach, which is recommended here, seeks a balance between these two approaches. This approach acknowledges the individual's rights but also takes the public into consideration. The individual's right to privacy is therefore the fundamental principle, but it might be overruled in cases where, for example, people's lives are at stake.

BASIC PRINCIPLES APPLICABLE TO PRIVACY

The Principle of Human Autonomy and Respect for a Person

This principle implies that every human being has a fundamental right to privacy. The right to privacy can only be limited when it infringes unjustly on the rights of other people. In relation to information records, this principle implies the right of informed consent in cases in which personal information is used; the prohibition of altering any records pertaining to an individual without his or her consent; the use of such a record only as agreed upon by the individual; the right of access to personal-related information in possession of an information service, the right to correct it and the right to verify the changes that have been made to it.

The Principle of Impossibility

This principle implies that under certain conditions the rights and obligations involving an individual's privacy cannot be exercised. For example, when the rendering of effective health services implies, under certain conditions, the access to patients' medical records (which are normally regarded as private), it might imply a prima facie right of access to those records without the consent of these patients (Kluge 1994, 341).

The Principle of Relevant Difference

This principle acknowledges that rights and duties pertaining to an individual's privacy are exercised and fulfilled in specific contexts. With regard to privacy, it implies that an information professional's use of information (e.g., personal documents) divulged within a specific context must be restricted. Private and personal information of users must be kept confidential. The conditions of use that are set by an individual when he or she makes personal documents available to an archive must therefore be respected. However, this principle also makes provision for possible overriding duties and rights—for example, when there are grounds to believe that harm is likely to result to another person due to a user's unwillingness to disclose confidential information.

The Principle of Best Action

This principle entails an obligation of information professionals to handle all private and personal information of users in the best possible manner. This "best action" pertains, among other things, to the implementation of measures to safeguard private information effectively and to get the consent of a person when her or his private information is being used for any other purposes than those it was gathered for.

The Principle of Priority

Rights may be prioritized. For example, it can be argued that the right to privacy outweighs the right of society "to know." Depending on the context, this process of prioritization can be executed by the user or the information professional. For example, a client can waive the right to privacy regarding his or her personal medical information when it can be to the benefit of medical research (Kluge 1994, 343). Emergency contexts also prove reason to prioritize rights. A medical doctor can, when executing an emergency operation, override a patient's right to privacy regarding his or her body. In this case, the right to life is ranked higher than the right to privacy. Based on this principle, the question can even be asked whether or not it is permissible for an archivist to make personal files accessible to the police when they are investigating a crime.

The Principle of Equality and Justice

This principle entails that all persons must be treated as equals. This implies that (irrespective of color, age or gender) every person's right to privacy must be treated and respected in the same manner. Negative discrimination is ethically indefensible. A library can therefore not treat the personal and private information of a child differently than that of an adult.

APPLICABLE NORMS

The norms of justice, truth and freedom have already been identified and described as applicable in information-ethical reasoning. In the following paragraphs it will be illustrated how these norms can be applied to specific privacy-related issues.

Commutative Justice

Commutative justice calls for fundamental fairness in all agreements and exchanges between individuals or social groups and is based on respect for the equal human dignity of all people in economic and other transactions. This form of justice can be applicable in cases in which libraries, archives or museums use personal information of clients (with their consent) for other reasons than those for which it was gathered initially. An example is the selling of addresses of clients to other libraries, archives or museums for marketing purposes. It can be argued that, in exchange for trading or selling such information, the library, archive or museum owes the client certain advantages—for example, a discount on the annual membership fee.

Contributive Justice

As has been indicated, contributive justice implies that a person has an obligation to be productive and active in society, and that society has a duty to enable individuals to participate in this way.

Contributive justice is of specific relevance to privacy issues relating to the delimited right of the state archive to have access to and gather a person's personal and private information. In the same way, a university library can be considered justified in gathering and using the personal information of students to ensure the effective management of the library. This form of contributive justice is, however, delimited insofar as the gathered information must only be used for the intended purposes.

Distributive Justice

This form of justice implies the fair distribution of information and can be used to justify the right of access of an individual to his or her own personal and private information that is stored and used by a library, archive or museum. This does not only imply the right of access to the information, but might imply the responsibility of an applicable information service to make the personal information proactively available (i.e., require its distribution) to the person concerned.

Retributive Justice

This category of justice, which justifies the punishment of the guilty, has specific bearing on cases in which private and personal information of users is misused or in which personal-related artifacts are exhibited in an inappropriate manner.

Freedom

Material freedom, which relates to the content of a choice that can be made, is of specific relevance to a user's right of privacy. Freedom *from,* which emphasizes the negative aspect of freedom, can be seen as a justification of freedom from intrusion by information services on the private lives of its users. This is applicable when information services gather personal information that they do not need (e.g., Social Security numbers). Freedom *to*, as the positive expression of material freedom, can—in terms of the abovementioned example—be formulated as the right to be private. It can further be argued that an individual must have the freedom of control over his or her personal information. This expression of freedom implies the right to know in which manner a library, archive or museum is using such a person's personal and private information.

Truth

Truth as a norm is of specific relevance to the accuracy and correctness of a person's personal and private information that is being used and processed by libraries, museums and archives. This norm, as with distributive justice, justifies the individual's right of access to personal information and to verify the correctness of that information. Truth acts also as a normative guideline when it comes to the notion of "contextual integrity," when personal-related artifacts are exhibited in museums.

PRACTICAL GUIDELINES

Applying these principles and norms from a rule-utilitarian perspective, the following broad guidelines pertaining to the handling of private and personal information can be formulated (Britz 1999):

- The acknowledgment of the autonomy and freedom of the individual. This implies the assumption that a person regards the handling of private and personal information as confidential in all cases. This is linked to the basic principle that an information user has, to a certain extent, control over his or her personal and private information.
- A person's private and personal information must be handled with the necessary confidentiality and respect. This implies security and control of access to private information, the right to use that information and the right to change or add any information.
- A person must, on a regular basis, have access to all his or her private and personal information that is kept and used. This provides the opportunity for a person to verify the accuracy of this information. Furthermore, it is the responsibility of the information professional to see to it that necessary corrections are made.
- When private and personal information of users is merged into a different database than the one for which it was originally collected, it must be done with the necessary caution and the assurance of contextual integrity. In cases of merging, relevant individuals must be notified about the nature and future use of their information.
- A user must be notified explicitly of the intended purposes of the use of all personal and private information. This also implies the need to acquire the person's permission.
- No unnecessary private or personal information must be gathered. This is necessary not only for logistical and administrative reasons, but also to prevent the unnecessary violation or exposure of a person's privacy. When personal and other private information is no longer of use, it must be destroyed.

- When the rendering of a specific service or product to a person is refused on the grounds of personal information, the reason for this denial must be made known to the person.

Apart from these general guidelines, it is also important to formulate a privacy policy comprising the following elements: the categories of information that must be regarded as private and personal, the levels of confidentiality (e.g., who has access to and use of which information), a clear explanation of the purposes of the use of the information and the description of the procedures to ensure the accuracy of this information.

Conclusion

Information professionals are confronted with ethical issues pertaining to privacy, access to information, intellectual property and the quality of information. This chapter has illustrated that the information professional's main ethical focus must be on the individual user's rights of access to information and of privacy. Ownership rights have to be protected and the information professional should be held ethically responsible for the quality of the information provided.

References

Bedford-Strohm, H. 1991. "Vorrang für die Armen: Auf dem Wege zu einer theologischen Theorie der Gerechtigkeit" (Preference to the poor: toward a theological theory of justice). Doctoral diss., Rupert-Karls University of Heidelberg, Heidelberg, Germany.

Britz, J. J. 1999. "Technology as a Threat to Privacy." In *Encyclopaedia of Library and Information Science,* vol. 63, ed. Allen Kent. New York: Marcel Dekker.

Capurro, R. 1985. Moral Issues in Information Science. *Journal of Information Science* 11:113–23.

Froehlich, T. J. 1992. "Ethical Considerations of Information Professionals." *Annual Review of Information Science and Technology* 27: 291–324.

Froehlich, T. J. 1994. "Re-Thinking Ethical Issues in an Online Environment." In *Online Information: '94 Procedings, 6–8 December 1994,* ed. D. I. Raitt and B. Jeapes, 415–22. Oxford: Learned Information.

Kluge, E. H. W. 1994. "Health Information, the Fair Information Principles and Ethics." *Methods of Information in Medicine* 33: 336–45.

Mason, R. O. 1986. "Four Ethical Issues of the Information Age." *MIS Quarterly* 10, no. 1: 46–55.

National Conference of Catholic Bishops. 1986. *Economic Justice for All. Pastoral Letter on Catholic Social Teaching and U.S. Economy.* Washington, D.C.: U.S. Catholic Conference.

Taylor, R. S. 1986. *Value-Added Processes in Information Systems.* Norwood, N.J.: Ablex.

Van der Hoven, J. 1997. "Towards a Theory of Privacy in the Information Age." *Computers and Society* 27, no. 3: 33–37.

Woodward, D. 1990. "Framework for Deciding Issues in Ethics." *Library Trends* 39, no. 1-2: 4–13.

Zipkowitz, F. 1996. *Professional Ethics in Librarianship: A Real Life Casebook.* London: McFarland.

CHAPTER 12

Organizing Ethics in Archives, Museums, and Libraries

CHALLENGES AND STRATEGIES

Elizabeth A. Buchanan

Introduction to Professional Ethics

As stewards of information and the historical and public record, librarians, curators, and archivists hold great power and influence in our societies. The information professions are typically service oriented, civil, and just—rarely do we encounter the "evil" information professional. Many of our organizations are nonprofits, which does not mean, however, that we do not face the many difficult decisions our counterparts do in the for-profit arenas. As professionals, we have many responsibilities beyond those typically recognized by the general public; a major component of such responsibilities is the urgent need for the understanding and practice of ethical codes of conduct. Finks (1991) describes a code of ethics as the embodiment of the ideals and responsibilities of a professional group. Finks stresses the importance of the true intent and practice of the code, as opposed to its face value or "public relations message." That is, we must not adopt codes of ethics because it will look admirable to others: belief in and reliance on such codes is imperative to their value and to the sound organizational culture for which organizations strive.

Such codes outline behaviors and relations that should exist among any given professional organization. Mason (1996, 150) rightly acknowledges that key principles or tenets of codes of ethics vary slightly across disciplines, with many embodying such ideals as "responsible professional behavior, competence in execution of duties, adherence to moral and legal standards, standards for making public statements, preservation of confidentiality, interest in the welfare of the customer, and the development and maintenance of professional knowledge."

While our disciplines are indeed unique in and of themselves, commonalities obviously exist. One such commonality revolves around the impact of professional or organizational ethics, which affect us in at least three interrelated ways: as individuals, as members of an association or organization, and as members of society at large. In each of these facets, a different sense of ethical responsibility resides. Moreover, these areas collide with each other, blurring boundaries and adding complexity to the already complex realm of ethics.

One can differentiate between professional codes of ethics and organizational codes of ethics on the basis that the former encompasses a larger population of individuals, while an organizational code of ethics may embody the professional code but stand unique as well. Kizza (1996, 213) has clearly defined this distinction:

> professional codes as disciplines . . . are intended to define the rights and responsibilities of professionals in their relationship with each other and with the public. The organizational code is too a set of guidelines laid down by one's employer, that all employees regardless of their professions must follow when making decisions.

For purposes of generality, I will use the two somewhat interchangeably, as we are not discussing individual organizations per se; much can be learned from looking at the intersection of professional and organizational ethics. Overall, professional and organizational ethics serve multiple purposes. Typically, in the form of a code or statement of ethics, professional ethics seek to identify and discuss "the most serious problems of professional conduct, the resolution of problems arising from conflicts of interest, and the guarantee that the special expertise of the members of a profession will be used in the public interest" (SAA 1992). Furthermore, professional ethics seek to fill a potential void that legislation may not cover. Ethics is distinct from law in that the law provides a structured context to which we look for "reasonable" decisions; the law does not necessarily tell us what is inherently good or bad. With emerging and ever-changing technologies facing us in the library, museum, and archives professions, legislation is generally a step behind, while it also fails to differentiate moral soundness. Legislation does not prescribe behavior for the purpose of morality but for the purpose of satisfying societal requirements or rules, which are dictated by authority, not necessarily morality. Therefore, professional ethical codes serve to assist professionals in making informed and just decisions, beyond that which the law mandates.

Ethical decision making is a part of everyday life. Ethics is generally defined as the philosophical study of moral behavior, of moral decision making, or of how to lead a "good life." Morality can be defined as the activity of making choices and of deciding, judging, justifying, and defending actions or behaviors called "moral." Brincat and Wilke (1999, 34) clarify the distinction between ethics and morality:

> Ethics is the study of morality; the study of what we do. Morality could exist without ethics (if no one investigated how morality is done) but there cannot be ethics without morality (we cannot study morality unless there is morality). . . . Morality is like eating; it is an inevitable part of everyone's life. Ethics, on the other hand, is like nutrition. It is crucial to living a good life but it is not an inevitable part of living or an activity engaged in by all.

The challenge facing professionals revolves around the establishment of a groundwork from which to judge professional actions and behaviors. Indeed, as Bodi (1998) has identified, "there is ambiguity about ethics, in large part because there is a weighing and balancing between competing interests." These competing interests may be intrinsic or extrinsic—or both—adding further complexity to ethics. As professionals, we have a duty to keep our personal opinions and beliefs distinct from our work; this is very difficult, since we as humans cannot compartmentalize ourselves that easily. Confronting our own personal biases and ideologies in tandem with our professional codes of ethics indeed proves challenging, but nevertheless, professional or organizational ethics provide a suitable groundwork or framework for us as we face difficult ethical dilemmas and decisions.

Overview of Information Ethics

The discussion of ethics is predicated on certain conditions. Namely, ethics and, subsequently, ethical behavior presuppose that individuals are free and want to do what is "right," and that informed, conscious and reflective decisions can be made without undue influence. When we engage in ethical discourse, we use two main approaches: descriptive ethics and normative ethics. With descriptive ethics, we are "simply" stating facts or observations: "archivists preserve the public record." A normative approach gets closer to the moral and ethical questions, whereas a descriptive approach tends to be less controversial and offers more straightforward or "factual" statements. A normative approach may question whether archivists are violating individual privacy by restoring, digitizing, and displaying personal letters and documents of an individual.

Libraries, museums, and archives each have unique ethical dilemmas and issues, although the information professions do share a set of issues. The field of information ethics itself is relatively new, first named by Robert Hauptman in the late 1980s. The information explosion of the 1990s has brought these general ethical issues to the forefront of our work. As outlined in Buchanan (1999), information ethics embodies such issues as:

- Privacy and confidentiality
- Access
- Ownership
- Censorship
- Freedom of speech and representation
- Information imperialism
- Monopolistic creation, control, and dissemination of information
- Morphing and manipulation of data
- Piracy and software crime
- Hacking (Goodrum and Manion, [2000], offer an interesting look at the "ethics of hacktivism," noting that computer attacks on unjust govern-

ments and their web sites should not be considered unethical, but a form of civil disobedience.)

- Rights versus privileges (For example, should access to the Internet be considered a right or privilege in American society? President Bill Clinton made this a public policy issue by mandating that every school and classroom be connected to the Internet. What about prisons and prisoners? If the Internet is indeed an educational revolution, should we restrict access to it by prisoners? This raises the distinction between negative rights or liberties, which are rights to act without interference. The right to "life, liberty and the pursuit of happiness" is a negative right; positive or claim rights are rights that impose an obligation to provide certain things to people. A positive right is the right to welfare, for example—but now, we are seeing that this, at least in Wisconsin, is not a positive or claim right. The question for us becomes: Is it a positive or negative right for all members of a society to have free access to information?)
- Erosion of personhood and cultural identity
- Distribution of power and power relationships
- Loss of reflective abilities (Computing in general facilitates instantaneous action and a sense of immediacy. Such immediacy denies the opportunity for reflection and conscious thinking. The phases of ethical decision making are often overlooked and in their stead, knee-jerk or uncritical decisions are made.)
- Depersonalization (Individuals who violate copyright law by copying software, for instance, often practice a depersonalizing rationalization. The idea that "no one" is really being hurt makes such violation acceptable, whereas the same principle of theft, when turned to a concrete object in a store, for instance, becomes something different. Another example, offered by Palmiter [1996, 240], typifies this depersonalization: "When enemies are simply blips on a computer screen, they become dehumanized. It's no longer a moral crime to kill them, since the 5th Commandment doesn't extend to computer blips.")

Many of these issues are analogous with the ethical issues faced in museums, archives, and libraries, though each of these institutions has its own unique set of issues and dilemmas. Overall, the ethical dilemmas can be understood, following Zipkowitz's schema (1996) as affecting colleagues, patrons, things, organizations, and vendors. An additional sector is the public at large, which adds to the ethical discussion issues of the public policy realm. As ethical issues are continually evolving, such lists should be seen as a starting point for discussion, and certainly not definitive. Conferences such as the Institute for Legal and Ethical Issues will promote significant research and practice in recognizing and working through the many difficult challenges facing these professions.

The following sections mention the important codes of ethics for museums, archives, and libraries; the issues facing each of these institutions; and sources that discuss these issues.

MUSEUMS

Edson (1997) asserts that "every administrative, curatorial, public relations, and fund raising decision includes the possibility of an inappropriate or unacceptable action" (11). We have seen the recent controversy surrounding the Brooklyn Museum of Art and the tension between public funds, artists' rights and freedom of expression, and censorship. Not every ethical situation facing us in museums will be as extreme, but such public cases open much-needed discourse around ethical issues in our institutions.

The standard code of ethics for the museum profession is the International Council of Museums' code. It is referenced in the resource list at the end of the chapter.

Important issues in ethics for museums are:

- Conflicts of interest
- Antitrust issues
- Political contributions
- Cultural sensitivity
- Indigenous knowledge and property issues
- Consumerism/commercialism
- Representational politics
- Responsibility to protect the social good
- Integrity in acquiring exhibits and collections
- Preservation or distortion of the historical record

Each of these areas is discussed in detail in G. Edson's comprehensive work, *Museum Ethics.*

ARCHIVES

In the United States, the Society of American Archivists' code of ethics is the operative code. It is referenced in the resource list at the end of the chapter. Important ethical issues for archives are:

- Protection of privacy
- Public right to access
- Preservation and conservation (see Baynes-Cope 1994 for an excellent discussion)
- Ownership
- Integrity in acquiring exhibits and collections
- Representational politics
- Indigenous knowledge and property issues
- Public funding of private collections
- Issues surrounding digitization
- Copyright issues
- Consumerism/commercialism
- Preservation or distortion of the historical record

H. MacNeil's *Without Consent: The Ethics of Disclosing Personal Information in Public Archives* is a notable source, and delves into many of these areas.

LIBRARIES

In the United States, the American Library Association (ALA) offers its code of ethics as a guiding set of principles. It is referenced in the resource list at the end of the chapter. However, as libraries evolve, other sets of ethical principles from diverse organizations apply. Ethical issues facing libraries are:

- Intellectual freedom issues
- Access rights and privileges
- Ownership
- Censorship
- Public funding issues
- Consumerism/commercialism

- Selection issues
- Copyright issues (which are growing at exponential rates, due to emerging technologies)
- Filtering

F. Zipkowitz's *Professional Ethics in Librarianship: A Real Life Casebook* offers a useful discussion of ethical dilemmas in librarianship, while other valuable sources include Stichler and Hauptman (1998), Severson (1997), Oz (1994), Lancaster (1991), and Hauptman (1988).

Codes of Ethics

In general, codes must provide guidelines for "justice, beneficence, nonmaleficence, independence, objectivity, and professionalism" (Mason 1996, 152). Furthermore, a code must not be a list of dos and don'ts—it must not be prescriptive—but must demonstrate the guiding ethical principles and why they are so. The efficacy of a code of ethics depends on how thoroughly it articulates the socioprofessional ideals of any profession or organization. The development and adaptation of a professional code of ethics is predicated on the

> normative purpose of the profession. It is the professional purpose that provides the filter through which principles are strained. . . . The purpose of a profession does not change. The purpose is itself a normative filter, the basic ethical conduit through which a profession's contribution to the welfare of society takes on additional importance and new responsibility. (Palmiter 1996, 230)

Consider a code of ethics as a set of "best practices." With this mindset, members of your profession will not feel the anxiety and pressure of "living up to" the code, but will look to it as a guiding set of principles from which they can make better, more informed decisions.

Johnson (1985) identifies four channels through which professional codes of ethics should be judged: obligations to society, obligations to employer, obligations to clients, and obligations to colleagues and organizations. However, many criticisms surrounding codes of ethics include lack of specificity, lack of "directions" about handling ethical dilemmas, lack of enforcement mechanisms, and lack of knowledge or understanding about the code *by* the actual professionals in the field. For these reasons, it is imperative that education about ethics begin before individuals enter the workplace—and continue well into one's professional career.

Many professionals enter the field with little or no ethical preparation or training. Many have never encountered the ALA's code or the International Council of Museums' code. Thus, it is highly important for professional schools and programs to begin to teach ethical responsibilities and allow students to "practice" ethics before they are faced with thorny situations in the workplace. In the ethics class I teach, each student works through various case scenarios after they have been armed with philosophical theories of ethics and evaluation procedures. Acting out ethical dilemmas encourages the processual thinking requisite to understanding the impact of each decision and action. An apt policy for libraries, museums, and archives includes training staff on ethical issues and appropriate responsibilities through cases and role playing. New hires should be made familiar with the appropriate code of ethics and how professional ethics are a part of the organization; likewise, stressing the currency of professional education for all members holds value. Ethical training and decision making must become systemically integrated into all aspects of the profession, so when the "hot" cases strike, every member of the team is ready and able to make sound decisions.

Strategies for Organizational Ethics

Ethical decision making involves a number of strategies. Many approaches can be found in the literature. Once a normative analysis is complete, individuals make decisions and "prescribe" what ought to be. Such prescriptive thinking seeks to answer the questions posed in normative analysis. Brincat and Wilke (1999) offer three criteria surrounding prescriptive thinking: it must not be random; it must include a system of rules or values that are the "machinery of prescriptive ethics" and work "to facilitate the judging, choosing, and justifying of ethical choices"; and it must be universalizable or generalizable.

How do we "do" normative thinking? Or, in simple terms, how do we assess the rightness or wrongness of a situation? Ethical codes of conduct provide guidelines and frameworks but, more often than not, fail to give us "answers." Thus, series of questions can be used in evaluating and justifying decisions and behaviors. I have divided such deliberations into two phases.

Phase 1: Issue Definition and Evaluation

- Define the issue or situation as objectively as possible. Then, define it with your own biases.
- Are you confident of your competence in the issue?
- Who are the stakeholders or affected parties?
- How would you describe the situation to an outsider and an insider?
- How did the situation or issue arise? What variables played into the issue?
- Separate the trivial from the significant in the situation—Are we understanding the situation fully? What is really important?
- Where do your loyalties fall? Is there any conflict of interest? Can you differentiate your decisions as a member of society and as a member of an organization?
- Do you understand all aspects and perspectives of the issue?
- Can you discuss the issue with the stakeholders before moving to phase 2 of the decision-making evaluation?

Phase 2: Action/Inaction Evaluation and Implementation

- Consider the boundaries of the actions and inactions. What is the intention behind an action or inaction?
- Evaluate alternatives and their repercussions. Try to establish believable alternatives and credible repercussions—Do you really believe your decision will result in X? Or, is X a long shot, and you are trying to convince yourself it will happen?
- Determine a course of action with which you are comfortable and can face yourself and those involved with or affected by your decision. Are you really considering how your decision will impact others? Can you live with your decision? Will you be confident disclosing your decision publicly?
- Under what, if any, conditions would you allow exceptions to your decision? Evaluate those exceptions closely.
- Decision making is cumulative: one decision often builds on previous. How does your decision fit in with the previous decisions? Also, your decision affects other decisions you will make—are you satisfied with the

course of actions you are taking? How will this decision impact how you proceed?
- Can you universalize the decision? If not, why?
- Before decisions are made, refer to codes of professional ethics. Is there consistency or conflict in regard to the codes and your plans?

To complement these series of questions, a strategy I suggest to organizations as well as individuals is to record the responses to these questions in a journal and have a "cooling off" period before actions are taken. After a day or two, revisit the journal and reflect upon the answers. Has a change in perspective or evaluation of the issue changed? If so, why? What factors contributed to that change? This strategy encourages the processual thinking requisite to ethical decision making.

Finally, Edson (1997, 11) offers a valid comment concerning ethical decision making: "The important measure of all decision making is that the seriousness of the risk is never to be out of proportion to the worthiness of the cause or the means of circumvention." By weighing and evaluating such proportions, individuals and organizations can take confidence in their decisions and actions.

Conclusion

We hear over and over that we are living in the information age. Our professions are indeed important to society and to the public good. We are often disillusioned that our decisions and actions are not as significant as those made by doctors, lawyers, politicians—that our decisions affect a few, but not the many. I maintain that this is inaccurate at best, and irresponsible at worst. Our contributions to our profession and our society are extremely important. The cost, as Zipkowitz says, of *not* making ethical decisions is too high a price to pay. The cost of not understanding the ethical ramifications of our actions and how they affect others is also too high. No decision is easy to make, and ethical decisions do put us through rigorous tests—personal and professional. As information professionals, we must have a good understanding of how ethics plays a role in both our personal and professional lives, and the requisite distinctions between the two. We must think about the implications of our actions or inactions and who we are impacting. By approaching dilemmas or decisions through a series of questions and strategies, we can be confident that our decisions are ethically sound.

For the information professions addressed in this chapter, Hauptman's (1998, 1) words are especially appropriate on which to conclude.

> Because information is power, it is necessary to regulate its production, dissemination, and application in some way, and since it is repugnant in a democracy for the government to control every aspect of its citizens' lives, self-regulation can be affirmed through a set of operative ethical principles:
>
> - Respect the integrity of data and information.
> - Do not purposefully or inadvertently distort, fabricate, plagiarize, or manipulate in order to give a false impression.
> - Do not attempt to control others' articulations and thereby control their thought.
> - Respect professional confidentiality.
> - Distinguish between personal commitment and professional obligation.

Given these principles, combined with a solid framework for analyzing and responding to ethical issues, and codes of professional or organizational ethics, we can be confident that in our actions and mind-sets we are in fact contributing to the just, democratic, and beneficent professions to which we belong—and ultimately, to the betterment of society as a whole.

References

Baynes-Cope, D. 1994. "Principles and Ethics in Archival Repair and Archival Conservation." *Journal of the Society of Archivists* 15, no. 1: 17–27.

Bodi, S. 1998. "Ethics and Information Technology: Some Principles to Guide Students." *Journal of Academic Librarianship* 24, no. 6: 459–65.

Brincat, C., and V. Wilke. 1999. *Morality and the Professional Life: Values at Work.* New York: Prentice Hall.

Buchanan, E. 1999. "An Overview of Information Ethics Issues in a World-Wide Context. *Journal of Ethics and Information Technology* 1, no. 4: 193–210.

Callahan, J., ed. 1988. *Ethical Issues in Professional Life.* New York: Oxford University Press.

Edson, G., ed. 1997. *Museum Ethics.* New York: Routledge.

Finks, L. 1991. "Librarianship Needs a New Code of Professional Ethics." *American Libraries* 22, no. 1: 84–92.

Gasson, M. 1997. "Business Archives: Some Principles and Practices." *Journal of the Society of Archivists* 18, no. 2: 141–50.

Goodrum, A., and M. Manion. 2000. "The Ethics of Hacktivism." *Journal of Information Ethics* 9(2): 51–59.

Hauptman, R. 1988. *Ethical Challenges in Librarianship.* Phoenix: Oryx.

———. 1998. "Information Ethics: The Challenge of Today. *MLA Newsletter* 25, no. 5: 1–3.

Johnson, D. 1985. *Computer Ethics.* Englewood Cliffs, N.J.: Prentice-Hall.

Kizza, J. 1996. "The Role of Professional Organizations in Promoting Computer Ethics. In *Social and Ethical Effects of the Computer Revolution,* ed. Joseph Kizza, 210–18. Jefferson, N.C.: McFarland.

Lancaster, F. 1991. *Ethics and the Librarian.* Urbana-Champaign, Ill.: Graduate School of Library and Information Science.

MacNeil, H. 1992. *Without Consent: The Ethics of Disclosing Personal Information in Public Archives.* Metuchen, N.J.: Scarecrow.

Mason, F. 1996. "Ethics and the Electronic Society. In *Professional Ethics in Librarianship: A Real Life Casebook,* ed. Fay Zipkowitz, 148–52. Jefferson, N.C.: McFarland.

Oz, E. 1994. *Ethics for the Information Age.* Dubuque, Iowa: Business & Educational Technologies.

Palmiter, C. W. 1996. "Personal and Sociological Ethical Amid Technological Change." In *Social and Ethical Effects of the Computer Revolution,* ed. Joseph Kizza, 230–47. Jefferson, N.C.: McFarland.

Severson, R. 1997. *The Principles of Information Ethics.* Armonk, N.Y.: Sharpe.

Stichler, R., and R. Hauptman. 1998. *Ethics, Information, and Technology: Readings.* Jefferson, N.C.: McFarland.

Zipkowitz, F. 1996. *Professional Ethics in Librarianship: A Real Life Casebook.* Jefferson, N.C.: McFarland.

Resources

American Association of University Professors Statement on Professional Ethics. Available: http://www.aaup.org/Rbethics.htm.

American Library Association Code of Ethics. Available: http://www.ala.org/alaorg/oif/ethics.html.

Association for Computing Machinery (ACM) Code of Ethics. Available: http://www.acm.org/constitution/code.html.

Canadian Library Association Code of Ethics. Available: http://www.cla.ca/about/ethics.htm.

Canadian Library Association's Copyright Resources (includes ample information on Canadian, American, and international copyright laws and issues). Available: http://www.cla.ca/resources/copyright.htm.

Computer Ethics Institute's "Ten Commandments of Computer Ethics." Available: http://www.cpsr.org/program/ethics/cei.html.

Computer Professionals for Social Responsibility Ethics Working Group http://www.cpsr.org/program/ethics.

International Council of Museums Code of Professional Ethics. Available: http://www.icom.org/ethics.html.

Society of American Archivists Code of Ethics. Available: http://www.archivists.org/governance/handbook/app_ethics.html.

Society of American Archivists Fair Use Guidelines for Digital Images. Available: http://www.archivists.org/statements/confu.html.

PART FIVE: COPYRIGHT AND OTHER OWNERSHIP ISSUES

CHAPTER 13

Copyright for Libraries, Museums, and Archives

THE BASICS AND BEYOND

Shelly Warwick

Copyright, even when restricted to library issues, is a vast topic. This chapter is not intended to exhaust the subject, but rather to explore the principles, laws, and guidelines relevant to libraries, museums, and archives. What is provided is a framework for examining copyright issues rather than definitive advice on specific practices.

To lay a foundation for this exploration a brief history of copyright is presented and basic doctrines are discussed. This is followed by a description of current U.S. copyright law as it applies to libraries, museums, and archives, and by a bare-bones listing of some of the special exemptions for libraries and archives, along with relevant guidelines and practices. A discussion of some of the pending copyright issues of importance to information resource institutions is then presented, followed by some concluding remarks.

What Is Copyright and Why Do We Have It Anyway?

The theoretical basis for copyright is debated. Two views dominate. The first approach posits copyright as a "natural" right based either on labor as per Locke or personality as per Hegel (Hicks 1987; Ginsburg 1992; Goldstein 1992). The second approach treats copyright as a state-created right that is part of a policy to achieve specific goals, such as public access to information (Litman 1992; Patterson and Lindberg 1991; Samuelson 1994) or to ensure an orderly market for works of the mind (Demsetz 1967; Gordon 1990; Landes and Posner 1989). In the United States, copyright protection has traditionally been considered an incentive to encourage authors to create so that the nation as a whole can benefit.

The incentive nature of copyright is stated in Article 1, section 8 of the Constitution, which empowers Congress to enact laws to "promote the progress of science and useful arts, by securing for limited times to authors and inventors the exclusive right to their respective writings and discoveries." Some scholars think that U.S. copyright law has not fulfilled that purpose. Branscomb (1984) maintains that U.S. copyright law contains a basic conflict between its ideal of shared resources and its practice of the principle of management of scarcity through the choices of the marketplace. Hettinger (1993, 35) sees a contradiction in a political system that places value on freedom of expression and then has intellectual property laws that make ideas and expression private. His central question is "Why should one person have the exclusive right to possess and use something which all people could possess and use concurrently?"

The inconsistencies in copyright can perhaps be attributed to the differing viewpoints on the theoretical basis of copyright, but can also be found in the law's confused parentage. Current copyright law is the offspring of an arranged English marriage of a sixteenth-century grant of a trade monopoly for the purpose of censorship and an eighteenth-century statute intended to promote trade and curtail that monopoly (Rose 1993). Is it any wonder that, with such a heritage, copyright does not function well in a twenty-first-century networked, global economy. To be more explicit: in 1553 Queen Mary Tudor granted a group of London printers an exclusive monopoly on the condition that they only print works approved by the Crown. This group, the Stationers' Company, developed among themselves a practice that whomever first printed a work would have the perpetual exclusive right to print that work. In the early eighteenth century the cost of books was considered too high and the Stationers' Company was no longer seen as serving a useful purpose, so their charter was revoked. After much politicking the Statute of Anne (8 Anne C. 19) was passed in 1709, granting a fourteen-year exclusive right to print a work to the first printer of that work. Authors were only casually mentioned in the act (Patterson 1968; Rose 1993).

In France, copyright took a different path, with authors being granted not economic rights, but *moral rights* (Birrell 1899). Moral rights differ from economic rights in that they generally cannot be sold or transferred. Moral rights are usually grouped into rights of paternity (or attribution) and rights of integrity (Jacobs 1993). These include the right to be identified as an author of a work, the right to publish a work anonymously, the right not to publish a work, and the right to prevent others from using a work in such a way that adversely reflects on the author (Nimmer and Melville 1995).

In 1790, when the first U.S. Copyright Act was passed, it appeared that the British had sorted the situation out properly, so an economic rights pattern was followed. The Copyright Act of 1790 mirrored the provisions in the Statute of Anne in great detail. The basic period of protection was fourteen years, with a possible renewal of another fourteen years.

Patterson (1968) identifies four goals in the development of copyright in America between 1783 and 1834: 1) to secure the author's rights, 2) to promote learning, 3) to provide order in the book trade by government grant, and 4) to prevent monopoly. During this period the United States did not extend protection to works published by citizens of other nations, first published outside the United States. This allowed the works of Charles Dickens to be freely published in America without any royalties having to be paid to the author or to the original publisher (Moss 1984). It was not until U.S. authors and publishers started to complain of their works being pirated abroad that Congress passed a bill in 1891 allowing the president to establish which countries would be eligible for reciprocal copyright recognition (Putnam 1891). During this period the creation of derivative works (such as translations, abridgments, and adaptations) was not considered infringing, but a transformative or productive use of a work that copyright was intended to encourage (Patterson 1968).

Major revisions to the Copyright Act were passed in 1870, 1909, and 1976, extending copyright protection to musical and dramatic works, photographs, sound recordings, and visual and pictorial works. Amendments after 1976 extended protection to software, computer mask works, and vessel hulls. The term of protection was gradually extended from fourteen years with one renewal to fifty-six years, to seventy-five years, to the life of the author plus fifty years, to life of the author plus seventy years. Until 1989 a notice of copyright on the work, registration of the work with the Copyright Office, and a deposit of copies with the Library of Congress were required for a copyright to be valid.

Though the United States started as a nation that did not recognize the copyright laws of other nations, by the mid–twentieth century it had become a major advocate of international intellectual property agreements and a foe of piracy. While it joined other conventions, the United States did not become a signatory of the 1986 Berne Convention for the Protection of Literary and Artistic Works until 1989, due to the convention's requirement to recognize moral rights. The United States now participates in the 1952 Universal Copyright Convention (UCC), the Berne Convention and related neighboring rights conventions, World Intellectual Property Office (WIPO) treaties, and the Trade-Related Aspects of Intellectual Property Rights Agreement (TRIPs) of the General Agreement on Tariffs and Trade (GATT). None of these agreements in themselves have the force of law in the United States, but copyright law has been consistently amended to bring it into conformance with these agreements.

Current U.S. Copyright Law

The 105th Congress passed three amendments to the Copyright Act: the No Electronic Theft Act of 1997, which provided criminal penalties for certain levels of noncommercial copying; the Sonny Bono Copyright Term Extension Act of 1998, which added twenty years to the term of copyright protection, including the terms of existing works; and the Digital Millennium Copyright Act of 1998 (DMCA), which implemented the recent WIPO treaties (the WIPO Copyright Treaty of 1996 and the WIPO Performances and Phonograms Treaty of 1996) by establishing criminal penalties for the circumvention of technological protections used by copyright owners. The DMCA also specifies actions that will provide a safe harbor for online service providers against liability for copyright infringement by their subscribers, allows libraries and archives to employ digital preservation methods, and charges the Librarian of Congress to develop guidelines for the application of copyright to distance education (Warwick 1999). The requirements of copyright law implemented by these amendments will be addressed within the general requirements of copyright law in relation to libraries, archives, and museums.

THE FAST OVERVIEW

U.S. copyright law currently protects original works of authorship fixed in any tangible medium of expression (17 U.S.C. § 102) for a term of the life of the author plus seventy years, with some adjustments for anonymous works, pseudonymous works, and works for hire (ninety-five years from first publication or one hundred and twenty years from creation, whichever expires first). Works created before January 1, 1978, but not published or copyrighted by that date receive the same period of protection as works published after that date, with the exception that in no case would the term of copyright expire before December 31, 2002, and if a work was published on or before December 31, 2000, the term of copyright will not expire until December 31, 2047 (17 U.S.C. § 302–304). Works published after 1989 do not have to be registered with the Copyright Office or carry a copyright notice to be protected by copyright, but a work must be registered before a copyright owner can sue for infringement. Copyright owners are granted the exclusive right to 1) reproduce; 2) prepare derivative works; 3) distribute copies to the public by sale, other transfer of ownership, rental, lease, or lending; 4) perform the work publicly; and 5) display the work publicly (17 U.S.C. § 106). Copyright protection only extends to expression, not facts. Copyright law is exclusively federal: states cannot grant or extend any right or equivalent right granted under the Copyright Act (17 U.S.C. § 301). Once the period of copyright protection expires, works enter the *public domain.* This means that anyone is free to copy them in any format or medium and to sell, rent, exhibit, display and distribute them in any manner or create a derivative work. The copyright bargain might be viewed as the federal government agreeing to grant and enforce a limited monopoly for a set period of time in exchange for total access to a work by all once the period of protection expires. The ability to use works in the public domain allowed Andrew Lloyd Webber to adapt for the stage, without payment or permission, Gaston Leroux's 1910 novel, *Phantom of the Opera.* The right to use works in the public domain permits scholars to create annotated editions of classics or for *Chambers Book of Days* to be scanned and placed on the web.

THE SUBJECT MATTER OF COPYRIGHT

Section 102 of 17 *United States Code* states that copyright protects original works of authorship fixed in any tangible means of expression, including

1. literary works;
2. musical works, including any accompanying words;
3. dramatic works, including any accompanying music;
4. pantomimes and choreographic works;
5. pictorial, graphic, and sculptural works;
6. motion pictures and other audiovisual works;
7. sound recordings; and
8. architectural works.

This list is meant to provide examples of the types of works protected rather than limit the types of works protected. Though software is not listed, it is protected; it is included because by definition it is a literary work (17 U.S.C. § 101). Copyright also protects compilations, including the original elements of factual works.

Copyright does not protect ideas, procedures, processes, systems, methods of operation, concepts, principles, discoveries, facts, and works by the U.S. government. This affirms an important doctrine, the *dichotomy between ideas and expression.* This means that while the exact words, picture, image, code, etc. used to express an idea, concept, or fact may be protected by copyright, the idea, concept, or fact is not protected. Where a fact or idea is so intermingled with its expression that using the idea or fact requires the expression, courts have generally found such use to be noninfringing. This approach has been questioned in relation to software, since there is controversy over what constitutes the expression in a computer program (Hayden 1991). Is the expression only the actual code, the actions performed by the code, that which is displayed on a monitor when the program is loaded, or some combination of these? This issue may be moot for libraries, since most vendors of computer programs now rely on licenses rather than copyright protection to determine the acceptable uses of a program. Though the code of a computer program is generally considered protected as expression, there is an exemption for reverse engineering for the purpose of interoperability, that is, looking at the code of one program so that another program or hardware can be made to work with the first program (17 U.S.C. § 1201). This is particularly important for institutions such as libraries that use multiple software packages and resources that must share data or an interface, since it permits the institution to bypass encryption to view a program's code in order to customize other programs to interact with it.

A second doctrine is implied in 17 U.S.C. § 102 and affirmed in 17 U.S.C. § 202, namely, that the ownership of a material object in which a work is embedded is distinct from the ownership of the copyright. An institution may own an original manuscript but the copyright still belongs to the author or his assigns, unless the copyright was transferred in writing to the institution. Under this doctrine the individual receiving a letter owns the letter, while the author of the letter owns the copyright. Letters, reports, drawings, and other works created as part of one's job are generally considered works for hire, which means that the organization for which the work was created owns the copyright. In such cases the organization, or its archive, would have the right to publish such works, including letters. If an organization wishes to publish letters received from persons outside the organization, it would have to seek the permission of the authors, unless the letters were in the public domain. Unpublished works created before 1978 are protected until December 31, 2002, or the life of the author plus seventy years, whichever comes first. Works created before January 1, 1978, and published between then and December 31, 2002, are protected to December 31, 2047, or the life of the author plus seventy years, whichever comes first. If the author is unknown, if the work is a work for hire, or if it is a pseudonymous work, duration is one hundred twenty years after creation.

THE RIGHTS OF COPYRIGHT OWNERS

The rights granted to copyright owners are stated in § 106 of the Copyright Act:

1. to reproduce the copyrighted work in copies or phonorecords;
2. to prepare derivative works based upon the copyrighted work;
3. to distribute copies or phonorecords of the copyrighted work to the public by sale or other transfer of ownership, or by rental, lease, or lending;
4. in the case of literary, musical, dramatic, and choreographic works, pantomimes, and motion pictures and other audiovisual works, to perform the copyrighted work publicly;
5. in the case of literary, musical, dramatic, and choreographic works, pantomimes, and pictorial, graphic, or sculptural works, including the individual images of a motion picture or other audiovisual work, to display the copyrighted work publicly; and
6. in the case of sound recordings, to perform the copyrighted work publicly by means of a digital audio transmission.

"Phonorecords" are material objects in which sounds are fixed. However, motion pictures and other audiovisual works are not considered phonorecords.

Authors of works of visual art are also granted the moral rights of attribution and integrity (17 U.S.C. § 106A). These include the right to be or not be identified as the author of the work; to prevent intentional distortion, mutilation, or other modifications; and to prevent the intentional destruction of a work of recognized stature. These rights do not apply to modifications for the purpose of conservation, or to the conditions of public display (such as lighting and placement) if these will not lead to the destruction of the work, nor do these rights apply to reproductions or depictions of the work. Only the author or authors of a work have these rights, and the rights cannot be transferred to the owner of the copyright in the work or the owner of the work, though the rights may be waived if done so in writing. These rights only apply to works of art created after 1990 or works still owned by the author in 1990, and expire at the end of the calendar year in which the last living author of the work dies.

PENALTIES FOR CRIMINAL INFRINGEMENT

Until recent years copyright infringement was a civil matter, with plaintiffs entitled to choose between seeking statutory damages or actual damages plus any profits made by an infringer. Now certain types of copyright infringement carry criminal penalties. A person willfully infringing copyright for financial gain, or reproducing and distributing works worth more than $1,000 in a 180-day period, can be imprisoned for up to five years as well as being fined $2,500 (17 U.S.C. § 506). This includes employees of a state or an instrumentality of a state acting in his or her official capacity. This means that if a person working in a library, museum, or archive places a work or a resource on an internal system or on the World Wide Web knowing that he or she does not have the requisite permission or license, he or she can be sent to prison as well as fined. While this provision was enacted to prevent piracy in electronic forms, it also applies to print copies.

LIMITATIONS ON THE RIGHTS OF COPYRIGHT OWNERS

Sections 107–112 of the Copyright Act list the exemptions to the exclusive rights of owners. Two exemptions that are available to everyone and that are very important to libraries, museums, and archives are the *right of first sale* and the *doctrine of fair use.*

First Sale

The first-sale exemption allows libraries to circulate materials. It provides, in essence, that once a person or an organization buys an object in which expression is fixed, that person or organization is free to do almost anything with the object except copy it (17 U.S.C. § 109). They can sell it or lend it or destroy it. This right was modified to prohibit disposal, lending, or leasing of phonorecords and software for direct or indirect commercial advantage, though an exemption was created for nonprofit libraries and nonprofit educational institutions. This means that nonprofit libraries or institutions, such as museums, can lend or rent lawfully made copies of videos, computer programs, records, and the like, but they are required to affix a notice specified by the Copyright Office. It is generally agreed that libraries can lend videos that are labeled for home use only if, when they bought the video, the vendor knew they were selling to a library (Reed and Stanek 1986).

One of the difficulties encountered with electronic resources is the fact that these resources are generally licensed, not owned, and therefore not subject to the right of first sale. If an institution wants to be able to sell or transfer the contract for a licensed resource, the institution must negotiate such a provision into the license agreement. Failing such a provision, the right of first sale does not apply to materials obtained via a contract. This means that while libraries can sell books that have been weeded from their collection, they cannot sell old software programs or data disks that were licensed, unless the license allows such sale or transfer.

Fair Use

The doctrine of fair use allows reproduction of protected works based on a weighing of four factors (17 U.S.C. § 107):

1. the purpose and character of the use, including whether such use is of a commercial nature or is for nonprofit educational purposes;
2. the nature of the copyrighted work (i.e., whether the work is a book, a poem, a picture, etc.);
3. the amount and substantiality of the portion used in relation to the copyrighted work as a whole; and
4. the effect of the use upon the potential market for or value of the copyrighted work.

While the statute lists criticism, comment, news reporting, teaching, scholarship, and research as examples of the purposes of uses permitted, not all nonprofit educational uses are automatically considered fair. For example, a library user cannot copy an entire book that is protected by copyright, since such copying would be found to be substantial, as well as having a negative effect on the potential market for the work. Likewise, a copy of an entire photograph or painting or design would be considered substantial, no matter how small the image. This applies equally to images from print and electronic resources. Even though an intended use may be educational, copying an entire image that can be licensed by educational institutions may well be found to be infringing. However, if a library made photocopies for an exhibit of the book jackets of some books that it owned, such use would probably be found fair, since the purpose was educational, a book cover is generally not considered a substantial part of a work, and there should be no negative impact on the value or market for the work, since it is unlikely that an institution would buy a work just to tear off its cover for a display. But if a library, museum, or archive decided they no longer wanted to deal with a slide projector, and that they would digitize their slide collection, and if the slides in that collection were protected by copyright, such copying would probably be found substantial enough to be infringing. This especially would be the case if the copyright owner was now offering the same slide collection on CD-ROM.

Exemptions for Libraries and Archives

Section 108 of 17 U.S.C. contains special exemptions for libraries and archives that are in addition to the general exemption of first sale and fair use. These exemptions make it possible to provide copies of out-of-print material to library users, make up to three facsimile or digital copies for the purpose of preservation, and provide interlibrary loans. (For a full discussion of these rights, see chapter 14 of this collection, by Dwayne K. Buttler and Kenneth D. Crews.)

The CONTU Guidelines

During the revision process that resulted in the Copyright Act of 1976, the new, big, threatening technology was the photocopier. Publishers were afraid that this new technology, coupled with the broad exemptions proposed by Congress for librarians and educators, would reduce sales and profits, and that libraries would cancel periodical subscriptions and rely solely on interlibrary loan to service their users. Congress gave the job of brokering agreement between publishers, authors, librarians, educators, printers, and users to the Commission on New Technological Uses of Copyrighted Works (CONTU). CONTU was successful in getting stakeholders to agree to a set of guidelines intended to identify "safe harbors," that is, the *minimum* amount that one could copy under the exemptions and not be liable for suit for copyright infringement (CONTU 1979a). These guidelines limit interlibrary loan requests for copies of articles in periodicals, up to six billed requests per year per periodical for articles that were published within the previous five years. Requests for copies from other types of works, including collective works, are limited to five copies per year per work for the entire period that the work is protected by copyright. The guidelines do not apply to requests for copies from works that a library owns, but which are unavailable. Libraries are allowed to request no more than five copies of articles from missing issues of a periodical to which the library subscribes. These guidelines also require that libraries keep records of requests and fulfillment for a three-year period from the date of the request. The guidelines specifically leave the status of periodical articles more than five years old to future determination. Though the CONTU guidelines probably prevented many legal battles between libraries and publishers, they also chilled exploration of what might be the maximum under the law. Since adherence to the guidelines is now standard practice, it is doubtful that they could be successfully challenged in court.

CONTU also developed "Guidelines for Classroom Copying in Not-For-Profit Educational Institutions with Respect to Books and Periodicals" (CONTU 1979b). Any nonprofit institution that provides any form of instruction should be familiar with these guidelines, which limit the extent of what can be copied, as well as the frequency. In general, multiple copies of works can only be made for face-to-face teaching if the decision to use the work is made too close to the moment of use to arrange permission.

CONFU Guidelines

In 1996 the Commissioner of Patents and Trademarks convened a Conference on Fair Use (CONFU) to bring together copyright owners and users to discuss fair-use issues with the concept of formulating guidelines for libraries and educators in regard to digital images, distance learning, educational multimedia, electronic reserve systems, interlibrary loan and document delivery, and the use of computer software in libraries. While draft guidelines were developed for digital images and synchronous distance learning, these were not endorsed. The group also concluded that there was no necessity to draft guidelines for the use of computer software in libraries, though a number of scenarios exploring acceptable use were developed (Lehman 1998). The Consortium of College and University Media Centers were active in drafting the Educational Multimedia guidelines (Lehman 1998), which they presented to the CONFU group. These guidelines were accepted by the publishers, authors, and media groups, but *not* endorsed by most library and academic groups, which considered the minimum use allowed to be too small, especially as they realized, based on the CONTU guidelines, how rapidly a minimum becomes a maximum.

Photocopying

Nonprofit libraries can make photocopies for their users consistent with the fair-use guidelines. They may make only one copy per user and the copy must become the property of the user. A copyright warning must be posted in any full-service copy center and at each copying machine available to the public (37 C.F.R. § 201.14). The form of this notice is prescribed by the Copyright Office, the text of which can be found in Circular 21 (U.S. Copyright Office 1998).

Public Performance and Display

FILMS AND VIDEOS

Films and videos cannot be publicly performed (shown) by institutions without specific permission or license, except for face-to-face instruction (17 U.S.C. § 110). It makes no difference whether a fee is charged or not. Institutions may set up viewing areas where a user can view a copy of a work owned by the institution. There has been some contention that if a work is viewed by more than one person at time, or that if the viewing area can be seen by the public, that such viewing constitutes a public display prohibited by copyright. As of this writing, this has not been tested in court, and most libraries with sufficient facilities allow small groups of users (two to three people) to view a performance of a work at the same time. The "ALA Model Policy" (Reed and Stanek 1986) suggests that viewing be limited to one person or one family.

TELEVISION AND CABLE BROADCASTS AND TRANSMISSIONS

Libraries or archives may reproduce on videotape (or any other media) local, regional, or network newscasts; interviews concerning current news events; and on-the-spot coverage of news events and lend copies of such programs (17 U.S.C. § 108(f)(3); U.S. Copyright Office 1998). Any other type of broadcast may be recorded as it is broadcast or transmitted by a nonprofit educational institution, but such recordings can only be retained for forty-five days after the date of the recording and can only be shown twice to the same class during face-to-face instruction, within ten school days of its broadcast taping.

DISPLAYS OF WORKS

Institutions that own the original or a copy of a work may display that work. This allows museums to mount shows and libraries to have exhibits. It also permits the display of books or video covers to encourage circulation. As noted above, showing a motion picture or audiovisual work is not a display, but a performance, and usually requires permission; however, individual frames of a film can be displayed. If a display includes an original visual work created since 1990, it is important to remember that it cannot be changed in any way that might be considered a distortion or mutilation, nor displayed in a manner that would lead to its destruction (such as placing some works in strong sunlight). The need to make sure that works are not destroyed through negligence also means that works that are not being displayed are properly stored.

As previously discussed, the acquisition of an object, such as a work of art, does not generally mean that the copyright is acquired. However, even without copyright ownership some museums and libraries choose to exercise control over images of works in their collection, even those in the public domain, by restricting user behavior (such as prohibiting users from bringing cameras or paints into the building). Others, in order to preserve works, limit the circumstances under which copying is permitted. This is not a matter for copyright, since institutions have the right to set the rules of access for works and objects they own.

If an institution creates reproductions or photographs of works it owns, those reproductions and photographs will generally be protected by copyright, even if the subject of the work is in the public domain. This allows libraries and museums to distribute such reproductions or photographs and to enjoin others from copying the photographs or reproductions without permission, except as provided by fair use. If a photograph is created by an agency of the U.S. government, such as the Library of Congress, the photograph will be in the public domain.

Trademarks

There is a very limited fair-use provision for trademarks. Trademarks function to indicate the provenance of an article in trade. One lawfully can use a trademark or service mark to indicate the goods or service with which the mark is associated. However, a logo, trademark, or service mark cannot be used to identify any goods or services not authorized by the trademark owner. If the trademark owner does not make sure that its mark is only associated with its goods, it will lose the exclusive right to the mark. Disney and other owners of licensed characters are known to be assertive in protecting their property, and have asked that unauthorized copies or drawings of characters be removed from the walls of schools and hospitals as well as from newsletters and web sites. One can display books or posters or other works created by the owner of the trademark.

Reserves

The American Library Association (ALA; 1982) has argued that the reserves section of an academic library is an extension of the classroom and as such is covered by the CONTU classroom guidelines. If this is true, the implication is that the provisions of the classroom guidelines apply to reserves, e.g., not available for use in subsequent semesters without permission. The ALA further maintains that those guidelines do not adequately represent the needs of college research, since university professors did not participate in the negotiation of the guidelines. For this reason, the ALA drafted model library reserve guidelines, which state, in essence, that the amount of material placed on reserve for one course should be reasonable in terms of the material assigned for the course, that the number of copies made for reserve should be reasonable in light of the number of students enrolled, that any reproduction of materials placed on reserve include a copyright notice, and that the library should own at least one copy of any work being used for a course. Many libraries also provide access to works supplied by instructors. While this practice is acceptable for books and some articles, it becomes problematic if the instructor supplies a printout of an article from a licensed database where no fair-use provisions were included in the license, and where the printout states that no further copies can be made. Many libraries require instructors to sign a statement affirming that the copies or originals supplied to the library have been legally obtained and are eligible to be placed on reserve and that permission has been obtained for the use of any restricted materials. This is especially necessary for tests, workbook pages, answer sheets, and other forms that were created by a third party and for which there is no fair-use right of reproduction.

Pending Issues of Concern to Libraries

DISTANCE EDUCATION

The DMCA included a provision requiring the Copyright Office to produce a study and recommendations regarding the use of copyright materials in distance education. This report (U.S. Copyright Office 1999) only addressed the use of materials in the course of mediated instruction, such as closed-circuit television or web broadcasts. It generally recommended that the Copyright Act be amended to broaden the concept of what constitutes a classroom, allow instructors providing distance education the same use of materials that they would have in face-to-face instruction (except that the use of movies and audiovisual works would be limited to clips), and ban students from keeping copies of any works received. The report also recommended that the Congress authorize the recording of distance education sessions and allow later transmission to enrolled members. While the issue of digital reserves was discussed, no specific recommendation was made. Legislation to extend the rights of educators in various distance learning situations is currently pending.

POSSIBLE EXPANDED PROTECTION FOR COMPILATIONS

In 1991 the Supreme Court issued its judgment in *Feist v. Rural Telephone Co.* (111 S. Ct. 1282; 1991 U.S. LEXIS 1856), which stated that the selection, arrangement, or coordination of a compiled work needed to be original not only in the sense that it was not copied but also in the sense that it exhibited at least a quantum of creativity, and that such creativity was a constitutional mandate. While the Court observed that most compilations would meet this requirement, it was clear that exhaustive listings of facts arranged alphabetically, or in some other standard manner, would not. This ruling has caused producers of databases to fear that they would have no recourse if their works could be copied in their entirety, and certain database producers have been pressing for new legislation that would provide protection beyond copyright to databases and collections of information.

This issue is important to libraries not only in terms of possible impacts on the cost and availability of databases, but also in the context of the protection of bibliographic records. In 1982 OCLC shocked the library world by applying for copyright protection for its database (Franklin 1993). Many libraries protested, saying that bibliographic records are a collection of facts that cannot be protected, that records were created by the individual libraries participating in the OCLC database, and that if the records could be protected by copyright, each library should have the rights to their own records. The Copyright Office did let OCLC register the database, but as a compilation, granting it no rights to the individual records (Franklin 1993). It is possible that in the wake of *Feist* that the OCLC database could be found insufficiently creative in its arrangement to qualify for protection, as would any library's catalog database. While librarians as a rule endorse freedom of access to facts, it may be that some libraries would object to having their records downloaded into a database that would be later sold to other libraries as a cataloging aid, especially if they were not paid a fee. OCLC has maintained that it is concerned about preserving the quality of the database, and that while it can do so through enforcement of contractual agreements with its regional networks and members, it needs the ability to pursue third parties for copyright infringement. (Franklin 1993).

Two database bills were introduced in the 106th Congress: H.R. 354, sponsored by the Judiciary Committee, which would provide sweeping protections for compilations, limiting the amount of data that could be used even by lawful users of the database, and carving out only a very narrow exemption for libraries. In addition, this bill, strongly supported by such database producers as LEXIS/NEXIS and Thompson, would have opened the door for perpetual copyright and the protection of facts. The other bill, H.R. 1858, was brought forth by the Commerce Committee and had the support of the library and educational community, as well as those data compilers that collect facts from multiple sources, including Yahoo. This bill took an unfair competition approach, and would only prohibit copying of a database for a competitive purpose. Neither bill was passed. As of this writing representatives of the Commerce and Judiciary committees of the 107th Congress are meeting to produce a comprise bill and it is expected that legislation will be brought to the floor. Everyone who provides access to informative works needs to be actively involved in educating their users and representatives about the need to leave facts unprotected and to ensure that fair use remains a viable concept in a digital environment.

OTHER ISSUES

Is a copy of a digital work into volatile memory (RAM) a copy under the Copyright Act? If so, if a resource charges a per-copy access fee, will there be an additional charge for the copy in RAM? Should it be legal to digitize text and send it via a computer to satisfy an interlibrary loan request as long as the sending and receiving libraries delete the file from their system as soon as the user has possession of the file? If not, how does this differ in principle from faxing copies of articles? Should transmission be one of the rights granted copyright holders? If so, how will transmission be defined? Will sending a fax be a transmission? If the right of transmission is granted to copyright owners, what exemptions need to be in place for libraries, archives, museums, and educational institutions? These and other questions have been raised by a study of intellectual property rights and the national information infrastructure, generally called the White Paper (Lehman 1995); by CONFU (Lehman 1998); by the *Report on Copyright and Digital Distance Education* (U.S. Copyright Office 1999); and by other concerned information professionals and scholars. One thing is sure, as technology and its creative uses increase, so will the issues. But will their resolutions be unambiguous? Will a definite "no" regarding certain activities be better than the current "maybe"?

Conclusion

For many years copyright has provided the basic ground rules for access to resources. It was considered an equitable rule of reason that balanced the need of publishers and authors for profits and the need of citizens for access. Some believe that with the advent of digital technology, and a greater reliance on networked electronic resources, that copyright legislation has become more focused on providing profits for publishers and vendors than on making sure that new works are created and that the citizens of the United States have access to information (Jaszi 1997). Even with this shift in the focus, many information vendors do not believe copyright offers them sufficient protection or ability to profit, and they have turned to licensing schemes that provide access to information under terms much harsher than those governed by copyright. Some believe that copyright cannot continue to exist in a global, networked environment and that "information wants to be free" (Barlow 1994). Others believe that technological protections will be instituted to protect copyrighted works, and that the doctrine of fair use will be eliminated, since the DMCA has made circumventing such devices a criminal offense, and since without the ability to access materials without paying a fee the right to make fair use of them becomes almost meaningless (Samuelson 1997).

Interesting and confusing times are ahead for copyright and all the institutions and individuals that provide access to intellectual works. Only by being aware of both the underlying principles and the current issues will information professionals be major participants in the ongoing struggle to make sure that copyright continues to "promote science and the useful arts," and that society as a whole benefits from such promotion.

References

American Library Association. 1982. "Library Reserve Guidelines." In *ALA Model Policy Concerning College and University Photocopying for Classroom Research and Library Reserve Use*, http://www.musiclibraryassoc.org/Copyright/guideres.htm.

Barlow, J. P. 1994. "The Economy of Ideas: A Framework for Rethinking Patents and Copyrights in the Digital Age (Everything You Know about Intellectual Property is Wrong)." *Wired*, March: 85–129.

Birrell, A. 1899. *Seven Lectures on the Law and History of Copyright in Books*. New York: Putnam.

Branscomb, A. W. 1984. *The Accommodation of Intellectual Property Law to the Introduction of New Technologies*. Washington, D.C.: Office of Technology Assessment of the U.S. Congress.

CONTU. 1979a. "CONTU Guidelines on Photocopying under Interlibrary Loan Arrangements." In *Final Report of the National Commission on New Technological Uses of Copyrighted Works, July 31, 1978*, 55–58. Washington, D.C.: Library of Congress, http://www.ifla.org/documents/libraries/policies/contu.txt.

CONTU. 1979b. "CONTU Classroom Guidelines." In *Final Report of the National Commission on New Technological Uses of Copyrighted Works, July 31, 1978*, 54–55. Washington, D.C.: Library of Congress.

Demsetz, H. 1967. "Toward a Theory of Property Rights." *The American Economic Review* 57, no. 2: 347–59.

Forester, T., and P. Morrison. 1990. "Software Theft." In *Computer Ethics: Cautionary Tales and Ethical Dilemmas in Computing*, 27–39. Cambridge, Mass.: MIT Press.

Franklin, Janice R. 1993. *Database Ownership and Copyright Issues among Automated Library Networks: An Analysis and Case Study*. Norwood, N.J.: Ablex.

Ginsburg, J.C. 1992. "No 'Sweat'? Copyright and Other Protection of Works of Information. After *Feist v. Rural Telephone.*" *Columbia Law Review* 92: 338–88.

Goldstein, P. 1992. "Copyright." *Law and Contemporary Problems* 55, no. 2: 79–91.

Gordon, W. 1990. "Toward a Jurisprudence of Benefits: The Norms of Copyright and the Problem of Private Censorship. *The University of Chicago Law Review* 57: 1009–1049.

Hayden, J. F. 1991. "Recent Development: Copyright Protection of Computer Databases after *Feist.*" *Harvard Journal of Law and Technology* 5 (fall): 215.

Hettinger, E. C. 1993. "Justifying Intellectual Property Rights." *Philosophy and Public Affairs* 18, 31–52.

Hicks, J. B. 1987. "Copyright and Computer Databases: Is Traditional Compilation Law Adequate?" *Texas Law Review* 65, no. 5: 993–1028.

Jacobs, R. A. 1993. "Work-for-Hire and the Moral Right Dilemma in the European Community: A U.S. Perspective." *Boston College International and Comparative Law Review* 16, no. 1: 29–79.

Jaszi, P. 1997. "Taking the White Paper Seriously: Library of Congress Network Advisory Committee Network Planning Paper Number 30" [Abstract], lcweb.loc.gov/nac/nac30/]aszi-1 html.

Landes, W. M., and R. A. Posner. 1989. "An Economic Analysis of Copyright Law." *Journal of Legal Studies* 28: 325–63.

Lehman, Bruce A. 1995. "The report of the Working Group on Intellectual Property Rights." Washington, D.C.: U.S. Patent and Trademark Office. ["White Paper"]

Lehman, Bruce A. 1998. "The Conference on Fair Use: Final Report to the Commissioner on the Conclusion of the Conference on Fair Use." Washington, D.C.: U.S. Patent and Trademark Office.

Litman, J. 1992. "Copyright and Information Policy." *Law and Contemporary Problems* 55, no. 2: 185–209.

Moss, S. P. 1984. *Charles Dickens' Quarrel with America.* Troy, N.Y.: Whitston.

Nimmer, M. and D. Melville. 1995. "Nimmer on Copyright: A Treatise on the Law of Literary Musical and Artistic Property, and the Protection of Ideas." New York: Bender.

Patterson, L. R. 1968. *Copyright in Historical Perspective.* Nashville, Tenn.: Vanderbilt University Press.

Patterson, L. R., and S. W. Lindberg. 1991. *The Nature of Copyright: A Law of Users' Rights.* Athens: University of Georgia Press.

Putnam, G. H. 1891. "The Contest for International Copyright." In *The Question of Copyright,* ed. G. H. Putnam, 376–98. New York: Putnam's.

Reed, Mary Hutchings, and Debra Stanek. 1986. "ALA Model Policy: Library and Classroom Use of Copyrighted Videotapes and Computer Software," http://www.ifla.org/documens/infopol/copyright/ala-1.txt.

Rose, M. 1993. *Authors and Owners: The Invention of Copyright.* Cambridge, Mass.: Harvard University Press.

Samuelson, P. 1994. "The NII Intellectual Property Report." *Communications of the ACM* 37, no. 12: 21–27.

Samuelson, P. 1997. "The U.S. Digital Agenda at WIPO." *Virginia Journal of International Law Association* 37: 369–439.

U.S. Copyright Office. 1998. "Circular 21: Reproduction of Copyrighted Works by Educators and Librarians," http://www.loc.gov/copyright/circs/21.pdf.

U.S. Copyright Office. 1999. *Report on Copyright and Digital Distance Education.* Washington, D.C.: U.S. Copyright Office.

Warwick, Shelly. 1999. "The New Copyright Laws: What They Mean in an Online Environment." In *Proceedings of the Twentieth National Online Meeting, New York Hilton, May 18–20, 1999,* ed. Martha Williams, 499–510. New York: Information Today.

CHAPTER 14

Copyright Protection and Technological Reform of Library Services

DIGITAL CHANGE, PRACTICAL APPLICATIONS, AND CONGRESSIONAL ACTION

Dwayne K. Buttler and Kenneth D. Crews

Libraries have played a crucial role in the development of American copyright law for many decades, and the law has in many respects responded to the changing needs of library services. The library is, after all, a generally sympathetic institution offering broad public benefit. Politicians and other elected officials may well be motivated to support, especially, the public and academic libraries that serve large numbers of constituents. At the same time, the changing role of libraries and the expanding scope of services made possible by means of digital innovations have begun to test the ability of the law to meet the demands of librarianship. The potential for digital initiatives and new services to encroach upon the central interest of copyright owners also is recasting libraries as potential infringers, or even scofflaws, rather than as agents of a larger public good.

Background of Section 108

The recent history of section 108 of the U.S. Copyright Act[1] reflects this changing relationship between libraries and copyright law and evidences something of the larger struggle that Congress faces as it addresses the potentials and particulars of digital technology.[2] Section 108 has been part of the U.S. Copyright Act since the act was last fully revised in 1976.[3] The statute allows libraries to make copies of certain works for specified purposes, and generally only under detailed circumstances. Subject to numerous conditions, the law generally allows an eligible library to reproduce and distribute works for purposes such as preservation of materials, use in an individual's private study, and interlibrary loan.

As enacted in 1976, the statute was "technologically neutral"[4] and made no specific references to the technological means by which reproduction and distribution allowed under the statute might be accomplished. That absence of any reference to technological methods generally has been interpreted as permitting innovative means to be utilized in furtherance of the statutory activities. However, some librarians and their professional associations have expressed concern that the lack of any reference to specific technologies means that section 108 applies in general only to those technologies commonly available for use by libraries and contemplated by Congress in 1976. Those technologies were typically photoreproduction and microfilming. Some readers of the statute, therefore, have concluded that digital reproduction and dissemination, even consistent with the specific limits of section 108, are not allowed.[5]

The Digital Millennium Copyright Act (DMCA), enacted by Congress in October 1998, addressed this issue in part by amending section 108 specifically to permit some digital reproduction and distribution. Those amendments, however, were made only to the subsections of 108 applicable to preservation copying.[6] The subsections applicable to copies for private study and interlibrary loan remained unchanged.[7] While the law now explicitly permits using digital means for preservation copying, other parts of section 108 remain ambiguous about whether digital applications might apply to other activities or whether the "technologically neutral" statutory language confines the law to the general methods and circumstances contemplated at the time of its passage.

This chapter will examine the meaning of section 108 as amended by the DMCA and scrutinize its application to a few scenarios common to libraries and archives. This examination will first reveal the potential interpretation and meaning of the plain language of the statute. Second, it will reveal the ongoing tension between innovation in library services and the ability of the law to adapt to changing needs. Third, this study will demonstrate the opportunities for librarians—as well as the responsibility of librarians—to work within the statutory language in a probative and flexible manner in order to best facilitate the growth of innovation in library services. Finally, this study will reveal the limits of the law as currently written and highlight the limits of Congress's ability to respond to technological change.

Scenarios to Test the Limits of Section 108

To explore the meaning of Section 108, consider these scenarios:

Scenario one: The library has a collection of books, audio recordings, and videocassette tapes, many of which have deteriorated over time or have been damaged through frequent use. The library would like to make copies of these works—preferably digital copies—to preserve the materials in the collection. The library would like to make those preservation copies as widely available as possible to library users. In particular, the library would like to allow researchers to use the materials on the library premises, to check out the materials for use or study at home, and to allow the items to be sent temporarily through interlibrary loan to another library for use at that location.

Scenario two: The library includes a sizable archival collection of unpublished manuscript materials. The items are unique and are naturally subject to the risk of irreplaceable loss with each use. The library would like to use digital means to make copies of the manuscripts available for study on the premises of the library and for transmitting copies to other libraries for deposit in those collections for related research.

Scenario three: The library offers a service of making copies of select journal articles on request through its interlibrary loan services. For many years the library has made isolated photocopies of articles and sent them by mail to other libraries for delivery to the researcher. The library would now like to make a digital image of the article pages and to transmit that file to the requesting library as an e-mail attachment. The receiving library would like to mount that image on a web server and allow the researcher who requested it to access only that item using a unique and secure password. The researcher would be able not only to view the materials but also to print a copy for private study.

Many librarians may be surprised to learn that it would not be much of a stretch—and sometimes no stretch at all—for the law to allow all of the services outlined in these scenarios. Nothing in the law, however, is quite so simple and direct. If these services are allowed, they are still subject to numerous conditions and limitations, which will be outlined in this chapter. Nevertheless, the law ultimately may permit a considerable range of library services on terms similar to those set forth in these scenarios.

The balance of this chapter will examine the structure and application of section 108 and in the end will consider its implications for the adoption of new technologies to provide important library services. This analysis will provide many examples for better understanding the ability of Congress to respond to the copyright implications of digital technologies. To accomplish this, the study necessarily will follow the structure of section 108. The fourth, and next, part of this chapter will survey the origins of section 108 and the general "ground rules" under which a library may make use of the statute at all. The fifth part will examine the current application of the law to specific library services and will, in particular, emphasize the revisions made in 1998 for the use of digital applications. The final part will make some general observations about the meaning of section 108 and the interrelationship of law, technology, and library services.

Overview of Section 108

Section 108 of the U.S. Copyright Act allows libraries, within limits, to make copies for purposes such as preservation, private study by users, and sending in the name of "interlibrary loan" (ILL). The statute may be best understood as having two general components. First, the law establishes several ground rules.[8] Under the law, before a library can have the benefits of section 108, it must comply with these general conditions. Most academic and public libraries will have little trouble meeting these requirements. Other types of libraries may meet them as well. The ground rules also define the types of works that the library may reproduce.[9] Some copies of some works may be lawful for some purposes, but not lawful for other purposes.

The second general component of section 108 sets forth the substantive standards under which a qualified library may make copies for the specified purposes. In these subsections, the law defines the parameters of allowed copying for preservation, private study, and ILL.

THE GROUND RULES

With some important exceptions, the original ground rules from the Copyright Act of 1976 remained essentially the same after the DMCA amendments.[10] These exceptions are:

1. The library cannot copy or distribute copies for the purpose of "direct or indirect commercial advantage."[11]
2. The collections of the library must be open to the public, or available to researchers outside of that particular library, archive, or other institution.[12]
3. The copy or distribution of the work must include a "notice" of copyright.[13]
4. The library may make only single copies on "isolated and unrelated" occasions and may not, under most circumstances, make multiple copies or engage in "systematic reproduction or distribution of single or multiple copies."[14]

Unlike the original Copyright Act, the DMCA amendments now allow libraries to make three copies of a work for purposes of preservation and replacement.[15] Libraries and archives may still make only one copy for patron use and for ILL.[16]

Section 108 also strictly limits the types of works that may be copied for some purposes. In particular, section 108 explicitly bars copying of the following types of materials for a patron's private study or for sending in interlibrary loan:

1. a musical work;
2. a pictorial, graphic, or sculptural work; or
3. a motion picture or other audiovisual work.[17]

While this prohibits copying and distribution of those works for the specified purposes, section 108 places no limits on the types of works that may be copied for preservation purposes. At the same time, the statute permits the library to copy these closely related works for patron study and ILL:

1. other types of works that are not specifically excluded (usually text or sound recordings);
2. audiovisual works "dealing with news"; and
3. pictures and graphics "published as illustrations, diagrams, or similar adjuncts" to works that may otherwise be copied. (In other words, if you can copy the article, you can also copy the picture or chart that is in the article.)[18]

THE SUBSTANTIVE STANDARDS OF SECTION 108

Preservation Copying

When may the library make copies for preservation? Consider the library that has a collection of badly worn videotapes, damaged books, or scarce historical documents. Under subsection 108(b), applicable only to unpublished works, a preservation copy is permitted, if:

1. the copy is solely for preservation or security, or for deposit at another library, and
2. the work is currently in the collection of the library making the copy.[19]

If the library is seeking to copy a work that has been previously published, subsection 108(c) allows a preservation copy, if:

1. the copy is solely for replacement of a copy that is damaged, deteriorating, lost, or stolen, or if the format of the work has become obsolete (e.g., a player for your collection of eight-track tapes is no longer manufactured or available for purchase) and
2. the library conducts a reasonable investigation to conclude that an unused replacement cannot be obtained at a fair price.[20]

Preservation in Digital Formats

After enactment of section 108 in 1976, librarians debated whether they might use digital technologies to make preservation copies, in the absence of clear language on this subject in the statute. The DMCA clarified this issue in part. Digital preservation copies may be made of both published and unpublished works under the conditions set forth above. In addition, "any such copy or phonorecord that is reproduced in digital format" may not be "made available to the public in that format outside the premises of the library or archives." To oversimplify, machine-readable formats must be confined to the building. As noted earlier, while rights to make copies under section 108 are often limited to textual works, the right to make preservation copies extends to other media. In summary, the statute now provides that libraries can make preservation copies, even in digital formats, of textual works, musical works, art, software, videotapes, and other works, as long as the library complies with all of the requirements described above.

Copies for Private Study

When may the library make copies for the library user to keep? Consider the library that offers a copying service. A user requests copies of manuscripts, journal articles, or even a book. For journal articles or other portions of larger works, such as book chapters, subsection 108(d) allows research copies, if:

1. the copy becomes the property of the user;
2. the library has no notice that the copy is for any purpose other than private study, scholarship, or research; and
3. the library displays a warning notice where orders for copies are accepted and on order forms.[21]

If the copy is of an entire work or a substantial part of it, subsection 108(e) imposes somewhat tighter constraints on the library:

1. the library conducts reasonable investigation to conclude that a copy cannot be obtained at a fair price;
2. the copy becomes the property of the user;
3. the library has no notice that the copy is for any purpose other than private study, scholarship, or research; and
4. the library displays a warning notice where orders for copies are accepted and on order forms.[22]

Copies for Interlibrary Loans

When may the library make copies to send elsewhere in the name of interlibrary loans? First, a copy made for ILL is essentially a copy made for a user's research or private study. Thus, the copying must ordinarily follow the requirements summarized above from subsections 108 (d) and (e). Second, the library receiving the copies must adhere to this additional standard: the interlibrary arrangements cannot have, "as their purpose or effect, that the library or archives receiving such copies or phonorecords" on behalf of requesting patrons "does so in such aggregate quantities as to substitute for a subscription to or purchase of such work."[23]

Third, to help clarify that limit on the ability to receive copies, the National Commission on New Technological Uses of Copyrighted Works (CONTU) in 1979 issued guidelines that generally allow a library to receive up to five copies of articles from the most recent five years of a journal title during one calendar year.[24] After that quota, the general expectation is that the receiving library will pay a copyright fee or purchase its own subscription to the journal.

THE DEBATE SURROUNDING "TECHNOLOGICALLY NEUTRAL"

The absence of any reference to specific technologies in the 1976 act has left open the need to infer from its language the applicability of section 108 to many increasingly common library activities, particularly those activities made possible by new technologies. Moreover, the DMCA's new restrictions on preservation and replacement copies made in "digital formats" may have muddled further the heritage of "technological neutrality" in copyright law. Much of this confusion emanates from different meanings, and resulting different interpretations, of the concepts "technology" and "formats." For example, in drafting the 1976 act, Congress appears to have valued some categories of works more highly than others, excluding, for instance, the copying of "a motion picture or other audiovisual work" for a patron's private study or ILL. That exclusion might relate superficially to a certain "technology" at a certain historical moment: a "motion picture," for example, might be recorded on "photographic film." Thus, a reader of the copyright statute might infer that the law is in fact not neutral regarding technology. However, that same "motion picture" might today exist on videotape, digital videodisc (DVD), or a media file on a computer. The definition of "audiovisual works" refers to a "series of related images," regardless of the "material objects, such as films or tapes, in which the works are embodied" and thus is not confined to any particular technology or format.[25] Other definitions in section 101 take a similar technologically neutral approach.

This confusion may suggest consequences for interpreting section 108 after the amendments made by the DMCA. For example, in revising the preservation and replacement provisions of section 108, Congress explicitly used the language "digital formats" in limiting the distribution of works reproduced in that format to the physical "premises" of the library. "Digital formats" also might seem tied superficially to a specific technology, "digital technology." But here, again, the language in fact may be technologically neutral. "Digital technologies" and "digital formats" may exist in many varieties and in many forms. CD-ROM, DVD, MPEG-3, and JPEG, for instance, arguably constitute different digital formats or, at least, different digital file structures. PCs, Macs, Unix, other computing platforms, and the "brain" within your car may encompass different digital technologies. In a strict sense, "digital" signifies more usefully how the information is gathered, processed, and stored. It does not represent a specific technology or format. The inevitable fate of most formats and technologies is that none is guaranteed perpetuity. Copyright law arguably adopted a neutral approach exactly because of this unpredictability. If Congress had defined the law through technologies existing at the time of its passage, the law likely would have rapidly become outdated and ineffectual.

With the DMCA, Congress made explicitly lawful those digital copying activities that might well already have been lawful under a reasonable interpretation of the 1976 act. This belief found its support in the technologically neutral approach of the act, and not in any congressional willingness to determine whether certain categories of works—for example, audiovisual—may be used in certain copying activities, such as patron study or ILL. Thus, in interpreting section 108 after the DMCA, one should be wary of arguments suggesting that only preservation and replacement copies may now be made with digital means by using "digital technology." The statute itself makes explicit reference only to use restrictions on "digital formats" made for preservation purposes and not to any specific technologies or means used to pursue affirmative rights of copying and distribution assured under section 108.

Subsection 108(f)(1) also adds important support for the argument that the law is technologically neutral and therefore can accommodate diverse and unspecified technologies. Subsection 108(f)(1) addresses the implications of "unsupervised" photocopiers on the premises and the liability of the library for infringements committed by the user of those machines.[26] Quite simply, the statute exonerates the library and staff from those infringements, but only if the library displays a notice informing users that making copies may be subject to copyright law. The user of the machine may still be responsible for any infringements. This provision remains unchanged after the DMCA.

Although subsection 108(f)(1) is usually applied with respect to photocopiers, the statute offers protection to libraries that post notices on unsupervised "reproducing equipment," not merely on photocopy machines. A library may post the notice on all unsupervised photocopy machines, as well as on VCRs, tape decks, microfilm readers, computers, printers, and any other equipment that is capable of making copies. Because the language of the law is technologically neutral, the library can secure protection against misuses of a wide range of machines and devices that are capable of making copies of copyrighted works.

Taken together, these allowances and limitations in section 108 may indicate that Congress is willing, with respect to library activities, to identify certain categories of works and formats with certain limits of copying and distribution. Under today's section 108, for instance, the library can reproduce a wide range of works for preservation and replacement in a wide range of formats, including digital. The scope of permissible categories becomes narrower for patron use and ILL, but the DMCA makes no mention of restrictions on formats or technologies in which the library may reproduce materials. A plain reading of the statute coupled with an understanding of the technologically neutral premise would suggest that Congress wanted the law to be dynamic and capable of addressing new technologies.

Returning to the Scenarios

From this broad and somewhat detailed framework of section 108, return again to the three scenarios described at the beginning of this chapter.

Scenario One: Under section 108 a library is allowed to make copies for published works for preservation purposes. Unlike for some other purposes, copies for preservation are not limited to certain categories of works. Accordingly, the library can copy videotapes, audio recordings, and many other types of works. Copies of these published materials are always subject to the "ground rules." They are also subject to the requirement that the library look first to the market for an unused replacement at a fair price. The DMCA amendments make explicit that the library can make the copies in a digital format, but that format must generally be accessible only on the library premises. In this scenario, however, the library wants to use the copies for many purposes, including allowing researchers to use the works off-site. Again, the DMCA offers an opportunity. While the digital copy must be confined to the library, copies in other formats do not have that restriction. Moreover, the DMCA added a provision to permit libraries to make up to three copies of the works for preservation purposes. Hence, the library could make a digital preservation copy that is available for study at the library. A second copy could be made in "analog" format, and that copy would be available for lending and for sending to another library through ILL. The third copy could be retained in storage for security purposes in the event of loss of or damage to the copies in use.

Scenario Two: Unpublished archival materials may also be copied under section 108; again the DMCA explicitly allows application of digital technologies, and the digital copy must generally be accessible only at the library. The library would like to make copies available for use off-site. Again, the DMCA allows the library to make three copies for preservation purposes and if one copy is made in analog format it will generally be allowed to circulate to users.

The most complex issue in this scenario arises when the library seeks to use digital technology to deliver a copy of the work to another library for deposit and use at that location. Section 108 permits a library to make copies of unpublished materials for, among other purposes, "deposit for research use in another library or archives." The DMCA in 1998 added the provisions for digital copying, but restricted that use to the library premises. Look closely at this statutory language:

> any such copy or phonorecord that is reproduced in digital format is not *otherwise distributed* in that format and is not made available *to the public* in that format outside the premises of the library or archives [emphasis added].

The statute generally permits the transfer of a copy of the work to another library, but pointedly uses the phrase "otherwise distributed" to limit the uses of the digital version. This language suggests that the restriction applies to *further* distribution of the digital copy beyond the distribution occurring when it is transferred from one library to another. Moreover, the restriction specifies that the digital work may not be *made available to the public* outside the library. By this construction, a library could therefore make a transfer of a digital copy to the receiving library. That initial transfer is not an *additional distribution* implied in the word "otherwise." The transfer is also not a distribution to the public, but rather is a private communication directed to a single, identified recipient—in this case, the library that will retain and preserve the copy. The language of the statute then suggests that the digital copy, once received, should be made available to researchers at that library only in an analog format, despite the use of digital technologies to transmit the work between libraries in an efficient and expeditious manner. Apparently, digital technologies may be used to make, deliver, and store the preservation copy, but the copy actually used by the researcher should be in an analog format.

Scenario Three: This situation turns attention to provisions of section 108 that the DMCA did not amend, and that include no mention of specific technologies. To apply digital technologies to ILL requires an interpretation of the technologically neutral language to encompass diverse media. While ILL arrangements are explicitly the subject of subsection 108(g)(2), the limits of copying are found in the provisions related to copies for an individual's private study or research. Ultimately, the purpose of ILL is to supply copies of individual items for a user's needs, when that person's local library does not have the materials in its collections. Subsection 108(d) applies when a library makes copies of journal articles, such as the copies in this scenario.

Some of the debate about using digital technologies prior to the DMCA arose from the purported implications of a phrase in the preservation and replacement provisions that limited the copy to a "facsimile form." Some in the library community inferred from this phrase that any resulting preservation copy must be identical in form and format to the original. Consequently, only an existing "digital" work copied in digital form might be acceptable under this interpretation. Regardless of the merits of that interpretation, however, the phrase never applied to patron and ILL uses, such as those in this scenario, and the DMCA deleted that requirement, lending further weight to the argument that section 108 copying activities are technologically neutral, and that Congress in fact has reduced ambiguity in the statute.

Because "digital formats" are explicitly allowed only for the preservation activities, those subsections of section 108 (b and c) are also the only provisions with limitations on the use of those formats. Thus, in this scenario, if section 108 is technologically neutral—which the plain language of the statute suggests—the library could make a lawful copy using digital technology. Moreover, the library would not need to confine that copy in "digital format" to the library premises. As a practical matter, the library could send that copy by e-mail to the requesting library, which might make it available to the researcher under password restriction on the receiving library's web site. Similarly, the lending library might retain the copy on its web site under password restriction for the researcher.

Although such innovations may well be within the construct of section 108, they are not without dispute and consequent risks. Many copyright owners undoubtedly would interpret the law so as not to allow such innovations, and many of them would in any event express grave concerns about the potential harm to their markets and the risks that the digital copy might be easily downloaded and further disseminated. To find an appropriate balance in the application of the law, the library may consider granting access only in a manner that allows the researcher to retain a print copy, not a digital copy. Access should be limited to the one researcher for a limited time, and access should come with general notices cautioning the user against misuse of the work. A deep concern permeates the thinking of content owners today about the availability of "digital copies" of their previously "analog" works. When a library takes meaningful steps to limit the final delivery of the work to a print format, the library is signaling an appreciation of the rights of copyright owners and a desire to minimize risks to them. The more effectively libraries can promote reasonable strategies to lessen those concerns, while ensuring fullest access to copyrighted works, the more likely that libraries and patrons will benefit from the adoption of those strategies. Like all ILL arrangements, this scenario also would need to consider the CONTU "rule of five" limits to help emphasize that the "purpose and effect" of the copying is not "to substitute for a subscription to or purchase" of the work, thus potentially violating section 108(g)(2).

Conclusion

The application of the revised section 108 to digital technologies suggests several implications about the general relationship between the law and the development of new technologies.

The law is slow to adapt to applications of innovations in technology. This proposition should be no surprise. The nature of the law is to evolve gradually, and the nature of lawmakers is to make changes with hesitation and caution. Seemingly isolated developments in the law have broad application to diverse situations. When Congress or a court seeks to extend the law, it can anticipate only limited consequences; yet in the unpredictable future we will look to each change in the law for meaning that may have been unintended or may become undesirable. To minimize the risk of these unintended consequences, lawmakers often choose to take no action until the pressure for change becomes irresistible or until the consequences have been satisfactorily explored. Congress was therefore apparently comfortable with amending section 108 under the DMCA in 1998, because the implications were generally focused, and libraries and publishers alike had demonstrated prohibitive constructions of the previous statutory language.

Congress has chosen to avoid addressing many details of new technologies by creating "technologically neutral" statutes and leaving to the courts and to the marketplace the duty of bringing some practical meaning to the code. The fact is, however, that lawsuits involving any aspect of section 108 are few, and no reported court decision expounds on the details of the law. Consequently, librarians and others are left to bring meaning to the law and to discover its potential application to new technologies. From that application can come the ability to make, store, and disseminate works in diverse formats in furtherance of effective library services.

When Congress has chosen to address new technologies, at least under copyright law, it has sought to find a balance or a compromise. Finding a balance between rights of copyright owners and rights of users has been a central tenet of the copyright law. Often that balance is a carefully crafted compromise. Section 108 is a clear example of that tendency. All of section 108 is a compromise. It exists to provide some limited right of use for libraries in the face of broad rights reserved to copyright owners under the Copyright Act. Each of the permitted uses under section 108 also manifests a compromise, as certain uses are allowed, but only subject to a variety of conditions. Most of those conditions are intended to assure acknowledgment of the owner's rights, preserve the market for current sales of the work, and prevent further misuse of the work once it has been copied and distributed to a user. The amendments to section 108, made by passage of the DMCA, emphasize the continuing quest for balance, as the law allows some application of digital technology, but only with yet additional restrictions on the use of the digital copy.

As Congress has sought to clarify the law, it inevitably has raised new questions about the law's meaning. Some concepts and terms in section 108 will always be open to reasonable interpretation, but with the advent of diverse and complex technology, the potential for creative uses of copyrighted works is giving rise to additional questions about the meaning of the statute. While the struggle for answers to some questions has led to amendment of some subsections of the statute, other subsections continue to beg the central question of whether they apply at all to digital technologies. If they do, librarians will continue to raise questions about the specific meaning of the statutory language. Without amendments and without court rulings, we will need to answer our own questions in a reasonable and good-faith manner.

The increasingly complex interrelationship between law and technology suggests two duties of increasing importance for librarians. First, librarians have the responsibility to keep current with developments in their own field and with developments in the law. They also need to nurture an appreciation for the relationship between the law's meaning and its application to innovative services. The law seeks to establish a balance, and librarians have to realize that sometimes they cannot accomplish all that they might desire, even when their goals are technologically feasible and in furtherance of the library mission. Second, librarians also have a duty to themselves to look critically, and at times creatively, at the law, in order to discern the law's practical meaning and find a reasoned interpretation of law that might not explicitly encompass new technology at all.

This examination of section 108 serves as a microcosm of the relationship between technology and the law. Section 108 embodies the dilemma of extending the law into new technologies when the law is not explicit. It also demonstrates the compromises that are necessary if Congress is to amend the statute to give explicit assurance of the law's meaning to new applications. Yet one overriding conclusion is clear for the individuals who need to work with the law—in this instance the librarians seeking to apply section 108. The law will never fully address future needs, and the law will never answer all questions that will arise. The law offers only limited specificity and, accordingly, some uncertainty. In the first analysis, the need to bring meaning to the law and determine the lawful course of conduct will reside with the librarian seeking to give the law practical meaning and meet the needs of complex and changing library services.

Notes

1. 17 U.S.C. § 108 (1998).
2. The Digital Millennium Copyright Act amended existing section 108 to allow preservation copying in "digital formats" and created new sections for providing "safe harbors" for online service providers, for prohibiting the "anticircumvention" of "technological protections measures," and for controlling the use of "copyright management information." Pub. L. No. 105-304, 112 Stat. 2860 (1998) (now codified in various sections of Title 17 of the U.S. Code as amendments to the Copyright Act of 1976). Like previous versions of copyright law, these amendments and new sections continue to focus on "technologies" in the abstract, not specifying technologies in most instances. Consistent with a "technologically neutral" premise, the user is left to interpret the meaning of the law through its plain language, inference, and careful legal reasoning.
3. Copyright Act of 1976, Pub. L. No. 94-553, 90 Stat. 2541 (1976).
4. For example, in section 101, the Copyright Act states that a "work is 'fixed' in a tangible medium of expression when its embodiment . . . is sufficiently permanent or stable to permit it to be perceived, reproduced, or otherwise communicated. . . ." Another example: "A 'device', 'machine', or 'process' is one now known or later developed." The act contains other definitions that demonstrate careful drafting to avoid tying the language to identified technologies. Such an association would arguably date the law quickly and might compel Congress to revisit the socially complex issues of copyright far more often than it might desire.
5. Robert Oakley has argued that Congress intended to limit preservation copying to the use of "microfilm or electrostatic processes." Oakley, *Copyright and Preservation: A Serious Problem in Need of a Thoughtful Solution* (Washington, D.C.: Commission on Preservation and Access, 1990). Oakley and others emphasize a brief statement in a 1976 report from the House of Representatives that, in explaining section 108, mentions without further detail that libraries may not make the materials available "for storage in an information system." H.R. Rep. No. 94-1476, at 75 (1976), reprinted in 1976 U.S.C.C.A.N. 5659, 5689.
6. 17 U.S.C. § 108(b) and (c) (1998).
7. 17 U.S.C. § 108(d) and (e) (1998).
8. 17 U.S.C. § 108(a), (g), and (i) (1998).

9. 17 U.S.C. § 108(i) (1998).

10. Portions of the following outline of section 108 also appear in Kenneth D. Crews, *Copyright Essentials for Librarians and Educators* (Chicago: American Library Association, 2000).

11. 17 U.S.C. § 108(a)(1) (1998).

12. 17 U.S.C. § 108(a)(2) (1998).

13. 17 U.S.C. § 108(a)(3) (1998). Since passage of section 108 in 1976, libraries and publishers have debated whether the "notice" on the copy must be the formal copyright notice found on the original (the "©" followed by date and name) or some general indication of copyright's application (such as "use of this material is governed by copyright law. . ."). The DMCA clarified the type of notice required on copies. If the original work includes a formal copyright notice, the library or archives must include that notice on any copies made. If no notice appears on the original work, the copy need only include "a legend stating that the work may be protected by copyright."

14. 17 U.S.C. § 108(g) (1998).

15. 17 U.S.C. § 108(b) and (c) (1998).

16. 17 U.S.C. § 108(a) (1998).

17. 17 U.S.C. § 108(i) (1998).

18. 17 U.S.C. § 108(i) (1998).

19. 17 U.S.C. § 108(b) (1998).

20. 17 U.S.C. § 108(c) (1998).

21. 17 U.S.C. § 108(d) (1998).

22. 17 U.S.C. § 108(e) (1998).

23. 17 U.S.C. § 108(g)(2) (1998).

24. National Commission on New Technological Uses of Copyrighted Works, *Final Report,* 54-55 (Washington, D.C.: GPO, 1979).

25. 17 U.S.C. § 101 (1998).

26. 17 U.S.C. § 108(f)(1) (1998).

CHAPTER 15

Legal-Technological Regulation of Information Access

David A. Rice

Copyright provides varying degrees of protection for digital works. It affords none whatsoever for information as such, limited protection for data compilations, and substantial protection for computer programs and digital audio, audiovisual, graphical, musical, and photographic works. The differences in copyright protection in different media are particularly evident in court opinions dealing with computer program and database copyright infringement. While a computer program may be protected by copyright, it is well established that a program's copyright does not create exclusive rights in the information content of data files. Likewise, it provides no protection for program-embodied ideas, methods, or processes—the products of innovation and invention, which are the province of trade secret and patent law.

None among us would deny the importance and value of either invention or information. My immediate concern is with just one of these: information. It is the common fiber of science, arts, history, culture, and even self. Knowledge, lore, and experience are the information links with our own heritage and, in turn, with generations to follow. Different cultures and ages illuminate our present, not just others' pasts. In our own social and political culture, we prize self-expression, communication, and the discourse through which it is shared and appraised. Indeed, First Amendment protection of speech recognizes that information and ideas, and their free expression and use, are cornerstones of our political and social order, and essential attributes of autonomy.

The newest of the many generations of information technologies presents the greatest opportunity thus for universal information access, diffusion, learning, and use. Like prior generations of information reproduction and distribution technology, and their commercial exploitation, this one also tests anew that balance of private and public claims accommodated in what we often call the "copyright bargain."

What differs with this generation is that recent developments in private contract law and public legislation emphasize and legally reinforce the private claim. The rationale is that such strengthening is necessary to assure realization of the increased consumer and other public benefits that digital information and communications technologies offer. The first of two notable features of these measures is common to both. It is an emphasis on regulating access to and use of factual and other information in which neither patent, copyright, nor other intellectual property law grants exclusive rights. The second notable feature is limited to new legislative regulation. It is a change in mind-set or perspective from that of infringement to one of theft. This is most, but not exclusively, evidenced by Congress increasingly criminalizing copyright infringement and violation of related new statutes.

This chapter first briefly discusses background intellectual property law and the demand for new protection. It thereafter surveys the origins and features of contractual and technological restriction of information use and access, and then reviews relationships between these measures and traditional copyright and neighboring rights. Finally, it considers and comments upon significant implications of contractual and technological regulation of access, in particular, and the tension between, on the one hand, the information society's promise of universal access to scientific, historical, and cultural knowledge and thought and, on the other hand, the effects of commercial legal-technological regulation of access to and use of that knowledge and thought.

Intellectual Property Foundations

Judicial recognition that computer programs are patentable subject matter has led to a dramatic increase in the number of computer program patent applications. A great many computer program method, process, and apparatus patents now issue. Some have been highly controversial, especially in the case of certain e-commerce business methods patents.

Still, neither patent nor copyright protect abstract ideas or fundamental principles. Specific to patent law, eligibility is limited to particular, useful, novel, and not obvious applications of ideas and basic principles.[1] Copyright, of course, protects only original expression. The required originality or creativity is minimal, especially when compared to the patent standards of novelty and nonobviousness. Still, facts themselves are excluded from copyright as well as patent protection.

Fact compilations or databases are protectable, but only if the data selection, coordination, or arrangement is original or creative. The originality or creativity must be significant, but not necessarily substantial. Indeed, the nature of facts makes substantiality a standard rarely met.[2] The Supreme Court made it clear in *Feist Publications, Inc. v. Rural Telephone Service Co.* that the same characteristics of data compilations dictate that any available copyright protection is "thin" compared to that accorded literary, artistic, and other traditional copyright works.

The failure of copyright to protect facts or their nonoriginal compilation reflects neither an economic nor a social value judgment about the importance of information. Some would argue that it is merely a constitutional artifact, a product of Article I, section 8, clause 8 of the U.S. Constitution, conferring specific power on Congress only to enact laws to "secure for limited Times to Authors . . . the exclusive Right to their respective Writings." Not similarly constrained, the European Union in its Database Protection Directive subsumes certain exclusive database extraction rights within a more broadly defined concept of copyright. In the United States, it is assumed that Article I, section 8, clause 8 does not inferentially preclude Congress from enacting database protection legislation as unfair competition law under the commerce clause. Although various of the database protection bills put before Congress in each of the last several sessions technically would amend the Copyright Act, the sponsors make it clear that this would be through exercise of legislative power under the commerce clause and the necessary and proper clause of the Constitution rather than the patent and copyright clause.

Regardless, copyright is important in letter and in spirit to the contractual and technological regulation of the use of a work and access to its informational content. In letter, it establishes that some rights exist in at least some digital information products. Although weak as protection, it provides a footing for presenting that the very technologies that promise so much to so many simultaneously threaten realization of that promise. The mere exercise of the exclusive right to distribute copies is an act that exposes each copy to exact, quick, and inexpensive unauthorized reproduction. The Internet makes easy the unauthorized and widespread distribution of myriad unlawful copies. Diffusion of downloadable copies across many servers and web sites multiplies the opportunities for relatively anonymous making of unauthorized copies. All require greater copyright owner vigilance and investment to identify download sites and to proceed against their operators for either unauthorized distribution of copies or contributory infringement—the latter based on facilitating unauthorized copying by others.

So viewed, the very information technologies and network that promise wide diffusion and universal access simultaneously make digital content freely and anonymously appropriable. Recent litigation concerning DeCSS (DVD encryption code descrambling algorithm), MP3, and other technological breaches of technology-based protection measures reflects that the greater the popular demand for particular content, the greater will be the effort to obtain it at the least cost—especially if that is near zero. It also indicates exposure of a major fault line, one which some tend to view largely in adolescent rebellion terms and others in terms of more fundamental values and rights.

Although there are many theories of copyright, U.S. copyright law usually is regarded as reflecting a utilitarian rather than a romantic perspective. Author rights are created as an incentive to produce creative works for the benefit of society, not primarily to recognize individual creativity and to protect the integrity of its product. Still, the essential legal rights contained in copyright do not vary much from one legal system to another. These include a copyright owner's exclusive rights to reproduce the original, distribute copies, prepare a derivative work, and to display or perform certain classes of works.

Software, database, musical recording, and motion picture publishers claim that digital information technologies render this insufficient—for reasons that I stated above. Their claim is not new. Copyright law itself developed in response to the emergence of new technology, and each new wave of copy reproduction, distribution, display, and performance technology has forced judicial and legislative adaptation of copyright in order to maintain balance in what we often call the "copyright bargain"—a term that itself sounds a utilitarian chord. The earliest, and many later, adjustments dealt with the effect of new technology and its market implications on so-called upstream relationships between authors and publishers. Others concerned intermediate and end uses of broadcast and cable transmissions, photocopy reproduction of works, and other downstream implications of new technologies.

Seeking additional protection is, in this broader view, not without precedent. What differs is the type of protection that is sought. Lawyers have fashioned contracts and terms designed to restrict computer program and electronic database use, access, and resale (or other transfer). Computer software and hardware have been designed and developed to restrict and regulate access to and use of both resident and online computer programs and electronic databases. It is but a short, yet important, leap to claim that state and federal law—and state and federal courts—must legally support and enforce information product publisher use of these contract and technological measures that leverage copyright protection of expression into content enclosure.

The New Protection Market

The information age is one in which digital representation and access technologies, and their convergence with telecommunications technologies, promise universal access to literary and artistic works, scientific knowledge, historical archives, and cultural lore. This promise is not yet realized, and its universal fulfillment may be more a vision than a prospect. First, its realization requires enormous additional investment in infrastructure extension. Second, digital information product creation and maintenance often is costly. At the same time, information technology makes the creation and distribution of copies as easy and inexpensive for third parties as it is for digital information product publishers.

Industry representatives and some economists contend that copyright does not provide protection sufficient to optimal investment in the creation and distribution of digital information products. More particularly, they urge that traditional copyright and related infringement remedies are ill suited to digital products and the network environment. Unauthorized copying is easy and inexpensive, and can occur almost anywhere. The Internet and World Wide Web facilitate widespread unauthorized distribution of illicit copies at a nominal cost. Although technological innovation has increased detection and documentation capability, posting on numerous web sites and development of track-covering encryption algorithms make it difficult to detect and document individual acts of infringement. Finally, the high cost of infringement litigation creates a barrier to even vigilant domestic enforcement, let alone remedy seeking in another nation under its copyright law. This legal transaction cost barrier is most formidable for individual and small computer program and electronic database product developers, whose work is as likely to be downloaded and used by others engaged in information product development as it is by end users.

Digital information content providers therefore look increasingly to contractual and technological regulation of use as a copyright enforcement supplement or substitute. In furtherance of this, they have sought legal support for the use of technological means of protection, and legal enforcement of contractual restrictions on digital information product use and transfer. The Uniform Computer Information Transactions Act (UCITA), the World Intellectual Property Organization Copyright Treaty, and the 1998 Digital Millennium Copyright Act amendments to the 1976 Copyright Act are products of those efforts. In each, copyright is shown to be essentially transformed from its origins as an instrumental incentive to create into the foundation for instrumentalities to control. Through each, the underlying claims of proprietary rights—principally stated in terms of protest against "piracy" rather than the grant of limited property rights as a means of expressing the copyright balance or bargain—stronger than copyright legal protection is extended to informational content that is explicitly excluded from the protection by the legislative grant or recognition of copyright in a work as a whole.

Contractual Regulation of Access and Use

Software publishers first licensed copies subject to reproduction, distribution, and elementary use restrictions at a time when copyright protection for computer programs was uncertain and patent protection seemed unavailable.[3] The copy licensing approach continued after copyright protection was confirmed, but with new emphasis on contractual control over individual copy use and transfer. Concurrently, its use was broadened to create protection for otherwise unprotected information content and to enhance existing, but limited, legal protection for databases as compilations.

Formally, granting a license or mere privilege to use does not convey title to a copy. It is reasoned from this that control over a licensee's copy use or transfer is inherent in the reservation of copy ownership. While copyright law generally bars such control following initial sale of a copy, use licensing is claimed to circumvent this "first sale" or exhaustion of rights doctrine, one of the principal limitations on copyright. In the United States, this often-disputed tenet is the cornerstone of UCITA (formerly known as Uniform Commercial Code, Article 2B) and its contract law rules governing software, digital information content, and related transactions.[4]

Software publishers expanded copy-use licensing objectives from protection against copying to shielding their programs from product-line competition, regulating development of interoperable products, and protecting information content not protected by copyright. Other use and transfer restrictions are employed to differentiate, and thereby price discriminate between, user markets. Such provisions also may foreclose the development of product resale or system maintenance competition.

News, stock, and commodity trading transactions, and other reporting services, have long employed short-term contractual restrictions on disclosure, and U.S. unfair competition law affords short-term protection against third party misappropriation of gathered and disseminated "hot news." Providers of this and other information in digital form recognized that the software license paradigm offered a contractual approach for protecting uncopyrightable content and for discriminating in price according to use.[5] Commercial credit rating and reporting firms also license information access subject to use, disclosure, and transfer restrictions for the more particular purpose of managing liability risk resulting from unprivileged disclosure. This differs in that it furthers the public policy to safeguard sensitive information privacy. In other instances, licensing online access and use offers a means to minimize risk of injury and liability resulting from error, e.g., avoiding harm to patients by assuring that only adequately trained or qualified persons can access and use a medical expert system for diagnostic purposes. A major failing during the development of UCITA is that these particularly appropriate uses have been presented and too readily accepted as showing that law must generally permit digital information product publishers to contractually regulate access to and use of computer information, including public domain knowledge.

U.S. courts first denied, and then some later validated, use restrictions in computer program copy standard form contracts. Most prominent among decisions supporting use restrictions came in the controversial *ProCD v. Zeidenburg*.[6] UCITA rejects the judicial view that prevailed prior to *ProCD v. Zeidenburg*. UCITA adopts the copy-use license paradigm, strongly supports contractual regulation of use, and legitimates traditional shrink-wrap and online click-wrap contract formation. Important to libraries, research archives, museums, and other institutions that provide access by the public and scholars to information resources, UCITA also validates use of electronic means to temporally regulate the term of use. Through this, it makes content a resource that must be renewed rather than collectable and archiveable. It also establishes, subject to few limitations, that access and use-regulation terms made available only after payment or other typical assent-manifesting conduct are enforceable as contract terms. UCITA also allows original contract terms to control use by third party transferees or, in the case of libraries and other institutions, end-user patrons. Finally, it makes a contractual prohibition against transfer of a fully paid copy enforceable even against a third party by making an attempted transfer wholly ineffective as a transfer of possession and use rights and a ground for terminating any further use by the original licensee.[7]

The Technological Regulation of Use and Access

In December 1996, the World Intellectual Property Organization (WIPO) completed work on a Berne Convention protocol concerning copyright in digital works. The adopted Copyright Treaty and the Performances and Phonograms Treaty each require contracting parties to

> provide adequate legal protection and effective legal remedies against circumvention of technological measures . . . used by

> authors in connection with the exercise of their rights under this Treaty or the Berne Convention and that restrict acts, in respect of their works, which are not authorized by the authors concerned or permitted by law. (Copyright Treaty, Article 11; Performances and Phonograms Treaty, Article 12)

Law thus was brought into step with the development of digital copyright management systems as means for protection of authors' rights, and it was expressly made applicable to Berne Convention works of authorship, including computer programs and compilations of data—though not to the data themselves.

Article 11 of the Copyright Treaty, the one most central to this chapter, requires protection and remedies directed to the act of circumvention. Its focus on conduct strongly differs from device-focused regulation, the approach strongly urged by the United States and, with some modifications, initially proposed by the WIPO Committee of Experts. The rejected approach required contracting parties to prohibit use, importation, manufacture, or distribution of any device that had the primary purpose or effect of circumventing treaty-covered technological protection measures.[8]

The United States implemented the treaties in the Digital Millennium Copyright Act of 1988 (DMCA), but went beyond Copyright Treaty requirements in important respects. Section 1201(b) of the act prohibits the manufacture, import, distribution, or trafficking in any technology, product, service, or device that "is primarily designed or produced for the purpose of circumventing protection afforded by a technological measure that effectively protects a right of a copyright owner," has only limited commercially significant purpose or use other than to circumvent such protection, or is marketed for use in circumventing such protection.[9] Although made subject to several specific exemptions before enactment, the DMCA establishes the strong device-focused protection that the United States and, in modified form, the Committee of Experts initially proposed and the WIPO Diplomatic Conference rejected in favor of focusing on conduct, the act of circumvention.

Two other DMCA provisions deal with circumvention of technological measures that serve a quite different purpose, technological management of access to a work protected by the U.S. Copyright Act. These include computer programs and data compilations that meet the minimum standards of originality set forth by the Supreme Court in *Feist Publications,*

Inc. v. Rural Telephone Service Co, and likewise come within the scope of Article 5 of the WIPO Copyright Treaty.

The first access-focused anticircumvention provision prohibits the act of circumventing a technological measure that effectively controls access to a work protected by the Copyright Act. The statutory text applies equally without regard to whether a work is highly original and expressive or principally factual and minimally original.[10] A second provision parallels the copyright protection anticircumvention provision. It prohibits manufacture, import, distribution, or trafficking in any technology, device, or service primarily designed or produced for the purpose of circumventing protection afforded by a technological measure that effectively controls access to a work protected under the Copyright Act, has only limited commercially significant purpose or use other than to circumvent such protection, or is marketed for use in circumventing such protection.[11]

The effective date of the copyright protection anticircumvention provision was deferred two years to allow sufficient time for the Librarian of Congress to define any class of otherwise noninfringing uses of copyright likely to be adversely affected by the prohibition, and to adopt rules that exempt those uses for a following three-year period.[12] The effective date of the access anticircumvention provision was not similarly deferred.

The Librarian of Congress is directed to rule whether any users of a copyrighted work "are, or are likely to be for the succeeding 3-year period, adversely affected by [the prohibition] . . . in their ability to make noninfringing uses . . . of a particular class of copyrighted works."[13] Factors to be considered in the rulemaking are the availability for use of copyrighted work; availability of works for nonprofit archival, preservation, and educational purposes; impact of the prohibition on criticism, comment, news reporting, teaching, scholarship, or research; effect of circumvention on the market for or value of copyrighted works; and other factors considered appropriate by the Librarian of Congress.[14] Public notice of that rulemaking was given in November 1999, and numerous comments and reply comments were submitted and are now under consideration. Any listing published by the Librarian of Congress is limited in effect to making circumvention permissible only for otherwise noninfringing uses.[15]

The access anticircumvention provision is subject to a number of exemptions, including a limited exemption for nonprofit libraries, archives, and educational institutions for the sole purpose of determining whether to acquire a copy of a work.[16] There is a broader exemption for governmental law enforcement and intelligence activities,[17] substantial exemptions for encryption technology research[18] and security testing of computers and networks,[19] a narrow exemption for identifying and disabling technological capability to collect and disseminate personally identifying information reflecting online activities of a natural person,[20] and a limited and highly conditioned exemption for reverse engineering that is directed toward achieving interoperability.[21] The latter federally legislates that, for purposes of state trade-secret law, circumvention of technological protection against access is an improper means for discovery of trade secrets embodied in a computer program or other copyright work, except where the purpose is to achieve interoperability of an independently developed computer program.[22]

The exemptions reflect an important distinction between the copyright protection and access prevention provisions. The former concerns use of technological measures to reinforce the exclusive rights of an author or copyright owner to reproduce or distribute copies of a work protected by copyright. The latter pertains to use of technological measures to exclude access to information, knowledge, ideas, and other content that section 102(b) of the Copyright Act expressly excluded from protection by the copyright in a work.[23] Congress was careful in this respect not to undo existing copyright law.

There has been little litigation to date. The most noted decision concerns the DeCSS software utility designed and distributed as a means for decrypting digital versatile disk (DVD) protection code to permit motion picture DVDs to be run under the Linux operating system.[24] The Federal District Court for the Southern District of New York issued a preliminary injunction, pending full trial and determination of rights, against further dissemination of the software utility at the behest of the Motion Picture Association of America and a number of its members. The program decrypted the industry standard content scramble system (CSS) code used to protect against unauthorized copying of copyrighted films distributed on DVDs.[25] In a many-faceted opinion, the court concluded that DeCSS was created, used, and disseminated for the purpose of circumvention of effective technological measures utilized to protect against unauthorized copying. It further determined that the defendants had not demonstrated that either the reverse engineering or security testing exemptions created by the DMCA applied in this instance. More generally, it rejected a First Amendment and another constitutional challenge directed to the validity of the statute itself.

The most important, and controversial, aspect of the case was the court's rejection of fair use as a defense. The historical backdrop includes motion picture industry attempts in the early 1980s to legally block real-time home recording of broadcast television programs. The argument was that Sony's retail sale of videotape recording devices contributed to unauthorized, infringing copying by VCR users, thereby making Sony a contributor infringer and its instrumentalities bannable from the market. The claim was rejected by the Supreme Court, which held that copying for time-shifted viewing was a common and, under section 107 of the Copyright Act, fair use of copyrighted television programs.[26] Fair, noninfringing use of the Betamax machine in turn saved Sony from contributory infringement liability, and the VCR from condemnation on the ground that they had no commercially significant use other than to make unauthorized copies of copyrighted works.

Judge Lewis A. Kaplan concluded in the DVD case that the fair-use defense is unavailable under the DMCA except as it is expressed in the form of specific statutory exemptions. This position underscores that the DMCA is constitutionally grounded in the necessary and proper clause rather than the patent and copyright clause, at least if one is of the view that some recognized fair uses shape the edges of copyright so as to keep it within its intended constitutional scope. Judge Kaplan's position on this issue is very controversial, and it can be strongly argued that this view cannot be reconciled with section 1201(c), which declares "Nothing in this section shall affect rights, remedies, limitations, or defenses to copyright infringement, including fair use, under this title." A more alarmist view is that, if upheld, Kaplan's interpretation allows that ownership of content and control over its publication and distribution preclude uses even of legally unprotected informational content so long as some technological measure to effectively control access is employed. The prospect that the super copyright protection may thereby be extended to content that is entitled to only thin, if any, copyright protection is deeply troubling.

The other principal decision[27] is less prominent, but significant. RealNetworks develops and markets products and services to audio, video, and multimedia content owners for streaming distribution of content to consumers over the Internet. It alleged that Streambox, Inc., violated the DMCA through its distribution of several products that impaired digital video and audio distribution, retrieval, and playing or performance control sought and expected by customers using RealNetworks' products and services.[28] It also complained that Streambox violated the DMCA by distributing another product that permitted conversion of digital audio and video files from one format to another, thereby making them compatible with and usable in various hardware and software system configurations. The trial judge preliminarily enjoined distribution of two of the three products pursuant to section 1201(b) on the ground that they were unlawfully designed and distributed for the purpose of allowing users to make unauthorized modifications to software programs in which RealNetworks owned the copyright. Such modification infringed the exclusive right of RealNetworks under section 106 of the Copyright Act to make, or authorize the preparation of, a derivative of its copyrighted program. On the other hand, the judge refused RealNetworks' application for a preliminary injunction against distribution of the file-conversion program, this based on a showing that the program had significant commercial use for purposes other than circumvention of technological measures that effectively protect the rights of a copyright owner.

The Relationship to Copyright Protection

The WIPO Copyright Treaty and DMCA predicate application of their provisions on the existence of copyright in the work in question. UCITA differs in that it purports to deal solely with contract rights in transactions involving computer information. It, however, assumes the existence of background rights or control sufficient to require entry into a contract in order to obtain use or access.

Copyright protects a broad range of works fixed in a tangible medium. These range from literary and artistic to some, but not all, data compilations. Authors are vested with limited exclusive rights in expression that is original to the author, principally the right to reproduce, distribute copies, display, perform, or prepare a derivative work. As earlier noted, the required originality is minimal and, except at the extreme of purely factual matter, it is of no consequence that the expressed ideas, thoughts, knowledge, or facts are not original to the author. Still, copyright creates no rights in the expressed ideas, knowledge, or facts or in any described discovery or invention.

Contractual and technological protection of computer software and other digital information thus have been floated on a broad and thin rights membrane, not footed on a strong rights foundation like that of patent. Copyright protection by anticircumvention technology adds a capability to generally or finely regulate, monitor, terminate, and even bill and collect payment for access to and use of the copyrighted digital works.[29] Technological means used to prohibit or regulate access to a copyrighted work, and its informational content, exceed this by engaging a merely potential user at a defensive advance perimeter, and there determining whether to generally bar, selectively permit, or generally permit access to all or some content without regard to whether the content is protected by the work's copyright. Contract terms, alone or in tandem with technological measures, offer much the same potential. Their distinctiveness is that the rules they express are judicially enforceable and regulate conduct by legal rules of more general application than those expressed in binary code.[30]

Technological shields and contractual regulation are controversial because they provide the owner of copyright with means to claim more than copyright law expressly grants. In particular, it is argued that their use to preclude or regulate fair use and other uses expressly privileged by copyright law alters the copyright balance and, in effect, creates "super copyright." Comparatively, technological regulation of access to content and legislative proscription against its circumvention might well be described as "extra super copyright" for what copyright itself does not protect. Such regulation statutorily leverages the existence of copyright and its protection for some elements into legal-technological barriers against study of commercially and widely distributed products in quest of understanding of how they work, and what trade secrets they make open to otherwise lawful discovery. Equally, it encloses purely factual content not protected by copyright within legal-technological walls so long as those facts are contained within a compilation that is entitled to at least thin copyright protection or contained within computer program data files.

Implications and Further Observations

The enhanced protections serve to make the digital information product world safer for publishers and distributors. The public return for granting these legal protections without substantial qualification is not, however, full realization of the information society potential that digital information publishers offer as the social justification for stronger protection.

Technological and contractual regulation of digital information use offer, at best, more universal dissemination in exchange for greater publisher control over individual use. The principal justification, reduction of losses resulting from piratical unauthorized copying, pales in comparison to the primary purpose of securing use-measured economic returns that, in many instances, incorporated technology will classify, measure, bill, and collect. This itself might be unremarkable except that substantially unqualified legal recognition of technological and contractual regulation of use imposes substantial costs additional to the use-based revenues that they better secure for publishers. The most notable is technological and contractual negation or limitation of privileged or fair uses that copyright law has evolved or created as limitations on the copyright franchise.

Access anticircumvention measures, and access-regulating contract terms, impose substantially greater social costs. The technology blocks access to information content of a copyright-protected work, even though copyright law makes it clear that the protection of copyright does not extend to the information itself. The very limited DMCA use exemptions provides another perspective on the costs of access anticircumvention measures. The nonprofit library, educational institution, and research organization exemption, for example, does not permit a library to circumvent access anticircumvention measures to permit a treating physician to search a CD-ROM containing information on toxic substances in hope of learning something from which to formulate a strategy for treating a patient who is allergic to conventionally prescribed medication. Concerning a quite different point, is it sound to indirectly prohibit reverse engineering of an unpatentable access anticircumvention measure given that scientific and technological advances, including anticircumvention technologies, build substantially on prior discoveries and knowledge?

Finally, consider a quite different dimension. Cultural teachings, legends, and lore are not copyrightable. They typically have no identifiable human author and originated, in any event, at a time more distant than the life of an original author plus seventy years (the limit stipulated under the recent Sonny Bono Copyright Term Extension Act). In addition, many such teachings are held and transmitted in an oral tradition. In some instances, writing or otherwise recording in a tangible medium may in fact be prohibited in general or with respect to the particular content. Yet a digital work produced by a researcher or a commercial digital content publisher that represents those teachings, legends, and lore in words, symbols, sounds, and images is protected by copyright. Section 1201(b)(1) of the DMCA makes it unlawful to manufacture, sell, or traffic in any technology, product, service, or device that is primarily designed or produced for purpose of making or distributing a copy of the commercial product. Section 1201(a)(1) makes it unlawful to manufacture, sell, or traffic in any technology, product, service, or device designed or produced for the purpose of giving even members of the indigenous culture access to the informational content.

Simply stated, access regulation technology and contractual regulation of access have the potential to exclude or control access to information about one's own culture and heritage, depending upon ability to pay or other terms. Copyright protection technology and use-regulating contract terms have the capacity to control how one uses the very same information, something far different from protecting against unauthorized copying of the digital work in which the information is contained. The DMCA supports the creation access barriers and seeks to prevent infringement by regulating other technology, by prohibiting its manufacture, exchange in market transactions, and distribution or dissemination. Limited exceptions do exist, the primary one being for technologies that can be shown to have commercially significant purposes or uses other than circumvention of an effective technological measure to protect copyright or prevent access to a copyrighted work and its informational content.

Conclusion

The press to privatize control over access to and use of digital information diminishes the luster of the late-twentieth- and early-twenty-first-century opening of the information society. It undermines, not furthers, realization of information technology's potential to provide universal access to virtually all information resources irrespective of geographic distance or location, or individual economic or physical limitation.

The commercialization of cultural knowledge, heritage, legends, and lore and the use of treaties, statutes, and contracts to regulate or even preclude access to that information by members of the represented culture is perhaps the most extreme and deeply troubling scenario. Maybe most digital information product publishers generously will at least provide access to their products by bona fide members of a represented culture, and even to their direct descendants, as compensation for use of an indigenous culture's distinctive knowledge and lore. No doubt, however, this would be done subject to contract terms that restrict access to and use of the information to strictly noncommercial purposes, and prohibit transfer of provided copies to any third party.

Quite different, but equally troubling, is that both the DMCA and UCITA are products of efforts to maximize the commercial value of digital information and related technologies through means that prohibit innovative use or development of new technology by others. UCITA enforces contractual prohibition or restriction of nonstandard use of computer information, including creative and innovative use of digital information in a manner that is characteristic of breakthroughs in scientific, technological, business method, and human understanding and development. UCITA and the DMCA effectively invest private commercial entities that substantially control the production and distribution of digital format copyrighted works with quasipublic authority to regulate use of and access to digital information products, including factual and other content that the law denies the right or power to appropriate against others or the world.

The 1999 Seattle WTO demonstrations and riots reflected many sources of discontent, some of which have information technology and society dimensions. Use of legal-technological protections of investment in commercialization of information is met with technology-savvy teenage hacking to reverse engineer CSS code and make it possible to play DVDs under the open-source Linux operating system, rather than only on proprietary and closed-code computer operating systems. The vast majority of comments and reply comments filed in the DMCA rulemaking being conducted by the Librarian of Congress and its Copyright Office do not address the questions posed by the rule making notice or section 1201(a)(1)(C). Rather, they protest use of the DMCA—and even contract terms—to substantially preclude reverse engineering of computer program code for the purpose of what used to be generically called "inventing around," and now is more particularly characterized as "hacking around," technological and legal-technological barriers to uses ranging from pedestrian to innovative. Many reply comments note that numerous initial round comments were not on point, and therefore should be "dissed"—a most apt, because many-layered, contemporary usage.

A recent feature by John Markoff in the *New York Times*[31] described the current digital music recording and DVD code decryption battles in U.S. courts against efforts of some programmers to deregulate the Internet through the use of software rather than legal code. In particular, the article concerned Freenet and Gnutella, already widely distributed programs that make it possible to acquire and exchange content anonymously, and make it impossible to determine the source—or multiple sources—from which an individual downloaded the information. When effectively joined with decryption programs directed against technological protection of digital information product copyright and content, such uses of technology set up a fundamental clash of top-down regulation by legislation and contract with more diffused bottom-up regulation by digital code. It sets the ability to secure favorable legal rules against winning favorable reviews and acceptance. Alas, this sounds far simpler than it is—and that is what makes it so much the subject of social, economic, political, and jurisprudential debate in which most of us are almost daily engaged.[32]

Notes

1. Patents often are described, in common discourse, in terms far broader than their actual scope. The statement that a wrench or a computer program is patented, or covered by a patent, means only that the Patent Office has granted exclusive rights to make, use, or sell concerning certain features specified in particular claims. These are further specified as pertaining to an article or apparatus, a process, or a means of producing a particular result.
2. *Feist Publications, Inc. v. Rural Telephone Service Co.,* 499 U.S. 340 (1991).
3. Mark A. Lemley, "Intellectual Property and Shrinkwrap Licenses," *Southern California Law Review* 68, no. 1 (1999):1239–94; David A. Rice, "Licensing the Use of Computer Program Copies and the Copyright Act First Sale Doctrine," *Jurimetrics Journal* 30, no. 2 (1990): 157–87.
4. David A. Rice, "Digital Information As Property and Product: UCC Article 2B," *University of Dayton Law Review* 22, no. 3 (1997): 623–48.
5. Yochai A. Benkler, "Free As the Air to Common Use: First Amendment Constraints on Enclosure in the Public Domain," *New York University Law Review* 74, no. 2 (1999): 354–446.
6. *ProCD, Inc. v. Zeidenburg,* 86 F.3d 1447 (US Ct App, 7th Cir., 1996).
7. David A. Rice, "License with Contract and Precedent: Publisher-Licensor Protection Consequences and the Rationale Offered for the Nontransferability of Licenses under Article 2B," *Berkeley Technology Law Journal* 13, no. 3 (1998): 1239–81.

8. Julie E. Cohen, "Some Reflections on Copyright Management Systems and Laws Designed to Protect Them," *Berkeley Technology Law Journal* 12, no. 1 (1997): 161–87.

9. 17 U.S.C. § 1201(b)(1)(A)-(C).

10. 17 U.S.C. § 1201(a)(1)(A).

11. 17 U.S.C. § 1201(a)(2)(A)–(C).

12. 17 U.S.C. § 1201(a)(1(A).

13. 17 U.S.C. § 1201(a)(1)C). This review is to occur thereafter every three years.

14. 17 U.S.C. § 1201(a)(1)(C)(i)–(v).

15. 17 U.S.C. § 1201(a)(1)(D) and (E).

16. 17 U.S.C. § 1201(d).

17. 17 U.S.C. § 1201(e).

18. 17 U.S.C. § 1201(g).

19. 17 U.S.C. § 1201(j).

20. 17 U.S.C. § 1201(i).

21. 17 U.S.C. § 1201(f).

22. The latter is a judicially recognized fair use under the Copyright Act. See *Sega Enterprises Ltd v. Accolade, Inc.*, 977 F.2d 1510 (U.S. Ct. App., 9th Cir. 1992); *Atari Games Corp. v. Nintendo of America, Inc.*, 975 F.2d 832 (U.S. Ct. App., Fed. Cir. 1992); *Sony Computer Entertainment, Inc. v. Connectix Corp.*, 203 F.3d 596 (U.S. Ct. App., 9th Cir. 1999).

23. 17 U.S.C. § 102(b).

24. *Universal City Studios, Inc. v. Reimerdes*, 82 F.Supp. 211 (U.S. Dist. Ct., SD NY 2000).

25. Each viewing of a film necessarily involves copying into random access memory as well as display, which likewise is unauthorized and protected against by use of CSS technology.

26. *Sony Corporation of America v. Universal City Studios, Inc*, 464 U.S. 417 (1984).

27. The DMCA also was interpreted and applied in *Sony Computer Entertainment, Inc. v. Gamemasters*, 87 F.Supp.2d 976 (U.S. Dist. Ct., ND Cal. 1999).

28. *RealNetworks, Inc. v. Streambox, Inc*, __ F.Supp. 2d __, 2000 WL 127311 (U.S. Dist. Ct., WD Wa 2000).

29. Mark Stefik and Alex Silverman, "The Bit and the Pendulum: Balancing the Interests of Stakeholders in Digital Publishing," *Computer Lawyer* 16, no.1 (1999): 1–15.

30. The point is at the heart of jurisprudential debate about the alternatives of top-down regulation of cyberspace through traditional legal rules and bottom-up regulation through use of binary code.

31. "The Concept of Copyright Fights for Internet Survival," *New York Times*, May 10, 2000.

32. The contending views are discussed and compared in Lawrence Lessig, *Code and Other Laws of Cyberspace*. New York: Basic Books, 1999; Dan L. Burk,

"Muddy Rules for Cyberspace," *Cardozo Law Review* 21, no. 1 (1999): 121; Tomas A. Lipinski, "The Developing Legal Infrastructure and the Globalization of Information: Constructing a Framework for Critical Choices in the New Millennium Internet—Character, Content and Confusion," *Richmond Journal of Law and Technology* 6, no. 1 (1999–2000): 19; Neil W. Netanel, "Copyright and a Democratic Civil Society," *Yale Law Journal* 106, no. 1 (1996): 283.

PART SIX: IMPLEMENTATION OF LEGAL AND ETHICAL CONCEPTS

CHAPTER 16

Getting Started

LEGAL AND ETHICAL RESOURCES

Jane Colwin

Primary Federal Legal Materials

Note: A good one-stop shopping web site for locating primary federal legal materials is lcweb.loc.gov/global.

LEGISLATIVE

Public Laws. Issued sequentially during a congressional session as individual numbered pamphlets called slip laws (e.g., Pub. L. 106-10 is the tenth law passed in the 106th Congress). *Public Laws* is prepared and published by the Office of the Federal Register, National Archives and Records Administration. "GPO Access" is a U.S. Government Printing Office site that contains the text of public laws enacted from the 104th Congress to the present. The *Public Laws* can be found on these web sites:

www.access.gpo.gov/su_docs/legislative.html
thomas.loc.gov

United States Statutes at Large. At the end of each session of Congress, the slip laws are compiled into these bound volumes, also known as "session laws." The *Statutes at Large* present a chronological arrangement of the laws in the exact order that they were enacted. Because the text of laws published as public laws and *Statutes at Large* are the same, there is not a *Statutes at Large* database on "GPO Access." However, users may perform a search by *Statutes at Large* citation in both the public laws and *United States Code* databases.

United States Code. Every six years, public laws are incorporated into this codification of all general and permanent laws of the United States. The *United States Code* is arranged by subject matter, and it shows the present status of laws that have been amended on one or more occasions.

The *United States Code* is prepared and published by the Office of the Law Revision Counsel, U.S. House of Representatives. It is maintained as a separate database on "GPO Access." See these sites:

www.access.gpo.gov/congress/cong013.html
www4.law.cornell.edu/uscode

U.S. Code Annotated (West Group) or *U.S. Code Service* (Lexis Law Publishing). Either of these sets provides access to the *United States Code,* and is current and annotated with history notes and extensive case law references. Both are much more useful for doing research than the official *United States Code.*

U.S. Code Annotated is available on Westlaw; *U.S. Code Service* is available on Lexis-Nexis. Both are also available on CD-ROM from their respective publishers.

Constitution of the United States. On the web, see supreme.findlaw.com/constitution/index.html.

ADMINISTRATIVE

Federal Register (FR). The *Federal Register* is published Monday through Friday by the Office of the Federal Register, National Archives and Records Administration. It is the official publication for rules, proposed rules, and notices from federal agencies and organizations, as well as executive orders and other presidential documents.

"GPO Access" contains *Federal Register* volumes from 59 (1994) to the present. See www.access.gpo.gov/su_docs/aces/aces140.html.

Code of Federal Regulations (CFR). A codification of the general and permanent rules published in the *Federal Register* by the executive departments and agencies of the federal government. See www.access.gpo.gov/nara/cfr

Agency Rulings, Decisions, Bulletins, Circulars, etc.

"Federal Web Locator," www.infoctr.edu/fwl. Service provided by the Center for Information Law and Policy and intended to be the "one-stop-shopping" point for federal government information on the World Wide Web. This site is hosted by the Information Center at Chicago-Kent College of Law, Illinois Institute of Technology.

University of Virginia School of Law, www.law.virginia.edu/admindec. This institution provides a nice web site with links to other administrative actions that are outside the scope of the CFR and the FR.

U.S. Copyright Office, www.loc.gov/copyright. Also see Decisions of the United States Courts Involving Copyright. Washington: Government Printing Office, 1928–85.

Office of Government Ethics, www.usoge.gov.
U.S. Patent and Trademark Office, www.uspto.gov

JUDICIAL

U.S. Supreme Court. See the following sites:

www.supremecourtus.gov
www.findlaw.com/casecode/supreme.html
supct.law.cornell.edu/supct

U.S. Federal Circuit Courts. See the following sites:

www.uscourts.gov/allinks.html#all
www.findlaw.com/casecode/courts

U.S. Federal District Courts, www.uscourts.gov/allinks.html#all.

Secondary Legal Materials

Secondary legal materials include encyclopedias, treatises, loose-leaf services, digests, citators, periodicals, and web sites.

AMERICANS WITH DISABILITIES ACT (ADA)

Accessible Museum: Model Programs of Accessibility for Disabled and Older People. Washington, D.C.: American Association of Museums, 1992.
ADA Library Kit: Sample ADA-Related Documents to Help You Implement the Law. Chicago: Association of Specialized and Cooperative Library Agencies, American Library Association, 1994.
Roehrenbeck, Carol. *Complying with the ADA: Law Library Services and Facilities.* Dobbs Ferry, N.Y.: Glanville, 1997.
U.S. Department of Justice. "Americans with Disabilities Act: ADA Home Page," www.usdoj.gov/crt/ada/adahom1.htm.

APPRAISALS

Johnson, Steve. *Appraising Audiovisual Media: A Guide for Attorneys, Trust Officers, Insurance Professionals, and Archivists in Appraising Films, Video, Photographs, Recordings, and Other Audiovisual Assets.* Washington, D.C.: Copyright Information Services, 1993.
University Libraries, University of Missouri, Kansas City, www.umkc.edu/lib/geninfo/00collec.htm#gifts.
"Your Old Books," www.rbms.nd.edu/yob.html.
Department of Special Collections, Memorial Library, University of Wisconsin-Madison, www.library.wisc.edu/libraries/SpecialCollections/aboutrb.html.

ART LAW

"Art Law on the Internet," www.hg.org/art.html.
Institute of Art and Law, www.ial.uk.com. An independent research and educational organization, founded in 1995, that analyzes the interface between the world of art and antiquities and that of law.
Lerner, Ralph E. *Art Law: The Guide for Collectors, Investors, Dealers, and Artists.* 2d ed. New York: Practising Law Institute, 1998.

COPYRIGHT/FAIR USE

Boorstyn, Neil. *Boorstyn on Copyright.* Deerfield, Ill.: Clark Boardman Callaghan, 1994–.

CNET, Inc., builder.cnet.com/Business/Law. Provides a simple overview of copyright, trademark, and libel law and is primarily intended for web page designers.

Copyright Law Reporter. Chicago: Commerce Clearing House, 1978–.

Copyright Permissions. Chicago: Intellectual Property Law Association of Chicago, 1995.

Epstein, Michael A. *Epstein on Intellectual Property.* 4th ed. New York: Aspen Law and Business, 1999–.

Fishman, Stephen. *Copyright Handbook: How to Protect and Use Written Works.* 4th ed. Berkeley, Calif.: Nolo, 1997.

Gasaway, Laura N., ed. *Growing pains: adapting copyright for libraries, education, and society.* Littleton, Colo.: Rothman, 1997.

Gasaway, Laura N., and Sarah K. Wiant. *Libraries and Copyright: A Guide to Copyright Law in the 1990s.* Washington, D.C.: Special Libraries Association, 1994.

Goldstein, Paul. *Copyright.* 2d ed. Boston: Little, Brown, 1996 (now published by Aspen Law and Business).

Patry, William F. *Fair Use Privilege in Copyright Law.* 2d ed. Washington, D.C.: Bureau of National Affairs, 1995.

Shapiro, Michael S. *Museum Guide to Copyright and Trademark.* Washington, D.C.: American Association of Museums, 1999.

Stanford University, "Copyright and Fair Use," fairuse.stanford.edu. An excellent university-sponsored web page.

University of Texas, Office of the General Counsel, www.utsystem.edu/OGC/. A great site, has everything from UT's comprehensive copyright policy to a virtual copyright class.

ETHICS

American Association of Museums. *Code of Ethics for Museums.* Washington, D.C.: American Association of Museums, 2000.

American Library Association, www.ala.org/alaorg/oif/ethics.html.

Association of College and Research Libraries. "Standards for Ethical Conduct for Rare Book, Manuscript, and Special Collection Librarians, with Guidelines for Institutional Practice in Support of the Standards," *College and Research Libraries News* 54, no. 4 (1993): 207–215. Also available at *www.ala.org/acrl/guides/rarethic.html.*

Butler, Shelley Ruth. *Contested Representations: Revisiting into the Heart of Africa.* Amsterdam: Gordon and Breach, 1999.
Center for the Study of Ethics in the Professions, Illinois Institute of Technology, www.iit.edu/departments/csep/.
Cutter, Mary Ann G. *Ethics and the archival profession.* Denver: Society of Colorado Archivists, 1990.
International Council of Museums. *ICOM Statutes: Code of Professional Ethics.* International Council of Museums. Paris: ICOM, 1996.
Porciau, Lester J., ed. *Ethics and Electronic Information in the Twenty-First Century.* West Lafayette, Ind.: Purdue University Press, 1999.
Society of American Archivists. "Code of Ethics for Archivists with Commentary," www.archivists.org/governance/handbook/app_ethics.html.

INFORMATION TECHNOLOGY

Millstein, Julian S. *Doing Business on the Internet: Forms and Analysis.* New York: Law Journal Seminars-Press, 1997.
Nimmer, Raymond T. *Information Law.* Boston: Warren, Gorham and Lamont, 1996 (now published by WestGroup).
Smedinghoff, Thomas J., ed. *Online Law : The SPA's Legal Guide to Doing Business on the Internet.* Reading, Mass.: Addison-Wesley, 1996.
Smith, Mark. *Neal-Schuman Internet Policy Handbook for Libraries.* New York: Neal-Schuman, 1999.

LEGAL PERIODICAL RESOURCES

Legal Resource Index (LRI). Published by Gale Group, this is a comprehensive online index to the legal literature of the English-speaking world. It provides subject, author, case name, and statute name access to over nine hundred journals, with coverage back to 1980.

Index to Legal Periodicals and Books. Published by H. W. Wilson Company, a "Readers Guide" to legal periodical literature, with coverage beginning in 1908.

"University Law Review Project," www.lawreview.org/. Provides links to many law reviews and journals, a search engine for electronically available law reviews, and a free abstract e-mail service. These free services have been set up by FindLaw and the Coalition of Online Journals with help from Verity, the Australasian Legal Information Institute, the Legal Information Institute at Cornell, Stanford University, JURIST—The Law Professors' Network, and many law schools and journals throughout the world.

Note: Neither LRI nor the Index to Legal Periodicals and Books is freely available on the Internet, but many university libraries make one or both accessible to their institutional users via local networks (one site to try out LRI is http://147.31.63.12:81).

LEGAL WEB SITES

"FindLaw," www.findlaw.com. The leading web portal focused on law and government. FindLaw provides access to a comprehensive and fast-growing online library of legal resources for use by legal professionals, law students, consumers, and small businesses. FindLaw's mission is to make legal information on the Internet easy to find.

"Hieros Gamos," www.hg.org. A comprehensive law and government portal with resources for business, attorneys, consumers, and students. Sponsored by Lex Mundi, Ltd., the world's leading association of independent law firms.

LIBRARY-RELATED LEGAL ISSUES

Allred, Carol B. "Negligence Law for Libraries," *Law Library Journal* 77, no. 2 (1985): 195–222.

Bielefield, Arlene. *Library Patrons and the Law.* New York: Neal-Schuman, 1995.

Helper, Kim R. "*Kreimer v. Bureau of Police for Morristown*: The Sterilization of the Local Library," *Stetson Law Review* 23, no. 2 (1994): 521–50.

Kaplan, Ruth L., ed. *Disruptive Conduct in Libraries: Legal and Practical Responses to Sexual Harassment and Problem Patrons: Educational Seminar of the Social Law Library.* Boston: Proprietors of the Social Law Library, 1993.

Morin, Philip J., III. "Why Kreimer Can't Read: Striking the Proper Balance between Library Access and Problem Patrons in *Kreimer v. Bureau of Police*," *Rutgers Law Review* 46, no. 4 (1994): 1845–88.

Oberstaedt, Mark J. "Constitutional Law: First Amendment—Public Library May Constitutionally Deny Access to Patrons on the Basis of Personal Hygiene," *Seton Hall Law Review* 22, no. 4 (1992): 1567–74.

Rubin, Rhea Joyce. *Defusing the Angry Patron: A How-to-Do-It Manual for Librarians and Paraprofessionals.* New York: Neal-Schuman, 2000.

Semitsu, Junichi P. "Burning Cyberbooks in Public Libraries: Internet Filtering Software vs. the First Amendment," *Stanford Law Review* 52, no. 2 (2000): 509–45.

Tedjeske, Julia M. "Mainstream Loudoun and Access to Internet Resources in Public Libraries," *University of Pittsburgh Law Review* 60, no. 4 (1999): 1265–94.

Wilhelmus, David W. "Interaction of the Americans with Disabilities Act, the Family Medical Leave Act, and the Pregnancy Discrimination Act and their Impact on Libraries," *Law Library Journal* 88, no. 2 (1996): 231–46.

LICENSING

Bell, Paul B. and Jay Simon, eds. *Law and Business of Licensing: Licensing in the 1990s.* Deerfield, Ill.: Clark Boardman Callaghan, 1990–.

Kohn, Al. *Kohn on Music Licensing.* 2d ed. Englewood Cliffs, N.J.: Aspen Law and Business, 1996.

Stanford University, Office of Technology Licensing, otl.stanford.edu.

MUSEUMS

American Association of Museums, www.aam-us.org. Very complete site, including papers on legal topics such as "The Double-Edged Sword: Museums and the Fair Use Doctrine" and "Museums and the Internet: Tax and Other Legal Issues."

Legal Problems of Museum Administration: ALI-ABA Course of Study Materials. Philadelphia: American Law Institute-American Bar Association (ALI-ABA) Committee on Continuing Professional Education, 1973–. Published annually to accompany the ALI-ABA course. Most recent is the 29th ed., which accompanied the conference held in March 2001.

Malaro, Marie C. *A Legal Primer on Managing Museum Collections.* Washington, D.C.: Smithsonian Institution Press, 1998.

Malaro, Marie C. *Museum Governance: Mission, Ethics, Policy.* Washington: Smithsonian Institution Press, 1994.

Phelan, Marilyn E. *Museum Law: A Guide for Officers, Directors, and Counsel.* Evanston, Ill.: Kalos Kapp, 1994.

CHAPTER 17

Designing, Drafting, and Implementing New Policies

Claire Weber

Designing, drafting and implementing any new policy is a method of problem solving. The purpose of designing, drafting and implementing a policy change is to develop an appropriate, legally sound and workable solution to a real problem.

This chapter focuses on style, not substance. Good drafting is preoccupied with nuts and bolts matters of form and minutiae. But attention to form almost always highlights substantive and policy considerations. Paying close attention to form has the beneficial side effect of clarifying and often improving actual policy decisions. This author's particular interest and experience is in writing—drafting—legislation and policy, and this chapter focuses primarily on that topic.

Considerations in Designing a Policy

Before drafting a policy, it is important to consider the problem through a series of initial steps.

First, *identify the problem* to be solved, and note examples of the problem. This may appear simplistic, but a clear description of the problem, with examples, is absolutely essential throughout the process of developing a workable new policy. Especially when there is a problem that requires immediate attention, it is easy to skip over this stage and formulate a solution without precisely articulating the problem. This often leads to an inadequate solution that must be fixed later. If the drafter is not personally involved in the situation that needs to be addressed, he or she should discuss the problem with the persons who requested the solution. If possible, write down a couple of scenarios that illustrate the problem and that the new policy is expected to solve. These can be used later to "walk through" the policy draft to ensure that the policy will achieve its goal.

Consider whether this problem can be solved without changing policy. Is there an existing policy that could apply to this situation? Policies that were created to meet past needs of an organization may also fit new problems and considerations, even unanticipated ones. Read over the existing policies to ensure nothing already on the books covers the situation. This will not take much time and could save a great deal of drafting time and unnecessary effort.

Check for already-written policy in other organizations. Make use of networks with colleagues in similar organizations. Another group has almost certainly faced the same situation, and may have written something that can be adapted. However, it is important to recognize that a policy from another organization can almost never be adopted without modification—there is no "one size fits all" in policy drafting. It is also helpful to talk to the person in the other organization who implemented the policy that will be adapted and to find out how it actually works. Ask the person who works with the policy whether he or she would make any changes to it—this may elicit great suggestions that can shortcut some work and result in a better final policy.

Drafting a Policy

Some general approaches and considerations apply when preparing the initial draft of the policy. These are described below.

Design and outline the policy. If an existing policy cannot be used and there is no appropriate policy from another organization, a new policy will have to be written. The first step in drafting any new policy, as previously noted, is to specify the problem that the policy must address. Next, it must be decided, step by step, precisely what the new policy will be and how it will work. Make an outline or flowchart of the new policy.

Actual drafting is a job for one person. Developing a new policy and deciding what procedures are appropriate clearly benefits from the contributions of many people—customers, supervisors, line staff, attorneys and others. The most thorough policy drafts are those that have been reviewed by a number of people. But drafting of a policy is best done by a single individual, with the draft policy subject to review and suggestions from others. Cogent, coherent drafting cannot be done by committees or small groups. The primary drafter will be responsible for taking all suggestions and either incorporating them into the draft or explaining why they are not included. The person who will do this best is a person who thoroughly understands both the problem and the setting in which its solution will be implemented. This is usually a person directly involved in the organization or institution and not an outside person, even an outside attorney. (Of course, a new policy that is complicated or has potential legal implications should be reviewed by an attorney before it is finally adopted, and the attorney's recommendations should be incorporated into the final draft.)

Follow appropriate techniques to facilitate drafting by one person. It may be difficult for a drafter to announce to policy makers, supervisors and others that he or she is the only person who will be involved in actually writing a new policy. When a drafter is dealing with a group that expects to actually write the words of a policy, there are a couple of techniques that can be followed that allow their participation and keep the process practical, still allowing the drafter to control the situation. First is the "single-document" approach to negotiation. This is when a person creates a rough draft "just to begin discussion." This draft is circulated to everyone involved, or perhaps discussed at a meeting. Everyone who reviews the draft will mark it up, criticize it and make suggestions for changes. The drafter will need to incorporate some of the recommended changes or point out why they are not appropriate. However, the basic framework of the original draft and the major issues for discussion have all been established by the drafter. In most cases, all subsequent discussion and refinements will continue to conform to that draft.

The second technique, which complements the single-drafter and single-document approach, is the use of extensive in-text annotation. During the process of drafting, the drafter encounters numerous major and minor questions that must be decided either by the drafter or by someone else. It is helpful to call attention to the question, or to the drafter's decision, by inserting a comment in the appropriate spot in the text. Using bold type highlights the comment. For example, a drafter could insert the following comment in the middle of the text of an appeal procedure: "The twenty-one-day appeal deadline was arbitrarily selected. You may wish a shorter or longer period of time." An alternative example clearly leaves the decision up to the reviewer: "Current appeal procedures provide either twenty-one days or fourteen days for filing similar appeals. This policy will need to adopt one of these periods." In-text comments can also address substantive matters. Regardless of the type of comments that are required, in-text annotation is particularly helpful when several people will be reviewing a policy draft.

Avoid having pride of authorship. It is helpful to the drafter's continuing sanity if she or he makes a conscious effort to have no personal investment in the authorship of a draft, especially one that will be extensively reviewed. However, the single-text approach leads naturally to a great deal of criticism of the initial draft. When the issue is important or controversial, the criticism may be sharp and even personal. A thick skin and a short memory for personal criticism are useful attributes for anyone who drafts policy for an organization.

Follow the well-established sequence of sections in a new policy. The customary sequence is shown in figure 17.1. This sequence is almost univer-

Figure 17.1. Usual Sequence of Sections of a New Policy

1. Title
2. Statement of purpose, if any
3. Definitions
4. Persons affected—to whom the policy applies
5. Most significant general rules
6. Secondary provisions
7. Significant exceptions
8. Sanctions or other consequences for violating the penalty
9. Any temporary provisions, including effective date and expiration date

Source: Reed Dickerson, *The Fundamentals of Legal Drafting* 2d ed. (Boston: Little, Brown, 1986)

sally followed by legislative drafters. The author has never encountered a drafting situation that required any other sequence of sections.

Definitions

Among all the components of drafting, definitions require special attention because they are both crucial and difficult. It is more difficult to define a term clearly and accurately than it is to use the term properly in a policy. The following considerations are useful when deciding what terms to define and how to define them.

Know when to define a term. The usual reason to define a term is to clearly specify what is included in the scope of a policy and what is not. It is also helpful to define a word, term or acronym if it will make text sentences more direct and easier to understand. For example, an entity with a particularly wordy name, such as "The Frostbite Falls City/Rocky Squirrel County Board of Public Libraries and Information Access," should be defined as "the board" to prevent having to use this wordy phrase throughout the text of a policy.

Remember that definitions are only descriptions, not policy. It is easy to write a definition that goes too far. For example, "Patron means a nonemployee who visits the library for a lawful purpose *and is either at least ten years of age or accompanied by an adult and who is not under the influence of alcohol or any controlled substance and whose behavior does not constitute a nuisance to other patrons.*" All the emphasized language should be moved from the definition section to the sections of the policy that establish age limits and unacceptable patron behavior. Those sections will then state something like: "No patron may:

1. Be under the age of . . . unless . . .
2. Be under the influence of . . .
3. Act in a way that constitutes . . .

The words "means" and "includes" are terms of art in legislative drafting. In a definition, "means" shows that the definition is complete and enumerates everything included in that definition. In contrast, "includes" in a definition shows that, although the included items are part of the defined term, there may also be other items that are included in the definition.

For example, "'Disturbance' means any act by an individual that is likely to disturb a patron's use or enjoyment of the library. The term includes swearing, repeated loud talking, playing music outside the designated library music areas and eating or drinking." Under this definition, an act cannot be a "disturbance" unless it is likely to disturb a patron—the "means" portion of the definition. An act that constitutes a disturbance may be one of the specific acts listed in the "includes" portion, but could also be one of many other similarly disturbing acts that are not enumerated in the definition.

Definitions can also point out items that are not covered. An example of this type of definition is: "Patron does not mean. . . " or "The term does not include. . . ."

Define terms of art that are commonly known in a specialized profession or other use, but may not be known to the general public.

Don't define the obvious. There is no need, for example, to define the term "form" (as a noun) as "a paper with blanks to be filled in by an applicant." The term "form" can stand on its own.

In wording definitions, avoid wordy introductions, such as: "'Patron' is deemed to mean . . . " or "The word 'patron' shall mean . . . " or "The term shall not be construed to include. . . ."

Use commonly understood terms in definition. If at all possible, definition language should not include jargon or specialized terms of art whose meaning is limited to a select group, especially when the policy affects persons outside that group. However, if a term of art must be used to convey a precise meaning, then use it.

Avoid circular definitions. Generally, don't use a word in its own definition—the result is circular. An example of this sort of definition is: "House means a *house,* building or other structure that is used for residential purposes." This definition works better with the italicized word deleted.

List definitions alphabetically when there are several.

Use context references carefully. Some definitions define a term and then add the phrase "unless otherwise clearly indicated by the context." This may be more confusing than helpful. If the context indicates otherwise, perhaps a different term is called for.

Definitions should make sense. This may seem obvious, but it is surprising how often a definition is tweaked and amended over time so that it becomes either incomprehensible or unrelated to the term purportedly being defined. With a few rare exceptions, a definition should make logical, intuitive sense to any literate person who reads it.

Use each defined term. This sounds elementary, but the drafter should check to see that every defined term is used. After review and redrafting, sometimes a term that has been painstakingly defined is not used.

General Drafting Rules

There are several generally accepted drafting conventions that assist the drafter in writing clearer and more thorough policies. Some of these are grammar rules and some are drafting customs. The more important of these rules follow.

Write in the singular and avoid use of the plural if at all possible. This may require some careful drafting to be gender-inclusive and avoid commonly accepted incorrect grammar, but it is still preferable. Use of the plural, except when unavoidable, can result in ambiguous language. An example of such ambiguity is: "Applicants for library cards shall complete application forms stating their name and address and shall pay the required application fees." This sentence is ungrammatical and alternates between singular and plural. It also makes the underlying policy unclear—is there one application form and one fee or are there more than one? Using the singular in drafting avoids such imprecision.

For grammar challenges resulting from use of the singular, avoid the ungrammatical use of "their" as a pronoun with a singular noun, as in this example: "Each applicant shall state their name and address."

Use gender-inclusive language. Use "his or her" when appropriate. Drafters are probably already familiar with the many straightforward words that are substitutes for non-gender-inclusive words, for example, "worker" for "workman," and "chair" for "chairman."

Divide the policy into numbered sections and subsections. A policy is easier to draft, easier to read, easier to amend and appears more logical if it is divided into numbered (or lettered) sections, subsections, paragraphs, subparagraphs and, if necessary, subdivisions. Each subpart may be indented beyond the next highest division. A useful system to divide a policy into subparts is the following:

Structural Divisions of a Policy

Chapter (not always necessary): roman numerals	Chapt. I.
Section: arabic numerals	Sect. 1.
Subsection: capital letters	Subsect. A.
Paragraph: arabic numerals in parentheses	Par. (1)
Subparagraph: small letters in parentheses	Subpar. (a)
Subdivision: small roman numerals in parentheses	Subd. (i)

Policy Structure Example

1. Library hours
   A. Main reading room
      (1) Weekdays
      (2) Weekends
   B. Rare book room and stacks
      (1) Weekdays
         (a) Summer
         (b) Winter
            (i) Officially declared snow days
            (ii) Nonsnow days
      (2) Weekends
2. Patrons
   A. Minors
   B. Nonminors

Include title and subtitle phrases when appropriate. A phrase at the beginning of each section or subsection makes a policy more cogent and is particularly useful in long, detailed policies. A title is a word or phrase, similar to those in the preceding structure example. The use or nonuse of titles should be consistent within each policy—if one subsection has a subtitle, all the rest of the subsections should have subtitles.

Allow for later additions. Policy sections should be created using only odd numbers, to allow space for new material to be added to the policy in logical sequence without changing existing section numbers that may have become familiar to policy users. This is particularly important for complicated policies. (There is no need to use only odd numbers for subsections, paragraphs or other smaller divisions.) This also reduces the need to renumber an existing part of a policy when it is being amended. Over time, people become familiar with a particular section or subsection number, for example, "501(c)(3) organizations" under the federal tax code is familiar terminology to many and it is better not to change such familiar references.

Use consistent terminology, the same word or term to convey the same meaning, throughout the policy. It is easy to start drafting provisions for "the board" and end up drafting for "the library board" or even "the commission."

Consistency also requires that words in a series always be in the same order throughout the policy. If the policy refers to "cats and rats and elephants," it should not shift to "rats and cats and elephants" in the middle.

Time and Likelihood Descriptions

Periods of time, i.e., with starting and ending dates and times, should be precisely stated. "January to March" or "January through March" are not always consistently interpreted. It is preferable to write "beginning Jan. 1 and ending Feb. 29."

Elapsed time should be precisely stated. A phrase such as "thirty days after [event] . . ." is not precise. Substitute "no later than the thirtieth day after [event]. . . ." It may also be appropriate to specify whether the calculation counts business days or calendar days. (It usually does not matter whether the policy counts business or calendar days, as long as it specifies one or the other.)

Effective dates and days should be included where applicable. Some policies become effective after a lapse of time, so elapsed time rules should be followed. A complicated policy or one that requires preparing forms or modifying facilities may need a delayed effective date. It is best to choose the first of a month, for convenience of administration., using the wording, for example, "This provision takes effect on June 1, 2000." In some circumstances, the policy may be effective only for persons who take certain actions, which should be specified, as for example, "This policy first applies to persons who apply for new library cards on June 1, 2000."

Describe ages precisely. Some phrases may not be clear, for example, "between the ages of seventeen and twenty-five." A better example is, "at least seventeen years old but not older than twenty-five," or "older than sixteen years and less than twenty-six," or "has reached his or her seventeenth birthday but not his or her twenty-sixth birthday. . . ."

Avoid the undistributed middle, designated as such by Reed Dickerson. An example of this is the clause that refers, for example, to persons "divided into two classes: persons born before January 1, 1974, and persons born after January 1, 1974." This wording fails to address the person born on January 1, 1974.

"When," "whenever" and "if" can be useful phrases if used properly. The likelihood that a contemplated event will actually occur can be precisely referenced in a policy by correctly using one of the these three words. Choose one based on the likelihood that the given event will actually come to pass.

Use the word "when" for an event that is certain to happen, as in "When the museum closes for the evening. . . ."

Use the word "whenever" for an event that may occur infrequently, as in "Whenever an employee requires assistance from security personnel. . . ."

Use the word "If" for an event that may never actually happen, as in "If the county library appropriation exceeds the aggregate total of all budgeted library needs. . . ."

Wording and Grammar

The following specific wording and grammar topics focus on very narrow areas of concern, but they are important in crafting clear, well-written policies.

Avoid "and/or," as these words are contradictory in meaning. Substitute " . . . or . . . or both." Instead of "cat and/or dog," for example, write "cat or dog, or both."

"Whether or not" is redundant. The word "whether" conveys the meaning of the alternative and is less wordy, as in the phrase "the board shall determine whether to suspend the patron's library privileges."

Avoid using "etc." in drafting policies. It is not at all clear what the term adds to a sentence's meaning and it often makes a sentence less clear. In a definition, use "includes" and omit "etc."

Other words and phrases to avoid. Although legislation and legal documents have traditionally used words and phrases that are not commonly used elsewhere, policy should be written with straightforward, contemporary English. Following is a list of words and phrases that have no place in policy or legislation. The list also suggests alternatives, where appropriate. Some of these words are so unnecessary that no substitute is suggested.

accorded = given
aforementioned
deem = consider
during such time as = while
effectuate = carry out
endeavor (verb) = try
has the duty to = shall
have knowledge of = know
herein
hereunto
in excess of = more than
in lieu of = instead of, substitute for, change to
is authorized to = may
is empowered to = may
is entitled to = may
is required to = shall
prior to = before
pursuant to = under
said (as an article) = the, those
same (as a pronoun) = it, he, her
shall be construed to mean = means
subsequent to = after
whatsoever

"Shall" vs. "may": "shall" is mandatory and "may" is permissive. Use "shall" instead of "must" when drafting mandatory language. In the negative mandatory, the author also prefers "shall," for example: "No person shall permit . . . " or "A person shall not permit. . . ." (However, some accomplished drafters and academics contend that negative mandates are better conveyed using "may"; for example: "No person may permit. . . .") Although there is some disagreement about the use of "shall" and "may" in negative mandates, their use for positive requirements and authorizations is unquestioned. Written policy should always use "shall" for required actions and "may" for actions that are permitted but not required.

The word "should" is usually not appropriate in written policy. It conveys a meaning of a recommendation but not a requirement. Writing policy is essentially writing a statement of what can and cannot be done, not what should be done.

Avoid passive voice. Draft in the active voice whenever possible. This prods the drafter to specify who is responsible for an action. For example, rather than "Requests for waivers shall be filed with the office of, . . ." it is better to say, "Any person who seeks a waiver shall file a request with the office of. . . ." There are rare occasions when the passive voice is better, but most circumstances work best with a direct subject-verb-object sentence structure. Using the active voice also may help the drafter avoid some strings of prepositional phrases, which can be confusing and unclear.

Ambiguous modifiers can create unclear policies. This problem is often solved by setting up the item as a list instead of in a sentence. Take the following example: "A patron must be accompanied by a librarian when accessing city records, historic documents or first editions in the rare book area." It is not clear whether this restriction applies to historic documents that are not in the rare book area. Clearer wording would be:

"A patron must be accompanied by a librarian when accessing any of the following in the rare book area:

1. City records
2. Historic documents
3. First editions"

Another example is the phrase "Representatives of charitable and educational institutions. . . ." It is not clear whether the institutions have to be both charitable and educational or if only one characteristic is sufficient. A better example is: "Representatives of an institution that is either charitable or educational, or both. . . ." (This is also an example where drafting in the singular helps remove some ambiguity.)

Use simple sentences, if possible. Use familiar words and phrases. If jargon must be used, define it in the definitions section. At the same time, no drafter can produce a simple rule to express a complex idea. An attempt to handle a complex idea with a simple, uncomplicated sentence will not solve the problem and will not be good policy.

Special Situations in Drafting

Intent statements are encouraging but not commanding. Generally, intent or purpose statements are not necessary, as they rarely add anything and may actually be in conflict with some of the policy language.

Incorporation by reference is when a policy refers to a standard established by an outside entity, and the policy therefore specifies the precise version of the standard that is being incorporated and whether subsequent changes to that standard will also be incorporated. The following are examples: "the education requirements of the American Library Association in effect on January 1, 2000" and "the education requirements of the American Library Association in effect on, . . . including any changes to those requirements that may be adopted from time to time."

Creating boards, committees or other groups is sometimes required. If the policy requires creating a board or committee, consider specifying all of the following:

1. The number of members, usually an odd number.
2. What individual or entity appoints or selects the members and by what time or date.
3. The length of terms for the members.
4. How vacancies are filled, usually in the same manner as the original selection.
5. Whether alternates can be appointed to serve for members who are not present and, if so, who selects the alternates. It is helpful to require the person who selects an alternate to notify the board of his or her selection. The member can also be required to notify the board when he or she changes the designated alternate. (If alternates are permitted, some meetings may be composed entirely of alternates. If alternates are not permitted, quorum problems may result.)
6. Whether members can be removed for failure to attend meetings or other causes and, if so, how this is done.
7. If members serve set terms, initial terms may be set at different lengths to provide for staggered expiration of terms.
8. If replacement members are not selected in a timely manner or do not agree to serve, state that current members shall continue to serve until successors are selected and qualified to serve.
9. Establish an achievable quorum for meetings.
10. Include sections providing for the duties and powers of the board. Duties are mandatory—what the board "shall" do. Powers are permissive—what the board "may" do.
11. Try to keep the number of board members relatively low—less than thirteen or fifteen members. If political or protocol reasons require a much larger group, consider authorizing (or mandating) creation of

an executive committee to handle day-to-day business and "screen" agenda items for the full board. If an executive committee is created, its membership must be precisely specified. One possible composition of an executive committee would be the board officers and a few additional board members selected by the officers or the board. The executive committee's scope of authority should also be specified. Committee duties customarily include routine ministerial tasks. The committee may also review substantive reports and formulate recommendations for action, which can be forwarded to the full board for its discussion and, in most cases, approval.

Keep policies in loose-leaf binders. Printing policies on loose pages and keeping them in loose-leaf binders makes it easier to amend a portion of a policy and not have to reprint entire portions that are unchanged. It is useful to print a date in the bottom corner of each page to identify the correct version of each page.

Identify different drafts. For internal discussion and review purposes, it is helpful to have a quick way to identify each new draft. It is sufficient to number or date the draft on the first page. This is particularly helpful when several drafts are circulated to various reviewers, when it helps avoid confusing discussions in which each person is referring to a different draft version.

Drafter's Checklist for Designing and Drafting a New Policy

The following checklist is a useful sequence to follow when drafting a new policy, particularly a complicated or controversial policy. It is adapted from Reed Dickerson's *The Fundamentals of Legal Drafting* (1986).

1. Write down the problem to be solved—a couple of examples will help later when reviewing the draft policy.
2. Determine whether the problem can be solved under existing policies.
3. Check with other entities to see if they have a policy you can adapt to your situation.
4. If a new policy must be created, decide precisely what the new policy will be and how it will work, step by step. Create an outline or flowchart of the new policy.

5. Draft the policy according to your outline or flowchart.
6. Keep a side list of questions that crop up as you go along and handle them later. Do not try to handle these as you are drafting.
7. Set the draft aside.
8. Reread the draft horizontally and vertically for logic and consistency. Horizontal checks require review of each definition and each use of a defined term. Vertical checks require reading the draft in sequence to ensure it is complete and logical. Add any questions to the side list.
9. Resolve the questions on the side list.
10. "Walk through" the draft with actual situations and scenarios, including the problems noted in step 1. Do any scenarios produce unintended consequences?
11. Have other people proofread and review the draft and make suggestions. Reviewers should include persons who will have to implement, enforce or explain the new policy. The draft may need to be reviewed by an attorney, depending on the subject matter.
12. Redraft as needed.

Considerations in Implementing a New Policy

Formally inform affected people as soon as the policy is adopted. If the policy has been well designed and well drafted, the requirements of implementation should be clear. Complicated policies should have a delayed effective date to allow time for persons who implement the policies to be trained and become familiar with the policies. Printed information sheets or bullet sheets, with the name of the individual or office responsible for a particular action, may help forestall confusion about the new policy.

Unintended consequences of the policy may require amending or tweaking the policy to correct the problem. Even policies that have been thoroughly reviewed and carefully considered may end up not working as they were expected to. When unintended consequences result from a new policy, it is time to "tweak" the policy by drafting an amendment to fix the problem. If the original policy is well organized and divided into sections and subsections, the amendment may be only a few lines of text addressing a particular paragraph or subparagraph. Most unintended consequences can be readily eliminated with one drafting fix.

Legislative Drafting Sources and References

GENERAL SOURCES

This chapter draws on many direct and indirect sources. State legislative sources include the invaluable instruction and mentoring of colleagues in various legislative arenas. State legislative drafting manuals were helpful, particularly those of Louisiana and Wisconsin. Primary academic sources are the works of Reed Dickerson and Elmer A. Driedger, which are highly recommended to anyone interested in a thorough and detailed examination of the theory and practice of legislative drafting. The chapter also draws on personal observations during twenty years of legislative drafting. All errors in this chapter are solely the responsibility of the author, who is still learning about legislative drafting.

SUGGESTED READINGS

The following sources focus on drafting legislation, so they all include distinctly legislative-oriented sections about constitutional provisions, delegation of authority, conference committees, appropriations requirements and other matters that are not relevant outside of the legislative arena. The portions of the following sources that are most useful for nonlegislative drafters are those addressing topics such as organization of a draft, the drafting process, grammar and drafting style. (The earlier works of Dickerson and Driedger generally precede modern consideration of gender-neutral language, and their comments on language gender are therefore no longer relevant to contemporary drafters. This deficiency is overwhelmingly outweighed by the scholarly precision and care with which both authors address all other issues related to proper legislative drafting.)

Dickerson, Reed. *The Fundamentals of Legal Drafting.* 2d ed. Boston: Little, Brown, 1986. Focuses on legal drafting in general, but very helpful in legislative and policy drafting as well.

———. *Legislative Drafting.* Westport: Greenwood, 1977. Reprint of the classic 1954 edition.

Driedger, Elmer A. *The Composition of Legislation, Legislative Forms and Precedents.* Ottawa: Department of Justice of Canada, 1976.

——. *A Manual of Instructions for Legislative and Legal Writing.* Ottawa: Department of Justice of Canada, 1982. May be difficult to find, but it is worth the effort, because Driedger is absolutely rigorous and precise. His drafting instruction is invaluable.

Mehlman, Maxwell J., and Edward G. Grossman. *Yale Legislative Services Handbook of Legislative Drafting.* New Haven: Yale Legislative Services, 1977. Covers basic legislative drafting techniques for nonprofessionals. Addresses grammar and sentence structure as well as bill construction.

Office of the Revisor of Statutes, State of Maine. *Maine Legislative Drafting Manual* (May 2000), http://janus.state.me.us/legis/ros/manual/contents.htm. The basic manual for drafters of legislation for the state of Maine. Particularly helpful for nonlegislative drafters are the following chapters in part III: Chapter 1, Style; Chapter 2, Word Choice and Usage; and Chapter 4, Punctuation.

CHAPTER 18

Agents of Change

PLANNING, COMMUNICATION, AND IMPLEMENTATION STRATEGIES

Thomas D. Walker

Institutions are bureaucratic by nature and not necessarily open to change. This chapter will help you function as a change agent within your organization by providing you with strategies for heightening awareness of legal and ethical issues among administrators and other colleagues.

In Chicago, almost fifteen years ago, I worked for a large national organization. Our information services unit had a "system" for the photocopy machine. For staff of our unit, there would of course be no per-page fee for photocopies. For higher-level executives, there were also no such charges. For employees of other units, the fee was twenty-five cents per page, which was high for the mid-1980s. For nonemployees—and there was a significant number who used our collection and had no alternatives to using our machine—the fee was fifty cents per page. It was a captive clientele paying an exhorbitant amount. One can construct a certain logic to this: for work-related use, the cost was included in the unit's overhead expenses; for other uses, funds had to be collected from the users. The money went not into a supplies and equipment (S&E) account, but rather into a little gray metal box in the director's office. This was the source for our more than monthly staff birthday parties and almost weekly pizza deliveries.

What was wrong with this scenario? What could have been done? I do not think any laws were broken, but it seemed to me to be an unusual practice. It was well entrenched in the unit; the employees and director alike considered it to be a normal daily practice. It is sometimes situations like this that cause people the most discomfort. One wants to "be a player," yet does not want to encourage unethical behavior. There are ways to handle such situations.

Goals and Coalitions

Every institution has a mission, whether or not it is formally expressed. Some purposes and goals are obvious even to people who have very little contact with an institution. An ethical approach to an organization's business may not be a formal part of a mission statement. Indeed, the presence of a clause about the need to be ethical might make one think that one would not otherwise run the business in an ethical way. The same applies to a statement about adhering to the law; seldom would it be necessary to state that a museum, library, or archive will carry out its activities within the parameters of the law. Both ethical and legal behavior, in their most general senses, are usually assumed. Ethical statements may become more visible in statements about institutional goals, for instance in wording about privacy or accountability. However, a distinction is sometimes made between publicly espoused goals and operative goals (Quinn 1996, 91–92). A university, for instance, may state that instruction comes first, when in practice it organizes its reward system around expectations for grant accumulation, research, and committee service.

In such an example, there is an obvious coalition concerned with the image and prestige of the university that is willing to overlook or deemphasize publicly espoused goals. Operative goals are usually congruent with the interests of the dominant coalition (Quinn 1996, 91–92). Sometimes the weakest constituency is that associated with the publicly espoused goals. In this example, it is the students who are associated with the espoused goals, and they may be the constituency that looses in the power struggle. Organizational coalitions can be a barrier to change. It is useful to be aware of the various coalitions before attempting to institute changes, whether at the macro or micro level.

Corporate Culture and Change

Corporate culture is the "collective beliefs that people within the organization have about their ability to compete in the marketplace—and how they act on those belief systems" (Want 1995, 18). Corporate culture cannot be changed quickly; it takes time to institutionalize organizational attitudes and behaviors. Corporate culture is palpable and some organizations build on their cultures to develop specific public perceptions. Having a knowledge of an organization's culture can be extremely useful when one attempts to institute change.

The literature about corporate change is large, but much of it does not address ethical change. One consultant defines "enterprise engineering as "an integrated set of disciplines for building or changing an enterprise, its process, and systems. It integrates the most powerful change methods and makes them succeed. The goal is a human-technological partnership of maximum efficiency in which learning takes place at every level." (Martin 1995, 58). This sounds reasonable, but does not specifically address instituting information policy changes.

It is useful to be aware that there are various change forces within organizations. One author suggests three first-order change forces: social, political, and technological (Want 1995, 4). For those in documentary organizations, such as information centers and museums, all three forces manifest themselves in ways that have legal and ethical implications.

Methods for bringing change are many:

- On the broad scale, an institution's mission may be the ideal locus for addressing ethical considerations in general.
- Changes to formal statements of policies and procedures are concrete actions and may have a more immediate effect on daily activities.
- Improving formal communication channels may also benefit attempts to change by allowing the change process to be more public and providing a means of announcing changes.
- Personnel practices, including training and continuing education, can be useful ways of implementing ethical changes.

- Lastly, a reward/punishment system may encourage and enforce ethical behavior within an organization.

Overcoming Resistance

When dealing with corporate culture, coalitions, and individuals, you are acting and reacting with people. You may have multiple and varied academic degrees and superlative subject knowledge, but you may spend more of your time exercising your interpersonal skills than your academic expertise.

Depending on your official role in an organization, there are several options available to you: you can demonstrate by example, suggest, persuade, mandate, or coerce. Coercion is perhaps used more often by organized crime or totalitarian regimes and is probably not easily adapted to libraries, museums, and archives.

In the situation mentioned above involving the photocopy money being used for pizza, I was not in a position to coerce anyone to do anything. Subordinates may find it most useful to show by example, suggest, or persuade superiors or colleagues that a change should be implemented. Showing by example is an approach that demonstrates ethical behavior in sometimes visible, sometimes invisible ways. If I do not use my phone for personal calls, I may be the only one who knows about my ethical behavior. But if an employee, especially a manager, is known for not stretching the rules for, for instance, expense reports, a larger group will be aware of the ethical activity. Showing by example may be silent and should represent the normal course of events in an organization, but it can be a strong approach to instituting changes in behavior.

Newcomers or entry-level employees may be the very ones who notice ethical inconsistencies. They are not yet part of the existing coalitions. Because they may not be in a position to demonstrate by example in an obvious way, it may be necessary for them to suggest or persuade. Appeal to the logic of the people or groups in question. It may be useful to demonstrate that unethical practices affect staff morale; it may be useful to point out potential penalties that exist for illegal practices. Realize, however, that a subordinate or newcomer is not in the most favored position to influence a dominant corporate coalition.

If you are in a managerial position, it is easier to effect change: mandate it. Issue a departmental memo regarding a new institutional practice that does not regard e-mail as private. Affirm at a staff meeting that conversations with patrons are to be considered strictly confidential. A manager is in an excellent position to create an atmosphere that provides for staff "buy in." Assign or encourage the assembly of a short-term committee to consider the legal and ethical issues surrounding a situation. If several individuals spend the time to convince themselves of the desirablilty of change, it will be more easily accepted by a larger group of people than a command from above may be.

Regardless of your role, you can have a positive impact on policies and practices by taking a visible and active role in decision making. In so doing you will likely fill the void left by people who are too busy or apathetic. Feeling strongly about an ethical issue can be a great motivation; seeing changes result from your actions can be extremely gratifying.

Tolerating Ambiguity

Should German archives release personal data collected during the Cold War by East German security informants who provided voluminous data on their coworkers, friends, and even spouses? On the one hand, this is extremely interesting data that illustrate the lengths to which the secret service went to gather information. On the other hand, releasing the data violates individuals' privacy. Should the files be destroyed? Should they be sealed for fifty years? It is a complex and ambiguous situation.

When we learn more about a subject or situation, we naturally form questions about it. The more we learn, the more we realize that the situation is not to be resolved in either of only two ways. Seldom does curiosity and learning lead to black-and-white distinctions. Instead, curiosity leads to *sfumato.*

Sfumato is an Italian term linked by Michael Gelb to Leonardo da Vinci in his 1998 book, *How to Think Like Leonardo da Vinci.* The term means, literally, going up in smoke. But in practice it is used by art critics to describe Renaissance painters' use of paints to depict various levels of color and hue, in order to show different levels of distance. It refers to the use of a spectrum of colors, or for a range of hues for one color. The term's adoption during the Renaissance suggests that painting during this time became more refined. It used fewer broad expanses of color than can be seen in medieval paintings, for example.

The world is filled with what seem to be opposites. Few things in life break down into black versus white, right versus wrong. The richness of life depends on shades of meaning. Is it always wrong to break the law? Ask highway drivers who edge above the speed limits. Ask students who photocopy entire books.

How does change take place in your institution? How do its employees deal with change? How do they handle ambiguous situations? Interestingly, it can be the most ambiguous situations that cause change in an organization. If there is doubt about the legality or ethical advisability of a practice, it can be removed or lessened by reducing the level of ambiguity or uncertainty. Some of the most creative geniuses in the world had a high tolerance for uncertainty. The more they explored and learned, the more complicated—not less complicated—their worlds became. It seems almost counterintuitive: by exposing ourselves to more knowledge, we don't simplify things, we complicate them! In other words, we should embrace ambiguity. People in many fields thrive with ambiguity. The more we deal with paradox, the better we become at decision making.

Returning to Leonardo: most people are familiar with the *Mona Lisa.* For some people, the woman represented in the painting is the supreme expression of paradox. In his book, Gelb mentions that Freud considered Mona Lisa to be the most perfect representation of the contrasts dominating the love lives of women. Her smile lies on the cusp of good and evil, compassion and cruelty, seduction and innocence, the fleeting and the eternal. She is the Western equivalent of the Chinese symbol of yin and yang (Gelb 1998, 178).

I would like to suggest an exercise adapted from one suggested by Gelb. Keeping Mona Lisa in mind, think about the one person or group of people at your institution who is the most serious barrier to ethical improvements. It could be an unethical coworker or boss; it could be a stodgy coalition of luddites; or it could be an eager, devil-may-care group of creative thinkers who routinely like to stretch boundaries. Do you feel unsure about how to deal with them? Now, try to smile like Mona Lisa. Get under her skin. Adopt her serenity. What do you feel now? If you are like her, you have a secret confidence that you can accomplish anything.

My overall advice: don't merely tolerate ambiguity and change: embrace them. They're here to stay!

References

Gelb, Michael. 1998. *How to Think Like Leonardo da Vinci.* New York: Delacorte.

Martin, James. 1995. *The Great Transition: Using the Seven Disciplines of Enterprise Engineering to Align People, Technology, and Strategy.* New York: Amacom.

Quinn, Robert E. 1996. *Deep Change: Discovering the Leader Within.* San Francisco: Jossy-Bass.

Want, Jerome H. 1995. *Managing Radical Change: Beyond Survival in the New Business Age.* New York: Wiley.

Appendix: Discussion Problems

DISCUSSION PROBLEM 1

You are an adjunct instructor at a local college and have developed and taught an online course in your specialty. You used an existing syllabus as your guide to conform to the requirements of the course and its fit in the curriculum. You created lecture notes, examples, and exercises and assembled supplemental readings and compiled a guide to relevant web sources. You organized the materials within the framework of existing courseware the college had obtained under license with a software company.

The course was a stunning success and you decide to approach another, more prestigious institution, hoping to teach the course you worked so hard to develop. Your original college gets wind of this and denied you access to the course site and materials and justified their decision by stating that it was a "work for hire." You maintain that the course is your own intellectual property and that you can take it anywhere you want and do anything you want with it.

Questions:

1. Why does this situation seem different from one that occurs in the private sector in which an employee bakes bread or writes computer programs?
2. How can the above situation be resolved?
3. How could it have been avoided?

DISCUSSION PROBLEM 2

Your boss, Margot, has suggested expanding an existing patron service: information packets on the twenty-five most frequently asked questions or research topics received by your staff. Samples of suggested topics are: "Are Birds Dinosaurs?," "Buying and selling a House," "How to Choose a College," and "Mummies." Each packet will be a collection, produced in-house, of photocopied articles from journals, newspapers, books, encyclopedias, and web sites. Each will be produced in sets of about fifty in anticipation of patron demand.

You know this is an illegal practice that violates the letter and spirit of intellectual property laws. You have brought this up to Margot and other senior staff, but always receive the same answer: we've done this on a smaller scale for years and everyone loves it. The patron benefits from the information and we benefit from the good PR and from not having to gather the information from scratch every time we get a query.

Questions:

1. Who does not benefit in this situation?
2. What is the major obstacle you have to overcome?
3. How could the situation have been avoided?

Index